MORTAL
RIVALS

MORTAL RIVALS

SUPERPOWER RELATIONS FROM NIXON TO REAGAN

WILLIAM G. HYLAND

RANDOM HOUSE/NEW YORK

Library of Congress Cataloging-in-Publication Data

Hyland, William, 1929–
Mortal rivals.

Includes index.
1. United States—Foreign relations—Soviet
Union. 2. Soviet Union—Foreign relations—
United States. 3. United States—Foreign relations—
1981–   . 4. Soviet Union—Foreign relations—1975–
I. Title.
E183.8.S65H93 1987   327.73047   86-27919
ISBN 0-394-55768-9

First Edition
2 4 6 8 9 7 5 3

DESIGN BY JO ANNE METSCH

FOR
MY WIFE, LYNN,
AND FOR BILL, JIM AND LISA

ACKNOWLEDGMENTS

I was encouraged to write this book by my two sons, William and James. They insisted that a memoir of the Kissinger era would be well received. I, on the other hand, felt that I should deal mainly with the Ford administration, because that was the period when I served as an assistant to the president, and the Ford period had been slighted, in part because of the fascination with President Nixon. Thus, I set out to write a small memoir, but along the way various people encouraged me to expand it, and the result is in the pages that follow.

I am especially indebted to my wife, Lynn, who faithfully reminded me to keep working whenever my natural tendency to procrastinate overcame me.

I also want to thank my friends who read part or all of the manuscript and gave me their usual invaluable advice: Strobe Talbott, in particular, for his encouragement and suggestions; Peter Grose, my colleague at *Foreign Affairs*; Brent Scowcroft, whose friendship I can never repay; the Council on Foreign Relations, which gave me the opportunity and time to write a book, and the entire staff of *Foreign Affairs*, who tolerated my preoccupation with completing these pages. I am especially grateful to my editor, Peter Osnos, who shaped and transformed a rough draft into a publishable book.

Every writer knows that special thanks are owed to the person who guides the manuscript from beginning to end and turns a jumble into a coherent book. In my case, this was Mae Benett.

Finally, I am indebted most of all to Henry Kissinger. The reader will understand that without his friendship, this book would not exist at all. He, of course, is not in any way responsible for the judgments in these pages, nor are the other friends and colleagues who have been so kind and helpful to me.

William G. Hyland

CONTENTS

Introduction		xi
I	THE GRAND DESIGN	3
II	OPENING MOVES	13
III	THE ROAD TO MOSCOW	36
IV	END IN THE CRIMEA	62
V	THE ROAD TO VLADIVOSTOK	76
VI	THE ROAD TO HELSINKI	98
VII	DEFEAT IN ANGOLA	130
VIII	THE END IN MOSCOW	148
IX	GERALD FORD'S DEFEAT	172
X	KISSINGER APPRAISAL	188
XI	JIMMY CARTER AND SALT	202
XII	REAGAN'S ROAD TO GENEVA	227
XIII	THE NEXT PHASE	246
Index		261

INTRODUCTION

Shortly before midnight on May 26, 1972, I walked through the corridors of the Kremlin to St. Catherine's Hall to witness the signing of the first strategic nuclear arms agreements by Richard Nixon and Leonid Brezhnev. Later that same night I rode with Henry Kissinger to a bizarre press conference, held, incongruously, in the nightclub of a Moscow tourist hotel, where he explained the significance of the agreements and the summit conference. It seemed to me in those hours that the vicious cycle of hope and despair gripping the superpowers had finally been broken. But I was wrong.

Only four years later, when Kissinger and his staff left Moscow for the last time, much of what had been acomplished in superpower negotiations was beginning to crumble. Then, in March 1976, Gerald Ford abruptly dropped "détente" from his political vocabulary—abandoning the term that aptly described the complex intricacies of the U.S.-Soviet relationship. We had reached another symbolic turning point.

This book focuses on what happened to the Soviet-American rivalry in those years and beyond, when I served in the Nixon, Ford and Carter administrations, on the National Security Council staff at the White House and at the State Department.

It is a memoir of the period still commonly known as détente, and inevitably it deals largely with the diplomacy of Henry Kissinger, who was my boss for much of that time, and became my mentor and friend. It is also a chronicle of superpower relations through late 1977 (when I left government), focusing on the interplay among politics, personalities and policies in Washington and Moscow. An appraisal of Soviet relations after that date, under Presidents Carter and Reagan, is a final section. As an interested observer I watched Soviet-American relations inexorably progress through further cycles of improvement and deterioration, anticipation and disappointment.

Despite Ford's banishment of the word, the policy of détente continued under Jimmy Carter. Even though I had been a deputy assistant for national security affairs under President Ford, I was asked to remain on the new White House staff until the fall of 1977. This time I worked for another friend, Zbigniew Brzezinski, who assumed Kissinger's position as national security adviser. By the time I left, Soviet-American relations had recovered from a stumbling start; my last trip to Moscow was in March 1976 with the new team of Secretary of State Cyrus Vance. The mission became a well-publicized failure when the Soviets dismissed a proposal for deep cuts in strategic arms. But after that setback, the Carter administration did make considerable headway on a second strategic arms control agreement. Indeed, I left government service on a day when President Carter and Soviet Foreign Minister Andrei Gromyko met in the cabinet room at the White House and settled many of the disputed points that had blocked an agreement on arms control for two years. It seemed an auspicious moment to depart.

Many of the patterns of Soviet-American relations have become eerily familiar in the past thirty years. The themes of the mid-1980s were strikingly similar to the themes of the early 1950s, when I joined the CIA as an analyst. They applied as much to Mikhail Gorbachev and Ronald Reagan as they did to Nikita Khrushchev and Dwight Eisenhower.

Could we do business with the new Soviet leaders?

Would they forge new foreign policies and break with the past?

Should there be a summit meeting?

Could the new Soviet leaders be persuaded to negotiate seriously about ending the arms race?

In 1955 President Eisenhower met with Nikita Khrushchev in Geneva. Not much was settled, but the two powers seemed to agree implicitly that war between them was not inevitable. Thirty years later in the same city, Ronald Reagan and Mikhail Gorbachev would agree that nuclear war could not be won and should not be fought.

In the intervening decades the relationship fluctuated between a new cold war and "peaceful coexistence"—a phrase as much disputed in the 1950s as "détente" came to be twenty years later. There were periods of hope, but more often there were dramatic incidents and genuine crises—the invasion of Hungary, the launching of Sputnik, tension in Berlin and the shooting down of the U-2. Nikita Khrushchev became the first Soviet leader to visit the United States. President Eisenhower wanted him to see this country in the hope that he might change his views, much the same motive as that for Mr. Reagan's invitation to Gorbachev to travel here.

When Eisenhower left office, the relationship was in dangerous disarray. A summit meeting in Paris that was supposed to settle Berlin issues was aborted when a U-2 spy flight was shot down over the Soviet Union just before the meeting and Khrushchev insisted that Eisenhower apologize to him before the session convened. The president refused, and the summit ended. That melancholy atmosphere of May 1960 would have been familiar to Ronald Reagan and his advisers, after their frustration in Reykjavik a quarter century later.

In the summer of 1960, after the collapse of the Paris summit, Khrushchev decided to wait for the inauguration of a new president before pressing his demands on Berlin. John F. Kennedy sought to head off a confrontation in a face-to-face meeting with Khrushchev in Vienna; he failed, and the last act of that crisis was played out during October 1962 in the waters around Cuba, where Khrushchev suffered a humiliating defeat. Two years later he was removed by a palace coup.

The cycle began again. Would the new leaders, Leonid Brezhnev and Alexei Kosygin, adopt new policies? Could the new administration of Lyndon Johnson do business with them? Could the two superpowers check the new arms race, in defensive antiballistic missiles, that was about to break out?

President Johnson sought the answers in a meeting with the Soviet premier, Alexei Kosygin, in a small college town, Glassboro, New Jersey; a year later the president was about to announce a more formal summit when his plans were wrecked by the Soviet invasion of Czechoslovakia on August 20, 1968. And once again the cycle continued.

Would the new president, Richard Nixon, meet with the Soviet leaders, as all his European allies urged him to do, when they gathered in Washington to celebrate the twentieth anniversary of the founding of the North Atlantic alliance? Could he make an agreement on arms control, on Berlin, on European security? Would he go ahead with the new antiballistic missile system, which would protect the United States, or should he use it as a bargaining chip—questions much the same as those that confronted Ronald Reagan in 1986, proof of how firmly the patterns are fixed.

But the situation Nixon inherited was radically different from those of other recent presidents because America was bogged down in Vietnam, and the Soviet Union had become enormously more powerful in the preceding years. Nixon had to end the war in Vietnam and deal with the new challenge from Moscow.

It was at this point that I joined Henry Kissinger's staff at the White House and began to participate in working out the answers to these perennial questions. Perhaps we should have asked ourselves one other question: could any unexpected incidents arise to wreck the plans for Soviet-American relations that we were trying to devise in the spring of 1969? Yet not even the most prescient among us would have believed that the answer to that question would turn out to be the name of an apartment-hotel-office complex in Washington—Watergate.

This, then, is an account of Soviet-American relations as I have experienced them, using events I know firsthand and others I have studied in an effort to explain why, time and again, things turn out in the confounding way they do.

MORTAL
RIVALS

1

THE
GRAND DESIGN

Richard Nixon came to office faced with the most disastrous international situation any president had confronted since Pearl Harbor. In the winter of 1969 America desperately needed a new foreign policy and a new strategy to cope with the global power of the Soviet Union. The first priority was to end the war in Vietnam, but to do so while preserving an international position strong enough to deal with both Russia and China after the war ended. Obviously this would be no simple task.

The divisions over the Vietnam War made the conduct of a normal foreign policy nearly impossible. Bipartisanship had been ripped apart. The White House and the Congress were virtually at war, and the nation was deeply torn. Even the bedrock of the Atlantic and Japanese alliances was beginning to suffer from the ravages of Vietnam. Perhaps most important, the war threatened to destroy the core of America's postwar foreign policy: the containment of communism.

Containment in one form or another had dominated American policy since it was proclaimed by the Truman administration. It was the rationale for the Marshall Plan, the Truman Doctrine, the founding of the Atlantic alliance, the war in Korea and the intervention in Vietnam. It was based on a simple assumption: that American power could block Soviet expansion. Now, in 1969, it was a casualty of Vietnam. If communism could not be repelled in Indochina, how would the United States deal with the much larger threats from China and the Soviet Union? These were not idle questions, for at this very moment the growth of Soviet power threatened to place the United States in a position of strategic inferiority. How could a crippled nation conduct foreign policy in such unprecedented conditions?

Over the next five years Richard Nixon and Henry Kissinger designed and implemented a new strategy to restore the power position of the United States. The core of the new policy was a classical reversal of alliances, in which China, in effect, joined the West against Russia. This in turn gave America the leverage to manage the emergence of Soviet power. The policy came to be called détente—much to Kissinger's chagrin. This traditional European concept was too limited to describe the new international structure that he hoped might be created but too grandiose for what was likely to be achieved.

What Kissinger did in fact achieve was a new balance of world power. In the late 1960s, Russia and America no longer enjoyed the dominance they had acquired immediately after World War II. Until the late 1960s, the United States had been the only genuine superpower, but the new Soviet leadership under Leonid Brezhnev had recovered from Khrushchev's defeat in the Cuban missile crisis. Steady increases in military spending had brought the Soviet Union to a position of equality with the United States; some feared it was superior in strategic arms. Moreover, in 1968, Brezhnev had sent his army into Czechoslovakia to crush the dissidence of the "Prague Spring," and had declared Moscow's right to intervene anywhere in the Communist world. This set off alarms in China, and fighting broke out along the Sino-Soviet border. The break between the two strongest Communist powers changed the postwar balance, and simultaneously the older centers of power were rapidly reviving. Both Japan and Western Europe had almost completely recovered from the war and were prepared to play a larger role in world politics. The new international constellation offered the United States an unparalleled opportunity to combine with the other major powers to contain the Soviet

Union. For a country bogged down in a disastrous war, this was a wildly ambitious scheme.

To a striking degree the new strategy worked. It suceeded in opening a line between Washington and Peking for the first time since 1949. It created the basis for a new American relationship with the Soviet Union that would, in essence, last for a decade and center on the first limitations on strategic arms. It helped to extricate the United States from Vietnam.

In the early spring of 1969 these achievements were little more than vague hopes; no one could have imagined secret trips to China and summits in Moscow with Brezhnev. It was clear that both Nixon and Kissinger wanted out of Vietnam, but not at any price, and both had concluded that one way out was to neutralize Soviet and Chinese support for Hanoi. Thus the policy of détente grew out of the ashes of Vietnam, but it worked mainly because it reflected the new historical realities. Kissinger was fond of quoting Bismarck to the effect that the most a statesman could do was to grasp the garment of history as it passed by. Détente also worked because it was implemented not by a cumbersome bureaucracy but by a small group, operating mostly in secret, with a relatively free hand, and backed by the immense authority of the presidency. Under Nixon the threads of all the major foreign policies were gathered in the White House, and in the National Security Council staff that Kissinger led.

The NSC had been created under Truman largely to avoid a repetition of the breakdown in communications between the diplomats and the military that had contributed to the disaster of Pearl Harbor. The NSC was presided over by the president. Its primary function was to "coordinate" policy at the highest levels; the NSC staff was to assist in this task. That was the original theory, but in practice the NSC was brushed aside when there were strong secretaries of state, Dean Acheson and John Foster Dulles. In the Kennedy administration the system was revived and became a major center of power in Washington. Kissinger extended its power far beyond the intent of its founding fathers.

He quickly recruited a staff composed almost entirely of professionals from different government departments: State, Defense, the military and the CIA. This was a shrewd decision because it gave him a ready-made battery of experts, who needed no break-in period and who had a sense of the continuity of foreign policy. While the new cabinet officers were feeling their way and hiring their political subordinates and aides, Kissinger had a staff that was, in effect, already taking control. Moreover, a staff of professionals posed no particular political threat. It had no political base and was beholden to Kissinger and, less directly, to Nixon.

The new president wanted this system of White House dominance. He was genuinely interested in foreign policy, intrigued by its techniques, but contemptuous of the bureaucracy and determined to bring policy under his control. Kissinger and his staff provided the vehicle.

It was this staff that I joined in late February 1969. I scarcely knew Henry Kissinger at the time, but I had worked closely with Helmut Sonnenfeldt, when he was in the State Department intelligence bureau and I was in the Central Intelligence Agency. His friendship with Kissinger dated back to World War II, and Kissinger had hired him immediately upon being designated national security adviser by President-elect Nixon. Sonnenfeldt had the responsibility not only for the Soviet Union but for both Eastern and Western Europe as well. This proved a heavy load, and Sonnenfeldt asked me to join him; I eagerly accepted and remained on the staff until late 1973, when I transferred to the Department of State, as chief of intelligence, thus following Kissinger, who had become secretary of state in September 1973.

In those years, fortune smiled on me. The Soviet-European account in the NSC turned out to be on the cutting edge of American policy. I was able to observe and participate in the development of the policy of détente, in all of the Nixon-Brezhnev summits as well as the Ford-Brezhnev meetings, and in a dozen Kissinger trips to Moscow. But I was also on hand to watch the policy come under attacks from both the right and the left and suffer a nearly irreparable blow from Watergate.

We worked in a majestic old Victorian building separated from the West Wing of the White House by West Executive Avenue; it had once housed the entire State and War departments, but we preferred to think of ourselves as part of the White House. This was not reciprocated by the White House staff, who regarded Kissinger's entourage as rude interlopers and liberals, if not outright Democrats.

Fortunately, we enjoyed the protection of Nixon, who was rather proud of Kissinger's staff of "intellectuals," as he somewhat sarcastically called us. At one point, to our horror, he even proposed that the NSC staff be outfitted in blue blazers with an NSC emblem; this idea died, to our great relief, but it was a small sign that Nixon in fact did regard Kissinger's staff as special—at least that was our interpretation, though others saw malign motives.

Nixon was a ghostly figure for most of us on the junior level. Occasionally we could observe him at a meeting of the National Security Council, but these were usually pro forma affairs. The real decisions were made by Nixon and Kissinger, and it was a heady experience to be asked to draft presidential decisions before the NSC meetings had even been held. Kissinger, however, monopolized the president and, probably wisely, shielded him from access by the NSC. We had some vicarious contact, because Nixon would scribble marginal comments on our memoranda, and his staff aides would mechanically return them through channels. Some of his more acid comments were quite revealing, giving a glimpse of the "real" Nixon that would not emerge until the Watergate tapes were publicized.

I benefited from Nixon's interest in Soviet affairs. He had long experience in dealing with the Soviet Union and had developed a good feel for Soviet attitudes and reactions; he had a natural instinct for manipulation, which served him well in foreign policy but was disastrous in Watergate. His interest in Soviet matters permitted us more than the usual staff contact, and as the summit of 1972 approached, Sonnenfeldt and I became more and more involved at the higher levels of American policy.

For the NSC staff, Kissinger was the dominant figure. He brought to office certain qualities that made working for him an intellectual adventure and a personal ordeal. He had an incisive mind and a quick grasp of the core of any issue. He suffered no fools but was surprisingly solicitous and kind when it counted. Much of the time it was a war of all against all: the NSC against the State and Defense departments and a struggle for power within the NSC staff for Kissinger's favor (a struggle won by Alexander Haig, who became Kissinger's deputy and,

later, Nixon's chief of staff and Reagan's secretary of state).
Kissinger drove the staff and oscillated between frustration and
exasperation over the incompetence of his subordinates. We,
in turn, counterattacked with an avalanche of paper—briefings,
reports, analyses and policy recommendations—all supple-
mented by debates, discussions and occasional shouting matches.
And out of the process came a foreign policy, and a reasonably
effective one. Much of it was secret, and only Kissinger and
Nixon knew the full design. But the personal rewards came
on those rare occasions when, after months or years of effort,
the carefully constructed components of national policy came
together at the right place at the right time. One such moment
was in the spring of 1972, when Leonid Brezhnev found
himself entwined in a web of tightly linked issues and policies
that Kissinger had been spinning for three years; the Soviet
leader had no choice but to go through with the Nixon summit
at the very moment when the United States was bombing his
North Vietnamese ally. It was not an "easy decision," Brezhnev
told Nixon, and he never tired of reminding Nixon of it.

Kissinger was a strategist, in the proper sense of the term.
Though he could juggle diverse issues—the strategic arms
talks, his secret negotiations on Vietnam and the opening to
China—he understood that the strategist had to provide a
longer-term vision for the country, mobilize all of the resources
of the United States and bring them to bear for an extended
period. This was the essence of détente with the Soviet Union.
It was a political, military and economic strategy to stabilize
relations. It was to be embedded in a new and more stable
international structure. It was sound enough in theory, but in
practice it depended heavily on Kissinger's talents. When his
position weakened, so did the policy.

I had the opportunity to be involved with Kissinger more
than most of the staff because my particular responsibilities,
SALT and the Soviet Union, were his own special interests. In
addition, once a year a small group would adjourn to San
Clemente to help write Nixon's long annual report on foreign
policy. There we were treated to Kissinger's impatience with
our inept drafting, but we were also treated to his monologues
on the state of world politics and American policy. These
interludes were a mix of policy debates, Harvard seminars and
classes in freshman composition, together with grades on each

draft—no A's were awarded. A frequent Kissinger written comment was "baloney," a line along the margin meant "interesting," and, rarely, "good" was scribbled, in a handwriting that often almost defied deciphering. The exercise produced some important state papers; stripped of their political hyperbole, these documents still give an insight into the Nixon and Kissinger strategy.

Contrary to the popular perception of Kissinger as a Spenglerian pessimist, he was in fact a determined foe of the inevitable. Even as his achievements began to erode in the wake of Nixon's resignation in August 1974 and the fall of Saigon the following spring, he conducted a masterly rearguard action to preserve American power. In this too he was remarkably successful. Compared with the ebullience of the early period, however, those last years were melancholy ones. By then I was at a much higher level in the hierarchy, as a deputy assistant to President Ford in the White House. As a result, I realized how dependent any president is on strong public and political support in the conduct of his office. This was painfully evident as I watched Gerald Ford struggle to win the 1976 elections, fighting off attacks on his foreign policy by Ronald Reagan on the right and Jimmy Carter on the left. These barrages seemed particularly unfair to Ford, who had salvaged so much from the wreckage of Watergate.

By the time I arrived on the NSC staff in 1969, the Soviet affairs section was already active. Planning had started for new strategic arms control talks, which had been proposed by the Johnson administration and accepted by the Soviet Union before the invasion of Czechoslovakia. We were pressing for early negotiations, even though we had not yet resolved the substantive issues among ourselves—unfortunately, a typical American approach to diplomacy. Strategic arms included land- and sea-based ballistic missiles on the offensive side; antiballistic missiles (ABMs) were the only strategic defensive weapons included in the negotiations. We had to decide whether the United States should match the Soviet Union's antiballistic missile defense system or negotiate a mutual limitation. Along with SALT there was the first sign of Soviet interest in reviving discussions about Berlin—a surprise that no one had planned for. SALT, Berlin, as well as the overall German "problem," would become key elements in the maneuvering between Washington and Moscow.

Within three years, resolutions of these issues would radically transform them from the source of East-West tensions to the basis for a new superpower accommodation. These breakthroughs, ratified at the first Nixon-Brezhnev summit, became the preconditions for a grand European conclave in Helsinki in 1975, which was in effect the long-delayed peace conference ending World War II. In seven years we had come from the Soviet invasion of Czechoslovakia to a full-fledged European détente.

Cynics claimed that détente was the cold war by other means, and even at times by the same means; others claimed that it was merely George Kennan's old policy of containment by another name. The Kissinger era did continue the basic policy of containment, but there were significant differences. After Kissinger's secret trip to China in 1971, the United States became engaged in something approaching power politics with Communist adversaries, rather than ideological warfare. But the chief difference between the 1950s and the 1970s was that an accommodation with Russia and China was no longer foreclosed as an outcome of the policy.

A dual policy of containment and coexistence had been sporadically pursued by the United States after the death of Stalin in 1953. Eisenhower, Kennedy and Johnson had all flirted with their versions of détente. What Nixon and Kissinger did was to achieve a new blend. In the name of containment, they refused to concede an outright defeat in Vietnam and contested Soviet advances in the Middle East and Africa; but in Europe and in arms control with Moscow they adopted the Churchillian formula: one did not have to settle everything to settle some things. As the Vietnam War ended, the focal point of American policy shifted from the periphery of Asia back to the central struggle in Europe.

The policy of détente eventually became too focused on Europe. The dangerous contests in the Third World could not be settled, and consequently détente was periodically subjected to shocks. In October 1973, Brezhnev threatened to intervene in the Middle East war and American military forces went on a nuclear alert. In 1975, Cuban troops acted as the surrogates for Soviet power, intervening in the Angolan civil war, a challenge that the American Congress refused to meet. Eventually, under Jimmy Carter, these Third World crises spread: Cuban troops intervened in the war between Ethiopia and Somalia; Vietnam invaded Cambodia with Soviet support and the government of Afghanistan was overthrown by Communists.

Détente was badly battered by these crises. But to those of us intimately involved in the policy, it was clear that Watergate delivered the most crippling blow. Only a strong president and a strong policy could have sustained the ambitious strategy of Nixon and Kissinger. A weakened presidency could not fend off assaults on a policy that depended on the president's ability to offer carrots and threaten sticks: in 1975 the Congress withdrew the carrot of economic concessions to the Soviets, but it refused to apply the stick when Moscow intervened with impunity in Angola. For much of his time in office, Gerald Ford tried to continue the policy of détente; indeed, he added to the improvement of relations in his arms control negotiations at Vladivostok with Brezhnev in November 1974 and at the Helsinki conference in July 1975. But he had to contend with rising domestic disenchantment over détente, and the pressures of American politics. He was outflanked on the right by Ronald Reagan during the presidential primaries of 1976, and so Ford made his public repudiation of "détente" in favor of a "policy of strength."

It may well be that this renunciation did not matter by then. Leonid Brezhnev had already become disenchanted. On a bright sunny morning in the Crimea, in June 1974, he had secretly offered Nixon an alliance against China. He was rebuffed, and a few months later Gerald Ford turned down the same offer. It was a great irony. Kissinger had played the China card to drive Moscow in the direction of détente, and Brezhnev had countered by insisting that the card be dealt away by trying to make the United States his partner in hostility to Peking.

Carter tried to revive relations with Moscow and succeeded in forging a new arms control treaty in June 1979. But then, a decade after it began, détente finally collapsed when the Soviet Union invaded Afghanistan in December 1979. Nixon and Kissinger were out of power, but it was their grand design that was attacked by the Red Army. It was their carefully constructed political encirclement of the Soviet Union that was broken in Afghanistan. It was appropriate that the price Brezhnev had to pay for the invasion was measured in the fruits of détente. Jimmy Carter abandoned the newly signed second strategic arms agreement, which was to have replaced the Nixon agreement of 1972; he also embargoed the sale of grain to the Soviet Union, which had also been a crucial element of the Nixon-Kissinger strategy. And most of the Nixon-Brezhnev agreements on bilateral cooperation atrophied. Both the foundation and superstructure of détente were gradually dismantled in the early 1980s.

Yet it is surprising how much survived. Three years after Soviet troops came across the mountain passes into Afghanistan, Washington was again conducting negotiations on arms control and even talking optimistically about reducing missiles. By the mid-1980s, grain sales to the Soviet Union were at new highs and were even subsidized by the American government. In November 1985 the president was chatting amiably in front of a fireplace in Geneva with a new Soviet leader. All of this occurred in the presidency of that inveterate critic of détente Ronald Reagan. Little wonder that Henry Kissinger was moved to write that for all practical purposes the policies the Reagan administration was pursuing were the equivalent of détente. Perhaps this outcome should not have been so surprising: Nixon and Kissinger revolutionized American foreign policy. What they helped to create, as they claimed they would, was in fact a new global "structure," which not only survived them but is still the fundamental feature of international politics. With the broad framework of these past two decades in mind, we can turn now to a detailed look at how events in the U.S.-Soviet relationships have unfolded since 1969—and their consequences.

II

OPENING MOVES

When I reported for duty at the National Security Council staff in February 1969, I was assigned three issues: an analysis of the dispute between Russia and China; the preparations for the negotiations on limiting strategic arms (SALT); and what might be discussed with the Soviets on the status of Berlin.

It was fortunate that at this time of America's deepest troubles, the Communist world was falling apart. The United States needed leverage against North Vietnam, and the fracture between the two main Communist powers offered one means of gaining the necessary leverage. A major break between Moscow and Peking had been gathering force for years, and following the Soviet invasion of Czechoslovakia, tensions had risen sharply. The Kremlin justified the invasion by proclaiming the infamous "Brezhnev Doctrine," which insisted on the right of the Soviet Union to intervene throughout the Communist world to protect the gains of "socialism" wherever established. This threat of permanent Soviet interference was especially ominous for China. The Chinese leaders had ample grounds for fearing that they might well be the next object of the doctrine; after all, if there was one place where Soviet-style communism was undergoing a radical revision, it was in China.

By the spring of 1969, after fighting had broken out between
Soviet and Chinese troops along the Ussuri River border, we
on the NSC staff began to worry about the possibility of a full-
scale Sino-Soviet war.

Ironically, it was the American war in Vietnam, being fought
by the United States in the name of containing communism,
that was preserving the last vestiges of unity between the two
Communist giants. Neither China nor Russia could afford to
abandon their support of the North Vietnamese lest one or
the other be accused of betraying a Communist ally. Thus the
Chinese grudgingly cooperated in shipping Soviet military
supplies across China to North Vietnam; while both competed
to win Hanoi's favor in their dispute, Ho Chi Minh wisely
avoided choosing sides, thus guaranteeing the support of both.
For the United States it was Catch 22: as long as the Vietnam
War continued there was little that the United States could do
to take advantage of the growing split within communism, but
one way to end the war was for the United States to take
advantage of this conflict among Communists.

The United States had an additional means of exerting
leverage on Moscow. This was the growing concern in both
Washington and Moscow over a new nuclear arms race in
antiballistic missile (ABM) defensive systems. The Soviets already had a small ABM system of 64 interceptor missiles
deployed around Moscow, and the new administration had to
decide whether to proceed with a full-scale development of its
own ABM.

As the Vietnam War worsened, President Johnson had made
a desperate effort to salvage something of a global policy by
proposing that the United States and the Soviet Union join in
an agreement to limit all strategic weapons, both offensive and
defensive. To this end Johnson had met with Soviet Premier
Alexei Kosygin, at Glassboro, halfway between New York and
Washington. (It was indicative of growing American weakness
and Soviet arrogance that Kosygin refused to come to the U.S.
capital.) At the Glassboro summit, Johnson invited his secretary
of defense, Robert McNamara, to state the case against ABMs.
McNamara made an eloquent appeal to Kosygin to join in an
agreement to limit defenses against ballistic missiles. The
argument was straightforward: if one side built up its defenses,
the other side would have to respond, first by building up its

offense to counter an ABM defense, and then by also strengthening its defense—the classic definition of an arms race.
McNamara's appeal was sharply rebuffed by Kosygin, who
claimed in private, and later in public, that limiting defenses
would be "immoral." Kosygin may well have believed this claim,
but more likely the Soviet Union was not yet ready to trade its
own small but real ABM system protecting Moscow for a ban
on an American system that then existed only on paper. Three
years later, after the United States had begun its own ABM
program, the Soviet leaders would completely reverse themselves and become the champions of limiting all antiballistic
missiles.

By the time I had arrived on the staff, Nixon had already
decided to proceed with an ABM system but to urge the Soviets
to begin the negotiations on strategic arms limitation. The
American ABM system would be a large one, protecting all of
the United States, and would be justified as a defense against
third-country attacks—i.e., by China—and against accidental
missile launches. The decision to proceed with the ABM set
off a debate in the Congress and within the executive branch
over whether the system should actually be built or merely
used as a bargaining chip in the talks with the Soviets. These
debates would become permanent affairs; every new weapons
system would provoke another round. The controversy over
Star Wars in the mid-1980s was a familiar echo of the fights
over the ABM from 1969 to 1972.

Thus the United States had two possibilities for restoring its
international position: exploiting the divisions between China
and Russia; and opening negotiations with the Soviet Union
on the control of strategic weapons. The general outlook for
American foreign policy in early 1969 was nevertheless gloomy.

Nixon had traveled to Europe one month after his inauguration. He always valued the NATO alliance, which he invariably called our blue chip; and he knew that he had to gain
some European support as soon as possible. American relations
with Europe were soured by the allies' disenchantment with
our Vietnam obsession. De Gaulle's first question to Kissinger,
on that trip, was "Why don't you get out of Vietnam?" European-American relations were also troubled by the state of
East-West relations, which were in suspended animation after
the Czechoslovakia invasion. In retaliation NATO had agreed

to a freeze on diplomatic contacts with the Soviets, but by early 1969 the Europeans were already restless and wanted diplomacy to resume. This was their message to Nixon, and surprisingly, one area for new discussions was Berlin. Nixon had paid a quick visit to the city, and the Soviets had protested, as usual. But afterward they had hinted that they might be willing to start new negotiations on the city, including freer access from the west.

This was important because relations with West Germany were strained by a ragged debate over the Soviet-American treaty of 1968 to prevent the spread of nuclear weapons. The Europeans, especially the West Germans, thought this nonproliferation agreement was aimed at them. When the idea was first broached, in the mid-1960s, Chancellor Konrad Adenauer had called the treaty a new Morgenthau plan, thus evoking memories of the time when the United States and the Soviet Union had toyed with the notion of turning Germany into a pastoral oasis in postwar Europe. Only Soviet intervention in Czechoslovakia had temporarily relieved the strains across the Atlantic.

American statesmen were constantly preaching unity to the Europeans and urging the NATO allies to take a greater share of the defense burden. The West Europeans, however, were still badly divided. General de Gaulle was determined to block the British from membership in the European Economic Community, ostensibly because of their initial coolness to the concept of the EEC, but also because of their "special" relationship with Washington. Nixon wisely stayed out of this dispute, even though we clearly favored British entry.

What worried the Europeans, including de Gaulle, was the possible withdrawal of American troops from the continent; after all, Mike Mansfield, the majority leader of the Senate, was regularly proposing such a withdrawal, and support for his position was growing in the Congress. This movement of opinion could not have come at a worse time. After a long debate, NATO had officially adopted a new military strategy, called "flexible response," which allowed for a defense without immediate recourse to nuclear weapons. This made the presence of American troops more, not less, important. The new strategy also included the possible "first use" of nuclear weapons against a Soviet attack in Europe, but the Nixon administration quickly discovered that none of the NATO allies knew what "first use" of nuclear weapons meant in practice and were not eager to find out.

All of the European leaders came to Washington for the funeral of President Eisenhower, and most came again, a month later, to mark the twentieth anniversary of the founding of the North Atlantic Alliance. De Gaulle did not attend the NATO ceremony, but at Eisenhower's funeral he was clearly the dominant personality. The Soviets sent retired marshal Vasili Chuikov, who had led the final attack on Berlin. This was irritating to the White House; Nixon had expected a higher-ranking officer, possibly Marshal Ivan Konev, whose rank was closer to Eisenhower's wartime rank. In any case, the European message on these occasions was that Washington should open negotiations with Moscow on arms control and security issues.

In the Middle East there was also pressure on the Nixon administration to "do something." The Arab-Israeli war of 1967 had ended in six days, but there was no peace. In fact, a war of attrition had broken out between Egyptian and Israeli forces facing each other along the Suez Canal. The sporadic fighting threatened to escalate, as Israeli air strikes went deeper into Egypt. Cairo, in turn, leaned more heavily on Moscow for equipment and political support. America was isolated in the area. Russia had almost fulfilled the czarist dream of becoming the predominant power in the Middle East.

Even the international trading and monetary system, created at the end of World War II and based on the permanency of a sound dollar, was disintegrating. Two years after Nixon's inauguration, America officially abandoned the gold standard, unlinking the dollar from the price of gold, an event many regarded as marking the true end of the postwar world and the end of America's world domination.

Perhaps worst of all, the nation was losing its confidence that the United States could conduct an effective foreign policy. The divisions over Vietnam were increasingly bitter and violent. There was scarcely a national security issue that was not immediately challenged from all sides—right and left—and subjected to the most vicious debate. Congress was determined to create a new legal and constitutional system that would prevent future Vietnams, but it had no idea how to end the real war. The country had repudiated the Democrats and

Hubert Humphrey at the polls but had given Richard Nixon
only a bare plurality and saddled the new president with a
Democratic congress.

This litany of troubles was repeated time and again as the
Nixon administration took office. New administrations always
paint the worst picture of their inheritance so that four years
later their record will seem to be a favorable one in election-
year comparisons. But in early 1969 there was an underlying
reality to the campaign rhetoric about the United States'
situation in the world. The dominant fact was that there were
500,000 American troops in combat in Vietnam—in a war that
could not be ended and, seemingly, could not be won.

This was the prevailing cliché in 1969, but it was misleading,
if not wrong. The war in Vietnam probably could have been
won by launching a massive military offensive. The Vietcong
and North Vietnamese forces were weakened and still recover-
ing from the disastrous bloodbath of their Tet offensive in the
spring of 1968. Or the war could have been quickly ended by
large American concessions that would have turned the country
over to the Communists. Either course was unacceptable for a
new administration, even though a new president has considerable freedom during his first year. A concessionary settlement
was out of the question for an administration led by a new
president who brought to the Oval Office a vast reputation for
anticommunism. On the other hand, an all-out military attack,
possibly into Cambodia and Laos, and even into North Vietnam,
was not tempting to a president who sensed the basic meaning
of Vietnam: that there were limits to American power. Nor
was either course likely to be recommended by Nixon's new
national security adviser, Professor Henry A. Kissinger of
Harvard, who by training and instinct could not conceive of
an international problem in which the only choices were defeat
or capitulation.

In retrospect, Kissinger often wondered whether seeking a
military decision would not have been the wisest and the most
prudent course. It would probably have been political suicide,
in view of the poisonous atmosphere of those days. Long before
a military decision could have been reached, the domestic
turmoil would have gone out of control. In the mid-1980s,
service in the Vietnam War has once again become a "noble"
cause. Veterans are honored; memorials are solemnly dedi-

cated. But the atmosphere of 1969 and 1970 was far different—
at least as far as the psychological effect on those involved in
making foreign policy decisions.

Two memories of that period are most vivid for me. First,
there was a near-riot in Washington, D.C., in which armed
soldiers with drawn bayonets were standing guard along the
Memorial Bridge connecting Washington to Virginia. Tear gas
was floating through Foggy Bottom near the State Department.
The narrow stretches of Canal Road were littered with garbage
cans rolled down by protestors from the heights above. Working
at the White House in such a climate was scarcely conducive
to reasoned judgment about Vietnam, or any other aspect of
foreign policy.

My second recollection is of the spring of 1970. On a Saturday
morning, I was to join Henry Kissinger in a meeting with the
British foreign secretary, former prime minister Alec Douglas-
Home. As I drove toward the White House, I was confronted
by a wall of buses drawn around the White House grounds,
preventing anyone from entering except through a controlled
entrance, a scene reminiscent of Checkpoint Charlie at the
Berlin Wall. After negotiating my way through the barriers, I
went to Kissinger's office, which was then still in the west
basement of the White House (before he moved into more
prestigious quarters one floor higher). During the conversation
with Home, one could hear sirens and a continuing commotion
outside. How could the United States preserve the credibility
of its foreign policy in such an atmosphere?

The harsh fact was that no one, neither Nixon nor Kissinger,
had a clear idea of how to extricate the United States from
Indochina. What they did know was that, however it was
accomplished, the solution to Vietnam had to contribute to the
recovery of America's international position and not simply
stop the fighting. What was needed therefore was a grand
strategy to end the war, not the famous "plan" that Nixon had
promised throughout the election campaign (he later admitted
he had no specific plan). Both Nixon and Kissinger understood
that the crucial question was whether the United States could
emerge from Vietnam strong enough to operate effectively in
a changing international environment in which American power
was seriously weakened and the power of its principal adversary, the USSR, had grown significantly.

If the Vietnam War was criminal, it was not because of the way it was conducted but because it led to the nearly disastrous neglect of America's power position relative to the Soviet Union. Suddenly, in the late 1960s, almost without warning, it seemed, the Union of Soviet Socialist Republics had emerged as America's equal in world affairs and was demanding recognition as such. Soviet demands were simple and straightforward: First, and above all, Moscow wanted American acceptance of Soviet parity in nuclear weapons. Second, Moscow wanted a more formal American recognition of the Soviet empire in Eastern Europe, including recognition of the permanent division of Germany, both to be codified at a European Security Conference. Finally, the Soviet leaders wanted the United States to acknowledge the Kremlin's right—and duty—to support "national liberation" struggles throughout the world. These had been Khrushchev's demands, but he was too weak to enforce them after his defeat in the Cuban missile crisis of October 1962. Now, when Nixon took office, Brezhnev not only had adopted these objectives but was moving toward a position of global power from which he might be able to impose his aims on the United States.

It was ironic that Nixon and Kissinger became so closely identified with the policy of détente, because initially, at least, neither saw much prospect for more than a narrow, limited accommodation with Moscow. Rather than proposing a broad settlement, they offered to resolve a number of specific issues (e.g., Berlin and arms control). Eventually, they hoped, a broader, more general improvement might take shape, and it was to this end that they devised the tactic of linkage: making progress in some areas dependent on progress in others.

Whether the results of such limited arrangements would lead to major changes inside the Soviet Union—a traditional justification for American policy—was always considered highly problematical by Kissinger, and to some extent even irrelevant. Kissinger was skeptical of the proposition that the objective of United States policy should be to induce changes in Soviet society in the hope that such internal change would, in turn, produce a more benign Soviet foreign policy. This proposition, linking internal and external Soviet policy, was used as an argument for détente, as well as for the opposite policy of putting pressure on the Soviet Union as a means of forcing internal reform; the latter became a favorite theory of American neoconservatives in the early 1980s. It did not work then and would not have worked in the 1970s. To adopt such an approach would be to evade the necessity for policy choices and rely on history for vindication. And while the United States awaited history's verdict, operational control over many factors essential to American survival would be given up. Rather than conducting foreign policy, America would risk becoming bogged down in an endless debate over the nature of change within Soviet society (which is roughly what happened in the first years of the Reagan administration).

Nixon and Kissinger recognized that the power positions of both superpowers were undergoing changes. Their nuclear arsenals were growing enormously in the 1970s, and the position of the Soviet Union relative to the United States was substantially stronger than in the early 1960s. Yet both superpowers found that their ability to translate military power into political influence was limited, and these limits were becoming more and more evident. Kissinger frequently argued that the nuclear age had destroyed the traditional measures of power and had altered the requirements for maintaining the balance of power. An increase of purely military strength could no longer confer an equal element of security in an era of nuclear vulnerability. Therefore, it appeared possible and necessary to "discipline power," as Kissinger put it, so that power would "bear a rational relationship to the objective likely to be in dispute." If Moscow also understood the limits and requirements of the nuclear era, then, in the circumstances of a rough strategic equality, some common ground for accord might be discovered and explored. This reasoning was the core idea of the negotiations that Kissinger conducted with Brezhnev. It was the rationale for the agreements limiting strategic arms and creating an agreed set of rules, or a "code of conduct," signed at the first Nixon-Brezhnev summit in May 1972. The thrust of these principles was that neither side would seek "unilateral advantages."

Kissinger always tried to stress the limited utility of any individual agreement with Moscow, whether the SALT treaty, or a set of written principles on international conduct. He was particularly frustrated, however, over the elaborate attention given the Principles of Bilateral Relations by the American press and political analysts after they were signed by Nixon and Brezhnev in 1972. The media ascribed to them a self-enforcing power that they never had, nor were intended to have. It is easy to forget that the various agreements, even the strategic arms accords, were conceived as instruments of a larger policy.

Indeed, Kissinger believed that relations with the Soviet Union were bound to be ambiguous, if only because the Soviets were persistent in confronting their opponents with ambiguous challenges. This tendency of Soviet policy was to be countered by what Kissinger called a policy of "precaution"—that is, meeting challenges early, before they could take more definite and dangerous shape; he always cited the British and French failure to recognize Hitler's invasion of the Rhineland in 1936 for the broad strategic challenge that it really was. Such a policy of precaution is difficult to pursue in a democracy, where at every point the statesman has to prove his assumptions to a skeptical public and Congress. Consistent with the policy of precaution was Kissinger's attitude toward negotiation. He believed that negotiations had to be decoupled from the domestic debate over Soviet intentions and capabilities. Negotiations need not await a change of heart in the Kremlin but could proceed on their merits, but within a framework devised and understood by all the participants. Thus, Kissinger foresaw that there could be partial accommodations irrespective of any Soviet grand design.

After taking office, however, he argued for the tactic of linking different issues, for two reasons: first, to prevent the Soviet Union from establishing its own agenda and concentrating only on those issues it wanted to negotiate; and, second, to ensure that one or two isolated issues would not be resolved in an atmosphere of underlying hostility, but would be embedded within a general improvement in relations. Kissinger saw the danger, however, that successful negotiations with the Soviet Union would be represented in the United States as Moscow's "permanent conversion to a peaceful course," and that there would be a temptation to "gear everything to personal diplomacy." His answer to such concerns was to insist on a program of concrete negotiations, including the issues that were the real source of tension and hence were truly difficult to resolve. Thus, if there was progress, it would be genuine.

In sum, the initial approach to the USSR of the Nixon-Kissinger period was to deemphasize the ideological element; to downgrade the likelihood of profound changes in Soviet society; to set aside the debate on the nature of Soviet intentions; and to exploit the opportunities to reach specific, even though limited accommodations. To a great extent this was the policy actually followed in the ensuing years.

By the spring of 1969, the Nixon administration had decided to seek a settlement in Vietnam rather than to fight to the bitter end. Moreover, the administration decided to withdraw American troops in an effort to placate the domestic opposition and shift the burden of combat to the South Vietnamese. Finally, it was decided to pursue secret negotiations. There was a conviction in the White House that such a complex strategy required that the United States try to weaken the support of Peking and Moscow for Hanoi, or at least persuade both powers that their own national interests, as opposed to Hanoi's interests, would be better served by dealing with the new American administration.

The idea was simple: an American rapprochement with both Moscow and Peking would undermine their support for Hanoi, at least psychologically. The North Vietnamese, worried about the waning support of their Communist allies, would have to negotiate the best settlement possible with Washington, but could do so in secret without losing face. Both Nixon and Kissinger had separately foreshadowed this approach in articles published in *Foreign Affairs* before they took office. In theory it was intriguing, but in practice it would be a difficult operation. Neither the Soviet Union nor China would want to be caught abandoning their small Communist friend and ally. Thus Hanoi still had a veto, and, of course, the North Vietnamese had no incentive to do anything other than sit tight while America gradually withdrew from Indochina.

The challenge for the new administration was to make a new relationship with Washington so attractive to Moscow as well as to Peking that their fears of being isolated would come to outweigh their loyalty to Hanoi. To achieve this meant that Washington had to engage in constant maneuvering: first hinting to Peking that the United States would not simply stand by if Russia tried to crush China; and then hinting to Moscow that an American rapprochement with China might well be concluded at Soviet expense. This is roughly what happened, but it took a full two years—until the summer of 1971—to work it out. In the beginning, during 1969, there was only a shadow play.

When I joined the NSC staff, I learned that the Soviets had already approached Kissinger, probing to discover what they could about Nixon's intentions. In the process they complained bitterly about the brutality of Chinese conduct in shooting incidents along the Soviet border. These complaints were relayed through Anatoly Dobrynin, the shrewd Soviet ambassador to Washington, who had been in the same post since the Kennedy administration. He was to become a key figure in the development of Soviet-American relations (and still is today). He was experienced enough not to simply repeat the party line to Americans; a conversation with Dobrynin could go beyond the banalities that too often characterize diplomacy. But he was also wise enough to reserve a few vital points from his instructions for the next round of discussions; thus, one could be reasonably sure that he had not presented the entire Soviet position. The price for learning the remainder of his position, however, was to give something in return. He covered a total commitment to his own system with a veneer of joviality and even a self-deprecatory humor. But he had a sure instinct for the center of power and soon settled on Kissinger as his interlocuter, which is exactly what Nixon wanted: to transfer the key channel to the White House.

Initially, however, Dobrynin outsmarted himself. After years of soaking up the bitter anti-Chinese atmospherics in Washington during the Johnson administration, and especially from Dean Rusk, Dobrynin assumed that complaints about Chinese behavior would continue to be sympathetically received. He claimed to Kissinger, for example, that China was the Soviet Union's "main security problem." This was clearly the wrong approach to a practitioner of realpolitik; Kissinger read these complaints as signs of nervousness and evidence that the split between the two Communist powers was becoming more serious than he had imagined. It whetted his appetite for triangular politics. By midyear, Kissinger was advising Nixon that perhaps friction between the two Communist powers was sufficiently severe so that the United States might be able to take advantage of it. Moreover, this Sino-Soviet contest led Kissinger to emphasize at every meeting with the Soviet ambassador that the development of superpower relations between Washington and Moscow depended on events in Vietnam. Kissinger's message to Dobrynin was that the United States wanted "strategic" help from the Soviet Union, not suggestions for settling marginal problems.

But the Soviets were not playing. They would not sell out Hanoi for only a vague promise of better relations with Washington. Indeed, at one point Dobrynin bluntly asked what was in it for Moscow if the Vietnam War ended. And Kissinger rather lamely suggested trade and a summit meeting.

Our staff appraisal summed up the problem as we believed it was viewed from Moscow:

> The Soviets are probably still basically of two minds on Vietnam. On the one hand, they could see the virtue in further stalling, in expectation that domestic pressures in the United States will force new concessions in Paris. On the other hand, they may recognize that Vietnam casts a shadow over relations with the United States and may stand in the way of proceeding on other issues. The Soviets may also be concerned that the lack of progress in Paris vindicates the Chinese criticism and reduces Moscow's influence in Hanoi. But Vietnam is still a critical issue over which the Soviets have limited leverage and no compelling incentive to exert pressures on North Vietnam.

One reason for Soviet stalling was the very fact that tensions along the Chinese border were dramatically increasing. Washington was receiving more and more reports of serious armed clashes. About mid-1969, there were some calculated Soviet probes as to what America's attitude would be if the Soviets struck out at China with full force. One was launched in Washington by an official of the Soviet embassy in a conversation with a State Department official in August. All such overtures were strongly rejected by the White House, but reports of Soviet rumors could not be dealt with, and Kissinger began to worry whether we could head off a Soviet strike. To counter Soviet rumors, he caused reports of an impending Soviet attack and of American concerns to be leaked to the press; one source was the CIA director, Richard Helms, whose position no doubt added an aura of unusual credibility to the leaks. At the same

time, Pakistan was brought into play by Washington as a possible
private channel to convey American sympathies to Peking.

I became more and more involved in the analysis of Sino-
Soviet relations. It seemed to me that it was naïve to believe
we could pick up Soviet concessions either by shading our
sympathies toward China or by pretending that we were strictly
impartial in the conflict. If the Soviets did use force against
China, American impartiality would be exposed as a myth. We
would have to decide whether to break off various negotiations
with the Soviets, perhaps over Berlin or strategic arms; and if
we did, we would not be acting impartially. On the other hand,
if we continued business as usual we would be condoning Soviet
actions. I concluded in a memorandum to Kissinger:

> The notion of extracting Soviet concessions, once major hos-
> tilites have begun, is extremely naïve. The Soviets are not going
> to attack China in some quixotic mood. If they take this drastic
> step, they will be fully and totally committed to pursue it to the
> end. They are already working up deep racial and political
> emotions in Russia. The Soviet leaders believe we should share
> their concern about China and expect, at the least, sympathy
> and understanding for whatever actions they might take. They
> will almost certainly regard American gestures to China as sheer
> hypocrisy.

Sino-Soviet tensions continued to mount through the summer. Subsequent evidence, from the memoirs (*Breaking with
Moscow*) of the Soviet defector Arkady Shevchenko, who was
then in the U.N. Secretariat, confirms that there was, in fact,
a serious debate in the Kremlin over whether to attack China.
The probing of U.S. attitudes and the negative American
response turned the debate away from an attack. This was our
impression at the time, though we could not be sure. A recent
book on the relations between Moscow and Peking (*China and
the Superpowers*) by the Soviet historian and writer Roy Medvedev also confirms that this general interpretation of Soviet
intentions was correct. By late September, Dobrynin asked
Kissinger directly whether he expected a Soviet attack on China,
and Kissinger replied that as a historian, he had to allow for
the possibility. Dobrynin did not scoff at this answer. And
Kissinger was becoming increasingly worried that the Soviets

were secretly implying that we were being consulted and would acquiesce in a strike. But then suddenly, without warning, in September 1969 the storm broke. The Soviet premier Alexei Kosygin paid a surprise visit to Peking on his return from the funeral of Ho Chi Minh. He held a dramatic meeting with Chou En-lai at the Peking airport, and there was a joint announcement that the two sides would continue their talks. It was a stunning turn. Nixon immediately called Kissinger, asking for his evaluation. Kissinger, correctly, indicated his doubts that it meant a basic change in Sino-Soviet relations. After mulling it over, we in the NSC staff concluded about the same. It appeared to us that the Chinese had "blinked" in the confrontation, but, we concluded, "there was no significant movement toward an accommodation."

This was correct. Not only was there no accommodation, but in the months that followed, the Chinese rather cleverly out-maneuvered the Soviets in their bilateral talks. Soviet pressures on China were relieved after the Kosygin-Chou meeting, and thus China had to make no further concessions. But the Chinese leaders must have been sobered by the crisis, because it was about this time, in the fall of 1969, that Peking began to show an interest in responding to various American gestures. In fact, the Chinese agreed to resume the ambassadorial talks with the United States that had been held sporadically in Warsaw since the late 1950s. These talks had begun as a face-saving device after a Taiwan Straits crisis in the 1950s, but they had long been sterile. From time to time they served as a barometer of relations. Now the public announcement of a new round of Warsaw talks pointed to fairer weather—at least that is what was thought at the time.

Moscow reacted almost immediately. Dobrynin proposed a series of secret direct talks with Kissinger. In his best, disin-genuous manner, he inquired of Kissinger whether the rumors that he had heard about a U.S. summit proposal for Moscow were true. This classic diplomatic ploy was accompanied by other, more serious Soviet moves. In particular, the Soviets agreed to open negotiations over the perennial problem of Berlin; and in the second round of the SALT talks then under way in Vienna the Soviet delegation offered a significant concession by accepting an American proposal to limit the size of ABM systems. But gradually, in the late spring of 1970, this thaw in Soviet-American relations slowed, and then relations again became frozen. There were new Soviet threats in the Middle East: Moscow sponsored Egypt in a growing confrontation with Israeli forces across the Suez Canal; more Soviet military personnel were sent to Egypt to help man a new air defense line fortified by the arrival of new Soviet missiles. Dobrynin's talk of a summit waned. The SALT talks became bogged down, and nothing serious was happening in the Berlin talks.

The reasons were plain enough. Moscow had found another, more ardent Western suitor to replace Washington. A new West German government, led by Willy Brandt, the former mayor of Berlin, and his Social Democrats, had taken office in October 1969. Within a few months Brandt had begun to unveil a new Eastern policy (*Ostpolitik*) that must have been of immense interest to the Kremlin. At long last, it looked as if the West Germans would recognize the political status quo in Europe, as Moscow insisted, including the division of Germany and even the legitimacy of a Communist government in East Germany. For a time, at least, this shift in German policy made the United States suddenly superfluous.

The second reason for Soviet stalling in discussions with Washington was that after the invasion of Cambodia by American forces in April 1970, the Chinese had pulled back from their own opening to the United States. China was still not ready to be trapped into moving toward Washington if Moscow could then attack Peking for betraying its Vietnamese brothers. The Warsaw talks with the United States were canceled.

But the Chinese understood the game quite well. When Nixon did finally visit China in 1972, the Chinese leaders explained what their assessment had been in 1970: they had concluded that the Soviets did, in fact, fear that the United States and China were drawing closer, and for this reason Moscow had sent Kosygin to Peking to meet Chou En-lai, according to the Chinese. Whereas Kosygin had been interested in solving problems with the Chinese, Brezhnev was not; he was more ambitious, and more emotional. Kosygin could talk reasonably, but he had a technical mind and was not farsighted. Because of Soviet nuclear power, Brezhnev's ambitions were growing. Nixon was told, at the time that the Soviets were predicting a Sino-Soviet clash within five years (i.e., by 1977).

It is interesting that in their account of Soviet policy, the Chinese were off by only one year: their crisis with Moscow came in the winter of 1978–1979, when Hanoi invaded Cambodia and China "counterattacked" against North Vietnam, thus risking a severe confrontation between China and Russia, which still supported Vietnam. The episode proved to be an anticlimax, because Russia did nothing.

In the summer of 1970, all of this was well in the future. East-West diplomacy was shifting to Europe, to the old problems of Germany and Berlin.

One of the early surprises for the Nixon administration had been Soviet interest in talking about Berlin. Dobrynin had said as much to Kissinger in early 1969. This was one of my first assignments on the NSC staff: to assemble some background on the history of the long, tedious negotiations over Berlin that had taken place at various times since 1945. One quick glance at the accumulated files indicated how encrusted the subject had become with complex legal theories and political positions. The entire city of Berlin was still occupied by the four wartime allies: the United States, the Soviet Union, Britain and France each had a separate zone of the city. The Soviets had relinquished their responsibilities in East Berlin to the East Germans, after the building of the Berlin Wall in 1961. The United States still insisted, however, that the Soviets take responsibility for East Berlin and acknowledge that Berlin remained under the four powers collectively. Moreover, we held the Soviets responsible for free access to the Western sectors, from West Germany and from East Berlin. The Soviets refused to accept these legal responsibilities, which they claimed were under the jurisdiction of the East German government, but in practice Moscow kept a tight rein on the East Germans. The various Berlin issues had been dormant since the crises of the Berlin Wall and the Cuban missile confrontation in the early 1960s.

The idea of new talks about Berlin appealed to Kissinger. Berlin was a concrete issue on which progress could be clearly measured. In other words, it did not involve a vague, abstract improvement in the atmosphere. And given the long history of Berlin, almost any progress would be a significant political signal that superpower relations were also improving. The United States began carefully reexamining the issues. The State

Department had the main responsibility and was extremely jealous of its monopoly over German and Berlin matters. These issues had been the road to promotion and power inside the State Department bureaucracy in the 1950s and 1960s. But one result of this monopoly was that the State Department had become jaded, and the Berlin and German experts were dubious that anything much would be accomplished by new talks with the Soviet Union. Consequently, what they defined as "progress" was negligible: the restoration of telephone links between East and West Berlin, for example.

The West Germans erred in the other direction, wanting an ambitious program for relatively free access to the city from West Germany and freer movement between Eastern and Western sectors of the city. The Soviets, of course, wanted almost exactly the opposite: to weaken the links between West Germany and West Berlin and make the wall a recognized international border. The United States had no special plan other than to remove Berlin as a perennial trouble spot by gaining some form of Soviet guarantee for access to the city, but without demoralizing the Berliners in the process of the negotiations. The eventual result in the agreement of September 1971 was to be a classic compromise: the legal link between West Germany and Berlin was indeed weakened, but the access of people and goods to Berlin from the West was guaranteed by the Soviet Union, a compromise that has stood for over fifteen years.

After some stalling, in early 1970 the Soviets agreed to formal negotiations about Berlin. By then there was a new element: the change of government in Bonn that brought to power Willy Brandt and the Social Democrats.

This was a truly historic occasion. Social Democrats had not governed in Germany since before Hitler. Now they were in power, led by a major figure of the postwar struggles, the former mayor of West Berlin. Since 1966 Brandt had been foreign minister in the so-called Grand Coalition of all three major political parties. But as a result of national elections in the fall of 1969 Brandt became chancellor, even though the Social Democrats had the thinnest of majorities in the parliament. It is sometimes characteristic of governments with slender majorities that they are willing to strike out far more boldly than those with comfortable margins. Brandt almost immedi-

ately launched a new foreign policy. He formally recognized
the Communist government in East Germany, satisfied Moscow
by signing a treaty of nonaggression and performed an act of
contrition by visiting Auschwitz in Poland, where he signed
another treaty with the government of Wladyslaw Gomulka.
And he did all of this within less than a year.

This was a shock to Washington. For years the United States
had rather comfortably assumed that the various German
governments had no real choice but to continue the conservative
line of Konrad Adenauer, especially refusing any recognition
of the other half of Germany. Even though Bonn's policy of
trying to keep East Germany isolated had begun to weaken in
the late 1960s, the United States was not psychologically
prepared for Brandt's dramatic changes. This caused some
serious strains and aroused gnawing suspicions that the Germans were up to their old tricks of conducting an independent
policy, creating an opening to Russia and maneuvering between
East and West.

It was interesting (and appalling) how quickly these old
suspicions of German maneuvers surfaced, despite fifteen years
of close alliance between Germany and the United States. The
White House was not alone in its concerns. The old guard of
German hands, especially John McCloy, the former American
high commissioner for Germany during the postwar occupa-
tion, was uneasy; Dean Acheson, Truman's secretary of state,
even went so far as to attack, publicly, Brandt's "mad race to
Moscow." (This pleased Nixon no end; he had come to dislike
Brandt). The situation was not helped by the arrogant style of
Brandt's subordinates, who treated the White House with some
disdain. Egon Bahr, for example, told Kissinger the Germans
were tired of apologizing for the past. While pretending to
consult, Brandt was in fact simply informing Kissinger and
Nixon of his moves. Neither could give vent to their true
feelings, but various critical remarks were nevertheless leaked
and, of course, found their way back to Germany, further
poisoning the atmosphere. And there was the further irritation
that while Kissinger was conducting a complicated policy, trying
to manipulate the China factor, negotiate with the Soviets and
end the Vietnam War, Brandt was easing through all of his
difficulties almost effortlessly by making concessions.

Matters came to a head in August 1970. Brandt had signed

a nonaggression treaty with the Soviet Union that recognized
existing European borders, and while in Moscow he had spent
four hours in private with Brezhnev. This German treaty
incidentally marked Brezhnev's emergence in the public eye as
the new master of foreign affairs, replacing Premier Kosygin.
Brandt wrote to Nixon proposing a Western summit to plan a
strategy for the next phase of East-West relations. The cool
French reception of Brandt caused a slight downgrading of
his proposal to a meeting of Western foreign ministers, and
the French response allowed Washington to avoid a clear rebuff
to Brandt. Brandt, however, badly needed a prop from Washington because his political opposition in Germany was becoming increasingly critical of his concessions to the East. The
Christian Democrats were demanding that there be an Amer-
ican-Soviet agreement on Berlin before they would consider
ratifying Brandt's treaty with Moscow in the German parliament.

   The effect of this demand was to put the burden back on
the United States to rescue Brandt's strategy by concluding a
Berlin agreement with Moscow. This both pleased and irritated
Kissinger. Brandt had warned the Soviet leaders of this new
linkage between the ratification of his treaty by the German
parliament and an agreement on Berlin. Now he was urging
Nixon into action. In one of his letters to Nixon in the late
summer of 1970 he claimed that on the basis of his conversations in Moscow, he had concluded that the Soviets wanted a
"general calming of the international scene."

   There were two problems for the United States. First, there
was the intrinsic difficulty of the Berlin question, which had
become an extremely complicated political and legal tangle.
Second, there was Washington's perception that Moscow was
not "calming" its line but hardening it. This was the period of
the confrontation between Syria and Israel over the Palestine
Liberation Organization attacks on King Hussein in Jordan.
Moscow was supporting Syria, and the United States was
backing Israel, in what came to be a truly tense confrontation
that threatened a new war. Moreover, it was in that autumn of
1970 that the Soviets challenged Washington by beginning the
construction of facilities that we believed would become a naval
base for Soviet submarines in Cuba. When confronted by
Kissinger, the Soviets backed down, and there was an informal

agreement that they would give up these facilities and not service any nuclear submarines from Cuba. It was our conclusion in the NSC that Moscow was acting with a new boldness, in part because it had nailed down its settlement with Germany, and in part because it was clear that we were not getting anywhere by playing the China card.

The upshot was that Nixon was cool to an acceleration of East-West negotiations. Washington would have a difficult time in trying to impose German demands for a favorable Berlin settlement on the Soviet Union; Moscow after all had already pocketed enormous concessions in Brandt's recognition of East Germany and of all postwar European boundaries. The only leverage that the Americans had (other than the China card) was the continuing Soviet insistence on holding a European security conference. What Brezhnev wanted was that all of Europe, along with the United States, would assemble in a grand conference, a kind of replay of the Congress of Vienna, to endorse what he had agreed upon with Brandt: the continuing division of Germany and of Europe into two parts. Kissinger decided to link a Berlin settlement to a European security conference, much to Brezhnev's annoyance. Kissinger also tried to whet Moscow's appetite by putting European security on the agenda for a possible U.S.-Soviet summit meeting.

The real problem was that the United States was in danger of being caught in the middle of German politics. If Washington failed to deliver a Berlin agreement, Brandt's treaties would collapse and his government would probably fall. If we did deliver a settlement on Berlin, it would immediately be weighed inside Germany against a set of ambitious German demands; these ambitions could not be imposed on the Soviets, and the Germans would then blame the Western allies for failure, or for collusion with the Soviets.

But it was the Soviets who miscalculated. The various pressures on the United States in 1969 and 1970, whether in Indochina, the Middle East, Cuba or Europe, had not brought the United States to any fundamental change of course. In the winter of 1970–1971 the United States was still determined to play the China card. Moreover, shortly before Christmas an event occurred in Poland that changed the situation for both Washington and Moscow. There were riots in Polish cities against food price increases, riots so severe that the government of Wladyslaw Gomulka was brought down.

For over a decade, since the Polish crisis of 1956 during the Hungarian revolution, Poland had been under the control of Gomulka. For a time, he had been regarded in the West as something of a model of a "liberal" Communist, but gradually his regime had deteriorated. He had engineered the treaty with Brandt that recognized Poland's disputed postwar boundaries, and it was thought that in Poland he would be hailed for gaining German concessions. What his quick downfall suggested to Washington, however, was that the Eastern settlement with Germany was too narrow. Moscow (and Warsaw) still needed to put the German settlement on a broader basis; they needed a European-wide détente, specifically endorsed and supported by the United States. As long as the United States was only an outside observer, the limited German agreements engineered by Brandt would not be entirely satisfactory to Moscow. If this was the Soviet interpretation, then the United States could exploit the new situation. This was our assessment in the NSC in December 1970, and Kissinger decided to act on it. Indeed, he was elated, because what had seemed a complicated, difficult winter suddenly looked quite promising for us. And this was confirmed when shortly before Christmas Dobrynin came in to propose some new, wide-ranging discussions with Kissinger.

At this point, December 1970, Kissinger and part of his staff (including me) adjourned to the western White House in San Clemente, to begin drafting Nixon's "State of the World" report. These annual interludes became a combination of pleasant winter vacations in southern California (including one trip to the Rose Bowl) and long, tedious hours of writing and rewriting. But there were also opportunities for some more relaxed discussions, and in the course of these talks, Kissinger indicated he thought that we had reached a turning point with the Soviets. And he plotted a strategy for his talks with Dobrynin. His plan was to bring matters to a conclusion in the German-Berlin negotiations, which he now took into his private channel with the Soviet ambassador. Second, he said he would try to negotiate a breakthrough in the SALT talks, which had become bogged down. And he intended to undertake this plan while signaling strongly to China that Washington was ready for a significant move. These signals to China took various forms. A small one was contained in Nixon's annual report, which mentioned China under its proper name, the People's Republic. Chou En-lai later said he recognized this signal. Matters moved rapidly: a U.S. Ping-Pong team was publicly invited to visit China; and far more important, Nixon received a message from the Chinese on April 27, 1971, sent through Pakistan, inviting Kissinger to visit Peking.

What made this so satisfying to us was that the Soviets had once again outsmarted themselves. A U.S.-Soviet summit to be held in 1971 had been tentatively agreed upon during Soviet foreign minister Andrei Gromyko's meeting with Nixon at the White House in October 1970; Gromyko had promised an early and definite answer on the date for the summit, but after his departure there had been months of silence. The Soviets were drawing back from Washington and beginning to link the summit to a prior Berlin agreement. It was a crude but typical Soviet tactic. All of this was to Kissinger's great annoyance, as he plunged ahead with a visit to China. Even at the very last moment, however, before taking off to fly from Pakistan into China, Kissinger offered the Soviets a moment to fix on a summit date. But in July 1971, Moscow blew its chance.

In little more than two years after Nixon took office, Kissinger had engineered a diplomatic revolution. The China trip took place in secret, of course, and was dramatically announced by the president in July 1971. When Kissinger returned to Washington and confronted Dobrynin, the ambassador was "ashen," according to Kissinger's account; he and his patrons in Moscow had been badly outmaneuvered. Playing the China card was clearly a success. Within a few weeks, there was a breakthrough in the Berlin talks, the SALT negotiations began to move again and the Soviets agreed to a Nixon summit in Moscow for the following spring. The United States was now in the catbird seat.

III

THE ROAD TO MOSCOW

In retrospect, the maneuvering in those early Nixon-Kissinger years leading to the Chinese and Soviet summits in 1972 was intricate and tactically brilliant. It put the United States in a pivotal strategic position.

Yet the heart of the relationship with the Soviet Union had become the limitation of strategic arms, and the success or failure of these negotiations was the crucial test of American policy toward Moscow. It was certainly not Kissinger's original design that SALT should carry such an immense burden in superpower relations. To put such weight on any single area of relations was risky, but it was especially risky if that one area was arms control. It was bound to be the most difficult, for it went to the very heart of each nation's security. Partly for that reason the Nixon administration had not been eager to move in this direction. Indeed, the accepted theory was that an improvement in political relations, or even in the atmospherics of relations, should come first, because this in turn would facilitate important agreements, including arms control. But in the conditions of 1969 and 1970, it made sense that the strategic arms negotiations should assume such importance. In the nineteenth century, power struggles had been settled by war.

In the 1950s and 1960s, strategic nuclear weapons had, in effect, become the surrogates for war. If one side surged ahead in numbers or quality of weapons, it was entitled to geopolitical gains. It was never that simple or automatic, but both sides became excessively preoccupied with weapons balances.

By the late 1960s, the superpowers were at a crossroads in the development of their strategic arsenals. If there was to be any sustainable improvement of relations between Washington and Moscow, neither side could ignore what was threatening to become a major new arms race. Two new weapons systems involved were: on the defensive side, the antiballistic missile, the ABM, in Washington jargon; and on the offensive side, the MIRV, the multiple independently targetable reentry vehicle. The MIRV was an intriguing new technology that allowed several warheads to be carried on the end of one missile but dispensed in such a way that each could be guided separately to different, even widely dispersed, targets. It was marvelously depicted by the *Washington Post* cartoonist Herblock as a hydra-headed bomb, with numerous venomous snakes crawling out of the top.

The Soviet Union's small, defensive ABM system, deployed around Moscow, was so primitive that virtually all American experts agreed that it would not be very effective. But it was psychologically worrisome that the Soviets were moving in this direction. The existence of the Soviet ABM had led the United States to develop the MIRV, as a means to overwhelm the ABM by exhausting it with hundreds of incoming warheads. The United States, under Lyndon Johnson, had started the development of its own ABM system, named Sentinel, which the Nixon administration inherited. It was a program without any missiles or radars yet in the field and with only a vague rationale. On the other hand, the United States had already tested an ICBM missile armed with MIRV warheads, while the USSR lagged behind, though how far was the subject of dispute among experts.

The two systems, ABM and MIRV, were organically linked, at least in theory: if one side had an effective defense (ABM) system, or threatened to have one, the other side would feel compelled to counter the defense with a more powerful offense (MIRVs). One obvious solution was for both sides to give up ABMs and MIRVs. But this was greatly complicated by the belief at the time (1969–1972) that once a missile armed with a MIRV was tested, say, a dozen times, it would not necessarily have to be tested any further and could be ready to be fitted into ICBM silos. This process of substituting a MIRVed missile for an ICBM without MIRVs was believed to be undetectable by the means available to American intelligence. Thus, once a certain level of testing had been reached, arms control limits on MIRVs would be difficult if not impossible to verify. (This conventional wisdom turned out to be untrue, because in installing MIRVs, the Soviets had to make large and obvious modifications in their ICBM silos.) Not surprisingly, there was a growing chorus in the public and the Congress that suggested a freeze: to create a favorable atmosphere for the negotiations, the United States should not pursue its own ABM and should halt any further testing of its MIRV system.

As the effects of the Soviet invasion of Czechoslovakia wore off and the Nixon administration began to prepare for negotiations, the Soviets appeared to be stalling. This confounded the experts, especially in the State Department and Arms Control and Disarmament Agency (ACDA), where it was an article of faith that the Soviets were eager to negotiate in order to halt our ABM and MIRV programs. The Soviets' stalling, however, suggested that they might want to await the results of the "freeze" debates in the Congress.

This interval in the early months of 1969 should have been put to good use by the government agencies involved in preparing the U.S. negotiating position. In fact, the first six to eight months of 1969 were wasted in foolish debates, largely about abstract issues. One favorite topic was whether the United States should start negotiations by proposing a comprehensive agreement or a limited one. The State Department and ACDA invariably favored developing and proposing a broad, comprehensive plan that would cover every aspect of strategic weapons, on the dubious theory that more arms control was by definition better; it was also argued that a comprehensive offer by Washington would be regarded as more serious by the Soviets. These arguments led to a further conclusion that the Soviets would be ready, indeed eager, to give up their ABM system in order to stop our own system (still on paper). And of course it followed in the minds of many that we should also give up our MIRVs. This dovish sentiment inside the administration outraged Nixon, who regarded it as weak. It simply raised his contempt for the bureaucracy to another order of magnitude.

Kissinger had contributed to the intellectual evolution of the theory of strategic arms control when he was at Harvard. He was also intrigued by the operational aspects of the different weapons programs. But in 1969 he was preoccupied with Vietnam, and he allowed the bureaucracy to proceed on its own with developing initial position papers for the negotiations. These turned out to be virtually worthless. We found ourselves in the situation so characteristic of American diplomacy: on the one hand, we were pressing the Soviets to set an early date for the SALT talks, but on the other hand, we had no idea what would be negotiated, and we were bickering among ourselves. This state of affairs provoked occasional Kissinger outbursts, but he did not intervene until later in the year.

In addition to the usual debates between the State and Defense departments, Kissinger's staff was divided. It was unclear who had the responsibility for coordinating the issues on Kissinger's behalf, and this led to endless petty arguments. At one point Kissinger called a breakfast meeting to make peace in his staff. He must have been both amused and appalled at the arguments that broke out. Most were attacks on others for encroaching on the speaker's terrain, and little of the debate concerned the actual SALT preparations. This situation, in turn, was complicated by the fact that one of the contenders for Kissinger's favor in the NSC was Morton Halperin, who had been in the Defense Department and had shepherded the previous administration's position through the interagency coordinating process, and had even obtained the approval of the Joint Chiefs of Staff. He was inordinately proud of the compromise that he had achieved (it was basically a freeze on missile launchers). Naturally, he tried to sell it again to the Nixon administration, but the new administration wanted to go through its own process, although ironically its final position was not far from the Johnson one. Halperin was eventually superseded by Lawrence Lynn, also in the NSC, who produced some extensive analyses that impressed Kissinger. These analytical papers challenged many of the conventional interagency beliefs and emphasized the importance of being able to verify each of the various types of arms control limitations then being discussed. This emphasis on verification gave Kissinger the rationale he needed to bring the entire bureaucratic process under his control in a new group, under the guise of analyzing the possibilites for verification. In light of later bureaucratic and personal animosities between them on arms issues, it is worth noting that it was Gerard Smith, as head of ACDA, who urged Kissinger to involve himself more in the planning process.

Some of us in the NSC staff questioned the State Department's highly optimistic assumptions about the Soviet interest in strategic arms control, especially Soviet interest in banning both MIRVs and ABMs. In particular, we thought that in view of the threat from China, it was not very likely that the Soviets would give up their ABM defense of Moscow under any conditions. In that event, the United States could not abandon its MIRV program, which was designed to counter the Soviet ABM defense. And many of us were also appalled at the idea of starting negotiations with the Soviets by freezing our own programs, a step the State Department was urging in the Congress. Infighting and maneuvering at the staff level became particularly sharp.

At the higher levels, the situation was not much better. The Pentagon could not decide what it wanted. There was only a limited interest in the ABM system, because it would soak up money the Air Force wanted for a new bomber (which would later become known as the B-1), the Navy wanted for a new submarine (which would become the Trident) and the Army wanted for a new tank (the Abrams). Moreover, there was heavy pressure to reduce the defense budget as the Vietnam War began to wind down. The new secretary of defense, Melvin Laird, was a former Republican leader in the House of Representatives, and he was unusually sensitive to congressional pressures for budget reductions. These he was able to deliver, but miraculously without sacrificing major weapons programs. Indeed, the core of the strategic arsenal of the United States in the 1980s, on which Ronald Reagan relied, was really created by the Nixon and Ford administrations, during the decade of "neglect," as Reagan was to describe it in his campaign in 1980.

The Pentagon had no clear idea of what it wanted out of the arms control talks. The Department of Defense's representatives took refuge in some wildly exaggerated estimates of Soviet capabilities, especially concerning what the Soviet ABM system could do and the allegedly rapid pace of the Soviet MIRV program. These Defense Department estimates were almost completely wrong on both Soviet ABMs and MIRVs. Their alarms, however, were made public in congressional testimony and all too often through leaks to the press. Such publicity had the effect of charging the political atmosphere, making it still more difficult to draw up a sensible SALT negotiating position.

By late September 1969, the new administration could no longer ignore the fact that the Soviets had failed to reply to the many American requests to begin negotiations. This long silence prompted a staff memo we wrote for Kissinger, which he sent on to Nixon:

> If they [the Soviets] were concerned over ABMs and MIRVs, as some observers claim, then their deliberate delays are baffling. If, on the other hand, they have doubts over the possibility of any agreement involving extensive control of their own programs, this would be consistent with their delays.
>
> It may be that with the 24th Party Congress looming over the horizon [March 1970] the Soviet leaders are reluctant to negotiate for a major agreement with us which might risk a setback if talks fail, or commit them to a brand-new course if they succeed.
>
> China of course figures in all their calculations, and until they make hard decisions to take military action or not, other issues are likely to be treated ambiguously and cautiously.
>
> . . . there is no persuasive evidence for being very optimistic about SALT, or other key issues. The Soviets have not been responsive to the concept of an era of negotiations, despite some moderately toned speeches. They remain a highly suspicious, unimaginative and extremely conservative collective. There is no reason to expect a dramatic change in our relations on the basis of the record of the past six months.

In retrospect, I believe we may have overanalyzed the Soviet position. It may be that the delay was simple prudence, probably to take the measure of a new administration; but it is also quite likely that once the American ABM was approved by the Senate in August, despite the very narrow margin (one vote), the Soviets had no incentive for any further stalling. Thus the first SALT negotiations began in early November. Nevertheless, Washington could not decide on a number of key issues.

Kissinger made a vain last-minute effort at the NSC meetings
to clarify the broad issues by stressing the key relationship
between ABMs and MIRVs. In one session he called attention
to the vast changes in the strategic situation. New, accurate
missiles made it possible to plan effective partial strikes against
ICBM silos without having to launch a massive attack. This
was becoming a plausible scenario for the first time in the
missile era.

The comfortable American strategic assumption that we
could deter the Soviets by simply threatening to retaliate was
coming under sharp questioning. There had always been some
concern about vulnerability; for example, a surprise Soviet
attack against bombers still on the runways was an old nightmare. But the new scenario for partial attack against ICBM
sites was the first blush of what in later years would become
the "window of vulnerability," which maintained that the
United States would be vulnerable to limited Soviet attacks
until the "window" could be closed by an American ability to
reply with a similar limited disarming strike. Critics who argue
that the "window" grew out of American complacency during
détente forget that the vulnerability of American ICBMs was
thoroughly examined in 1969, including the countermeasures
that would later evolve; even the idea of developing a new
ICBM, the mobile MX, dates from this period. A number of
staff analyses were conducted on questions of strategic vulnerability. Of special concern was the impact of a new vulnerability
on the behavior of both sides during a crisis. If one side could
in fact launch an effective strike against the other side's missile
silos, would the temptation prove irresistible?

In the late 1960s, all of this was a heretical challenge to the
prevailing doctrine of deterrence through the guaranteed
ability to inflict an assured level of destruction on an opponent.
Hints of a new doctrine provoked a strong reaction within the
government. Gerard Smith, who was both head of ACDA and
the leader of the SALT delegation, wanted to hear none of it.
The result was that the question of the vulnerability of our
ICBMs was relegated to a secondary issue in arms control
planning and was subordinated to various negotiating formulas.
The only reflection of the broad strategic problem of ICBM
vulnerability was a preoccupation with reducing Soviet heavy
missiles, which would form the backbone of a strike force

against our missiles. Gradually, however, the strategic justification for this position was lost, and reducing Soviet heavy missiles became an end in itself. Thus resolution of the strategic debate over missile vulnerability, which should have been achieved in 1969 or 1970, was delayed for almost a decade.

Each of the possible solutions posed too many new problems for an administration trying to get ready for an early negotiation. Hardening our missile silos was one possibility, but this would require relocating many of the missile sites to harder, bedrock soils, which would be costly and take years to complete. Making missiles mobile was also possible, but many believed the difficulty of working out a reliable method of locating and counting such missiles would jeopardize an arms control agreement. Protecting each missile field with ABMs was also considered, but the ABM was already in political trouble. Finally, MIRVs could be banned on both sides, and the threat to American ICBMs thus reduced.

Refusal to ban MIRVs was the key decision in the entire history of SALT. Both Nixon and Kissinger thought it would be a weak move at the outset of a new administration and the opening of a long negotiation. And it would have provoked a bloody fight inside the administration and in the Congress. It was a truly fateful decision that changed strategic relations, and changed them to the detriment of American security. But I doubt that Nixon and Kissinger could have forced through the Pentagon both a ban on MIRVs and a sharp limit or ban on ABMs, and then persuaded the Soviets to agree; certainly this could not have been accomplished by the fall of 1969.

Nixon had to accept early negotiations. Largely because of Vietnam, he had to prove his good faith to the various critics who feared that the "old" Nixon was going to be too harsh. Thus, our delegation departed in November 1969 for the first round of SALT negotiations in Helsinki with only the vaguest of guidelines. Nixon and Kissinger preferred it that way because they wanted maximum flexibility. If given precise instructions, the delegation would be determined to put forth every last detail. As it turned out, our delegation did a highly competent job of probing the Soviet position. Moreover, the Soviets were operating in about the same mode, probing the American position without giving anything away.

An amusing sidelight for me was the task of drafting a public letter from Nixon to Gerard Smith, as leader of the delegation. These are usually boilerplate letters, routinely approved, wishing the delegation Godspeed. This time I put in some padding about the historic nature of the occasion. To my surprise, the astute *Washington Post* diplomatic reporter Chalmers Roberts wrote an analytical article drawing a number of implications about our probable position based on the phrasing of this letter. I must have subconsciously written more into this missive than I realized. But I am still amused that the usual bureaucratese could lend itself to such sophisticated analysis.

The talks in Helsinki went well. After some exchanges of generalities, the sides adjourned in a good atmosphere, much to everyone's relief. Both delegations promised to get down to business in the spring. In fact, the real action was not in Helsinki at these preliminary negotiations but in the Congress back in Washington. For it was there that the political battle lines were drawn on ABMs and MIRVs.

The ABM system, as noted, had almost been defeated in August 1969 in the Senate, where it passed by only one vote, a harbinger of continuing close calls. The effect of this narrow escape was that the Pentagon leaders backed even further away from the ABM; they feared that repeated political battles on the hill with key senators would jeopardize the remainder of the defense budget. And this was correct. Indeed, Senator John Stennis, chairman of the Armed Services Committee, finally had to warn the administration that the ABM issue was poisoning the defense debate. ABM stayed alive just long enough to become a major bargaining chip in the SALT negotiations. There was debate and confusion, however, over how to play the ABM card. By the spring of 1970 it was clear that the United States would be likely to deploy two or three ABM sites. The agreement finally reached in 1972 settled for no more than two ABM sites on each side. The United States had to choose between one site around Washington plus one around an ICBM field in North Dakota, or two around ICBM fields. The United States completed only one site, operated it briefly and abandoned it. No site was ever begun around Washington.

MIRVs fared better. Repeated congressional resolutions were passed urging that all MIRV tests be stopped before it was too late to reach an agreement with the Soviets to ban them. But they were ignored or resisted by the administration. The Pentagon was intrigued with MIRVs, not for their original purpose of overcoming ABM defenses, but because MIRVs would rapidly expand the U.S. strategic arsenal and offer much wider target coverage. Moreover, it was feared that the Soviets would go ahead with their own MIRV program. In fact the United States enjoyed about a five-year lead.

In sum, the ABM system was dwindling from a full-scale defense to little more than a token: MIRVs testing was continuing and thus the chances that MIRVs would be banned were also dwindling. What this process of elimination pointed toward was a treaty limiting ABMs to a low number, but not eliminating them altogether, plus a rough freeze in numbers of missiles. This did not rule out reductions of weapons. However, it was much too early in the thaw in Soviet-American relations to think seriously about cutting down weapons, even though our delegation made a proposal for some reductions. Thus the idea of a comprehensive arms control package gradually faded, and the final outcome at the 1972 summit was to freeze the numbers of ICBM silos, and, in effect, the numbers of submarine-launched missiles as well, in a five-year interim agreement. ABMs were limited, but in a permanent treaty, with no termination date.

All of this could probably have been agreed to in 1970. It took two more years largely because the Soviets, in their typical bargaining mode, decided to try a squeeze play to push through an early agreement that would limit ABMs only, while leaving all offensive weapons open. Public pressures gathered momentum to buy this poisonous offer of an immediate ABM treaty. The columnist Joseph Kraft called it "attractive"; Senators Hubert Humphrey and George McGovern came out in its favor; *The New York Times* editorialized that it would be "self-defeating" to wait for an offensive agreement, and *The Washington Post* also began to editorialize for the proposal. Congressional pressure built up.

A separate agreement on ABMs would have been a disaster. The Soviets would have been free to build all categories of offensive weapons, and at a time when the United States was still not ready to build any new systems. The political result would have been an immediate backlash against any arms control, and therefore pressures would probably have grown to repudiate the ABM treaty. The Nixon administration argued that offense and defense had to be linked. They could not be separate categories; if there was a buildup of defense by one side, the other would reply by building its offense; and as the ABM itself demonstrated, if offensive forces were growing, there would be pressures to build up defenses against them. To sign a treaty giving up ABMs without checking the Soviet missile buildup would have been political suicide. All of this created a stalemate with the Soviets, which could not be easily broken at the working level in Geneva. Kissinger decided that he had to intervene. He made the SALT stalemate one of the topics in intensified negotiations with Dobrynin, along with his accelerated negotiations on Berlin and a continuing byplay on a summit meeting in the Soviet Union.

In the Kissinger-Dobrynin negotiations in early 1971, Kissinger took the position that the relationship stood at a crossroads—a fairly standard cliché, but this time it had some meaning. The two sides had been through some difficult moments in late 1970, and Kissinger could claim that without an effort to reverse trends, conflicts would continue and would feed on each other; the relationship could slide into a serious deterioration. This same theme—that it was an important moment for progress—was also stressed publicly.

One reason for emphasizing this line was that the Soviets were approaching their party congress, which had been scheduled for March 1970 but had been postponed for one year. As the congress approached, we assumed Brezhnev had to think about his overall position at this event, as well as afterward. Soviet party congresses in the past had assumed unexpected importance; sometimes they became historic turning points. Stalin had used his speech at the party congress in 1939 to signal to Hitler his readiness for a bargain. Khrushchev had used the congress to launch de-Stalinization in 1956.

In March 1971, Brezhnev would hold his second party congress since the overthrow of Khrushchev in 1964, but it would be the first congress that Brezhnev would clearly dominate. This gave Washington some bargaining room, especially since it turned out that Brezhnev did use the congress to launch what became known in the Soviet Union as his peace program. For this program, a show of progress in the arms control negotiation was necessary. At first, Dobrynin sought a quick agreement before the party congress but was resisted by Kissinger. At the end of the congress our analysis in the NSC staff was that Brezhnev had a new incentive to improve relations with the United States, in order to help him achieve his domestic program and to control "divisive tendencies" within his empire. We still expected that he would stall while he evaluated the growing impact of the "peace issues" in the United States as we moved closer to the 1972 presidential elections. Nixon, in a comment on our memorandum, predicted a Soviet overture within thirty days, and he was right. Nixon's long experience in dealing with and watching the Soviet Union gave him a good sense of Soviet tactics.

When Dobrynin returned to Washington from the party congress in April 1971 he brought with him an offer of a summit meeting the following September. The Soviets were calculating that a summit in late 1971, before the presidential election year, would be so appealing that Nixon would make concessions to get it. Having thrown out this tempting bait, however, Dobrynin then began to stall; in his talks with Kissinger he tried to make a prior agreement on Berlin the condition for a summit.

But it was SALT, not Berlin, that was clearly the main issue. The SALT deadlock seemed to be a procedural impasse because the Soviets wanted to sign an ABM treaty and then quickly negotiate about offensive weapons, but we still insisted on linking offense and defense. In early 1971, Kissinger proposed that the negotiations on the ABM treaty be finished, but that before it was signed, an interim agreement on offensive weapons also be completed. Kissinger believed that in negotiating with the Soviets it was better to stake out a position and stick to it than to start high and bargain downward. The Soviet negotiators, however, invariably believe that no matter how adamant their adversary seems to be, there is probably one last concession to be achieved. This makes them maddening bargainers. They can never be sure that they can prove (to their superiors) that all possible concessions have been extracted; so to be safe, they will stall for an interval longer than any reasonable person can endure. This was one reason why negotiating with Brezhnev was faster and more likely to lead to results; he had to satisfy only himself.

As usual, Dobrynin waffled in the face of Kissinger's new offer. Then he replied solemnly, on behalf of the Politburo, that they wanted an agreement, and the sooner the better. They wanted a formal treaty on ABMs but would agree to a tacit freeze on offensive weapons (i.e., ICBMs); they preferred to discuss submarine-launched missiles later. As for the ABM treaty, the Soviets preferred an agreement that would limit missile defense to protecting the national capitals, Washington and Moscow. They did not want to do away with ABMs altogether. Thus, the Soviets virtually accepted the American position, but it was typical of the Soviet style that hard, irritating bargaining remained before the agreement announced on May 20, 1971, finally broke the deadlock.

Dobrynin tried several times to weasel out of the bargain, by shading the meaning of the Soviet commitment to work out an offensive agreement along with an ABM agreement. Kissinger at one point threatened to make the dispute public, and Nixon, as usual, urged Kissinger to hit hard. It was Nixon's style to take a hard line, knowing that Kissinger would use his own judgment; thus Nixon would have a tough position on the record and could distance himself from any of Kissinger's concessions, which he invariably approved. The secret talks between Kissinger and Dobrynin in Washington gave rise to a ludicrous situation when the Soviet delegation, then in Vienna, proposed to our delegation a bargain that Kissinger had already rejected a few weeks earlier in private with Dobrynin. Kissinger had to restrain our own delegation's enthusiasm and upbraid Dobrynin, who claimed ignorance of any chicanery.

The Kissinger-Dobrynin agreement of May 20 ended the deadlock and thus should have been welcomed. On the whole, the Kissinger agreement was well received—it was a "major step forward," according to *The New York Times*. But Kissinger's secret negotiations strained his relations with the SALT delegation, because they had not been consulted. They were informed only at the last minute and reacted peevishly. The head of the delegation, Gerard Smith, as well as his deputy, Paul Nitze, were critical. The agreement was, of course, what we had been trying to achieve for a year, but in Washington the question is who gets the credit.

The more serious charge from the American side was that Kissinger had failed to secure Soviet agreement to include a limit on submarine-launched missiles. And this myth has persisted. The fact is that Kissinger put the Soviets on notice on two separate occasions that we intended to include submarine-launched missiles in the final agreement. The Soviets subsequently tried to water down their commitment to include these weapons. The American delegation, angry at being excluded by Kissinger, made only a minimal effort to refute the Soviet version. Thus, a new deadlock began to develop. Moreover, since Kissinger and Dobrynin had not discussed precise levels of limits on ABMs, another deadlock emerged over how many ABM sites would be allowed on each side. Kissinger and Dobrynin had broken the stalemate on their level, but it continued on the second, operational level.

One reason for the problem was the chaotic state of the American position on ABMs. Kissinger rather wryly pointed out the confusion in our position to the policy group that was determining SALT strategy: the administration originally favored a large system for defense of the entire United States, but we were now beginning to build a defense of ICBM sites only. In the negotiations with the Soviets, however, we had proposed an ABM system that would protect only Washington, D.C., and the Soviets had accepted the proposal, but we had no plans to build such a system. The Pentagon was one source of indecision. The secretary of defense, Melvin Laird, changed his position almost every month, as did the deputy secretary of defense, David Packard. Even the senators who supported the ABM did so only on the understanding that no sites would be built in their own home states. Eventually the Pentagon settled down and decided to ask the Congress for the additional funding necessary for a new site to be built around Washington, D.C. Almost every dollar for ABMs caused a new round of fighting in the Congress. In mid-1971, one site was in an advanced stage of construction and another was just beginning. Both were abandoned, in 1974 and 1975.

This vagueness at the policy level allowed the American delegation in Vienna to resurrect its favorite proposal, a complete ban on all ABMs. In retrospect, this might have been a good idea, since the United States wound up with no more than a token program. But until the full link between offensive and defensive weaponry had been settled, the United States, or at least Nixon, was against a complete ban on ABMs. It turned out that the Soviets were also against it. Our persistence in hinting at an ABM ban finally caused Dobrynin to react and appeal to Kissinger to ask that the Americans stop "playing games." At the same time, Kissinger had to intervene with Dobrynin to stop the constant speculation that we would give up limitations on submarine-launched missiles. In the end Kissinger had to go directly to Moscow on a secret trip in April 1972 to break the new stalemates.

Kissinger worked out a final compromise with Brezhnev, to be signed at the summit, now scheduled for May 1972, with only a few changes. The Soviet leader finally conceded that submarine-launched missiles could be limited, as we had insisted. The final bargain was a virtual freeze on the total number of ICBMs and submarine-launched missiles. An exception was made for old ICBMs, which could be dismantled and, in effect, traded in for new submarine missiles, up to a level of 920 such submarine-launched missiles. The United States, however, had only 656 submarine-launched missiles, compared with the 920 ultimately permitted for the Soviet side. This was criticized as a great inequality; but the American missiles were being armed with multiple warheads, whereas the Soviets were five to six years behind our program. I was always convinced that Brezhnev rationalized this inequality in submarine missiles as compensation for giving up on trying to include the nuclear weapons of the French and British in the U.S. total.

This final breakthrough, in Kissinger's secret trip, was also received badly by our SALT delegation. Once again they had been excluded, but this time they had ample opportunity to complain before the summit, and to appeal the Kissinger package. In fact, after some maneuvering the American side settled down and accepted the Kissinger-Brezhnev outline. The delegation, now in Helsinki, put all but the final touches on the first SALT agreements. Clearly, the Nixon summit would be a triumph.

But suddenly matters took an unexpected and dangerous turn. At the end of April, the North Vietnamese launched a major offensive, and Nixon retaliated by ordering the mining of Haiphong harbor and the resumption of American bombing. It looked as if the summit would never take place. The summit was clearly going to be an acid test for the strategy of linkage.

Most of the betting in Washington, including Nixon's and Kissinger's, was that Brezhnev would cancel. But for the Soviets, too much had come to rest on Brezhnev's meeting with Nixon: not only the SALT agreement, but the German treaties and the Berlin agreement and, by implication, a European security conference. All of these had been carefully linked by the American side. Without a summit the structure would come crashing down. At that very moment, in early May, the West German parliament was meeting to consider the ratification of Brandt's Eastern treaties with Moscow and Warsaw. If the U.S.-Soviet relationship collapsed, the two German treaties would also be rejected. In that case, it was almost certain that the final Berlin agreements would not be signed either. Brezhnev's German policy would disintegrate. Finally, there would be no chance for a European security conference, which Kissinger had made clearly conditional on the Berlin agreements. Brezhnev might have gambled and risked his German policy and even the SALT agreements, and apparently he was under some pressure within his own Politburo to do so. But beyond all of these intricate linkages was one outstanding fact: Nixon had already been on his triumphant visit to China.

So the Moscow summit proceeded. And on the whole it went off quite well. Gromyko had to spend most of a late night–early morning session with Kissinger trying to straighten out a Brezhnev blunder, made earlier in the day during his meeting with Nixon. Brezhnev had suddenly and surprisingly accepted our position that when "modernizing" a missile silo, the silo could not be changed. He was apparently trying to show off his mastery of the subject, but he had taken the wrong position, and Gromyko had to undo it by arguing for the acceptability of some small changes in a modernized silo. Kissinger perversely let Gromyko stew in Brezhnev's juice for an hour during a very late night session before relenting. Then it was the American turn to create confusion. Our SALT delegation, still meeting in Helsinki, tried to abandon some of our own positions, making for a few more chaotic hours. Both sides returned to the previously agreed upon positions.

Despite delays in finishing the SALT agreement, the Soviets insisted on their self-imposed deadline for signing it. They had scheduled the ceremony for Friday, and when the last issue was resolved in the early afternoon, they insisted on signing that evening, even if it had to be after dinner. This led to frantic telephone calls to our delegation in Helsinki to get them to Moscow on time. They even had to give the Soviet delegation a ride in the U.S. aircraft.

For me the summit was memorable for the serious results, but it had its bizarre moments. Kissinger and the staff worked out of an "office" that was in fact a converted bedroom in the Kremlin. It was nicely furnished with period pieces but was short on functional furniture such as typing tables and file cabinets. The Soviets graciously offered to store our classified papers in their safes, which they assured us would be securely locked. We declined. Our crude filing system used the top of the upright piano for SALT documents and the deep window ledge for Vietnam. We had an antiquated copying machine, which broke down regularly, but which we finally figured out how to fix. The malfunction led to the spewing-out of poor copies, which we crumbled in one corner until they could be collected into the classified "burn bags." Periodically, Soviet waitresses would appear at the door with trays of tea, cookies, lemon and milk. We would allow them in, but usher them out quickly. (The room was guarded by U.S. marines.) This so-called office was next to the bedroom of Mrs. Nixon's hair-dresser, Rita de Santis, who was baffled by the Soviet electrical system and would ask at least twice a day for help in stringing together various transformers and extension cords. This led to the spectacle of Kissinger's staff crawling about the floor with string wire searching for electrical outlets. Our demeanor in those moments confirmed Kissinger's view that we were not taking the summit seriously enough.

Shuttling between the meeting rooms and this office, I came to know various labyrinthine passages of the Kremlin. I mem-orized the different carpet patterns to find my way back and forth; and occasionally I would encounter a Soviet guard, who seemed to think it almost natural that an American should be charging along the corridors of this ancient fortress. It was eerie, nonetheless, to pass by the dimly lit chapels where various czars had prayed. Once, when there was a delay in a meeting, I offered to take Nixon and Kissinger by my back-corridor short cut, but they had no confidence in my ability to come out at the right room.

The night of the SALT signing turned out to be particularly

strange. Once the documents were exchanged, assuming that the action was over for the evening, most of the staff had departed for relaxation around town. Then H. R. Haldeman, Nixon's chief of staff, persuaded Kissinger that he had to meet again with the press, despite the late hour, to fill in some gaps in an earlier briefing by Gerard Smith. So Kissinger grabbed me, and while he shaved and changed shirts we discussed what he should say about various issues in the agreement. I then went with him to the downtown Intourist Hotel, where the briefing took place in a large bar. Kissinger occupied the dimly lit stage, with a strange mural of flickering stars in the background. His masterly and humorous performance earned him at least one comparison in the press with Frank Sinatra.

The next morning I had breakfast with Paul Nitze and General Royal Allison of our SALT delegation before they returned to Helsinki. Haldeman, sensing that the delegation was unhappy about being bypassed during much of the summit, asked that I brief Nitze on what had gone on. I gave him the details of our sessions and added some color about our strange working conditions, the last-minute rushing about and so forth. To my surprise, he later described our adventures to his colleagues but converted them into a sarcastic attack on how not to negotiate with the Soviets.

And so the first "historic" summit ended. I did not go on to Iran, the next stop for the president's party, but returned to Washington to help prepare the formal briefings on the SALT agreement, which would have to take place immediately on Nixon's return. While we were in Moscow we were bombarded by alarming telegrams from Haig in Washington, who, as Kissinger's deputy, was predicting the worst (his natural style). But little opposition developed. There was some muttering by Senator Henry Jackson, but he called Kissinger and offered to cooperate. The agreements were generally well received. In time they passed the Senate by an overwhelming vote of 88 to 2.

In the event, these first agreements freezing offensive strategic missiles for five years remained in force for the next fifteen years. The ABM treaty had no terminal date. Their significance was quite simple: the two superpowers had agreed that they would remain vulnerable to a nuclear attack and would not attempt to build a significant defense against it. If possible, they would try to limit and reduce their offensive weapons. Both sides thus were groping for a concept of a stable strategic relationship. Given the deep, long hostility between the United States and the Soviet Union, the agreements were a profound accomplishment. That the United States and the Soviet Union have stuck to this basic bargain, despite major changes of leadership on both sides, testifies to its underlying validity. Neither side wanted the uncertainty of unbridled competition in *both* offensive and defensive weapons. They agreed that such competition would be more dangerous than exposing their countries to continuing vulnerability.

The situation did not change until March 1983, when Ronald Reagan abruptly revived the broad question of whether the United States should erect a space-based defense of the entire country—the Strategic Defense Initiative, widely known as Star Wars. In 1972 that question was ruled out on both strategic and technical grounds. The defensive weapons systems were much too primitive and ineffective to defend the entire land-mass of the United States. It is a commentary on the durability of the original bargain that Reagan's SDI proposal was not unanimously embraced, even though the new technology of lasers is far more promising than the technology available in 1972. In fact, the Star Wars plan has provoked another divisive debate, still to be resolved. And even in this debate, the fifteen-year-old ABM treaty finds strong defenders.

On the other hand, the 1972 turning point did little to stop strategic offensive arms. In the years that followed, these weapons (bombers and missiles) were frozen in number but not in quality. Thus single-warhead missiles were replaced with multiple warheads. The MIRV explosion was especially dev-astating and discouraging. The United States increased from about 1,700 missile warheads to about 10,000 warheads. The Soviets eventually reached about the same figure. Indeed, to persuade the Congress that the United States could safely ratify these SALT agreements signed in Moscow, Defense Secretary Laird asked for an accelerated offensive program (the B-1 bomber, the Trident submarine), and the Congress was quick to give him almost everything he asked for. Thus, the first strategic arms control agreement actually produced a sizable buildup in strategic weaponry. In this strange way—through a combination of arms control limits on the one hand, and unilateral military programs on the other—the two superpowers built into their relationship a new strategic foundation that survived the dangerous political turmoil that followed a few years later.

Unfortunately, these agreements also prompted a burst of undue optimism about the future. No one in the Kissinger or Nixon entourage believed in the rhetoric about "transforming" the Soviet-American relationship that was used in public statements. There was a belief that we could develop a broader and safer relationship, especially with Brezhnev in power. He had, after all, gone ahead with the summit, despite the mining and bombing of North Vietnam. He had signed a statement of principles concerning the conduct of relations, which we interpreted as a willingess to practice some restraint in his policies. Most important, inside the Soviet Union he started to declare a major commitment to the "irreversibility" of détente.

This was also the American intention—to make the gains irreversible. But it was not to be. While Nixon was basking in the postsummit sunshine in Key Biscayne, shortly after he had returned to the United States via Teheran and Warsaw, a "third-rate" burglary occurred in an office in the Watergate complex.

Détente did open a new era in relations between the superpowers and marked the closing of an old one, reflected in the Berlin and German agreements. Of course, Europe remained divided, but ties between the two parts would grow substantially. Trade increased, as did the other trappings of normal relations in Europe. Over the years, détente became more and more of a European phenomenon, which was its strength. But the focus on Europe would also prove to be one of détente's principal weaknesses. What was not settled in the 1972–1973 heyday was how the superpowers would relate in Third World conflicts. Thus détente was still vulnerable to crisis outside the main arena of confrontation—Central Europe.

Looking back now, I realize that Soviet-American relations were altered in this period not by a better "understanding" or more contacts but by a change in the raw balance of power in favor of a new anti-Soviet coalition. Soviet motives in pursuing détente, while related to their objectives in Central Europe and to the limitation of strategic arms, also reflected their concern that *two* separate fronts—in Europe and in Asia—were coalesc-

ing against the USSR. As a consequence, for the Soviets a U.S.
willingness to drop the China option and take up a semialliance
with Moscow gradually became a critical test of détente.

For the United States, détente achieved one of its original
purposes when the war in Vietnam was officially ended by the
Paris agreements of January 1973. It is highly unlikely that
this point could have been reached without the prior American
rapprochement with both China and the Soviet Union. The
ending of direct American involvement in Indochina permitted
a focus on the more fundamental strategic questions that still
remained in Soviet-American relations. Without Vietnam, could
a basic U.S.-Soviet accommodation be developed?

Contradictory aspects of American policy began to emerge.
On the one hand, Washington would be free of some of the
political divisions created by Vietnam. On the other hand, an
accommodation with Moscow, which had been justified by
Vietnam requirements, would now come under more stringent
scrutiny by critics. And Soviet-American relations would have
to encompass some new and difficult elements. European
military relaxation to complement the political accommodation
of the German treaties, for example, would have to include
some significant reductions in Soviet military predominance in
Central Europe. This would require major Soviet concessions—
which were never forthcoming. Long-term stabilization of the
strategic nuclear balance would also involve extensive concessions by both sides. And building a bilateral relationship would
have to include a new policy on trade and credits. These
concerns became general American objectives. They required
an increasing Soviet acceptance of the status quo—an acceptance at the very geopolitical moment when the Soviets were
claiming and achieving a strategic equality that they believed
entitled them to political gains in the conflict with the United
States.

Would Leonid Brezhnev be disposed to engage in the
accommodation that the United States required? In many ways
he was ideally suited to pursue a policy of détente. He was a
prudent, conservative political leader; he was drawn to pragmatism. He was the son of a steel worker, had been one himself,
and had served as a soldier. He was not an intellectual but
rather was an activist who had the stamina and nerve to rise
in Soviet politics during the 1930s and after the war. He was

personable enough to make a career in politics. He was certainly
no liberal-minded dove, as some Americans were disposed to
think. On the contrary, he had achieved high office in Stalin's
time and even occupied a junior position on Stalin's last
Politburo. After the war, he had administered the newly
occupied former Romanian territories of Moldavia, not a
position Stalin would assign to a civil libertarian. For a brief
time he was commissar of the Soviet navy. His career had
prospered under Khrushchev's patronage, but eventually he
had turned on his patron and joined, or led, a conspiracy to
remove him from power in 1964.

Brezhnev's own policies had been carefully conservative in
almost every sense. He ended Khrushchev's de-Stalinization
and partially rehabilitated Stalin's reputation. He brushed aside
the idea of major economic reforms but was a sporadic advocate
of consumerism. He reassured the party bureaucrats by guaranteeing their tenure in office, and he campaigned against
dissidence of every stripe. Above all, he unleashed the industrial
forces that would make the USSR a nuclear superpower—at
an eventual cost to a vulnerable Soviet economy. And he
continued a strong, unyielding anti-Chinese policy, much as
Khrushchev had. But Brezhnev went even further: he added
a massive buildup of Soviet military power along the border.

Détente appealed to Brezhnev for several reasons. He naturally wanted the prestige of being treated as an equal by the
leaders of the West. But this was largely psychological. More
concretely, he wanted a period of calm in the West while he
tried to deal with China, preferably in alliance with the United
States but unilaterally if necessary. He wanted to achieve in
Europe what had eluded both Stalin and Khrushchev—a peace
settlement, including recognition of the division of Germany.
And, obviously, he wanted the material benefits of détente—
trade and assistance from the West. For this he was prepared
to pay, though only in carefully arranged installments.

Brezhnev could be charming and even persuasive. Once,
after a tough negotiating session, he began ruminating on his
wartime experiences and about his father. He told a rather
touching anecdote about the old man and his desire for peace.
His father had wanted to know the highest point in the land,
he recalled, so that Hitler could be hanged from it. There was
scarcely a dry eye in the room. Afterward, I rode back from

the Kremlin to our lodgings in the Lenin hills with Kissinger, who looked at me with a slight smile and asked if I could believe that this was the same man who had ordered the invasion of Czechoslovakia. It turned out that the story was a staple; it was repeated to President Carter six years later.

Nevertheless, we all came to like him, to the degree that was possible given the political circumstances. Brezhnev had a particular fondness for the small black binder-clips that we used to hold our papers together; he would surreptitiously pilfer them, and occasionally reach across the table and snatch one. During a week we spent with him at his dacha in Zavidovo, a small suburb outside Moscow, we gave him a box of clips wrapped as a present. He was delighted. The personal relationship even reached the point where he felt free to tell anti-Semitic jokes to Kissinger. Once, possibly sensing our discomfort at these jokes, he said, as translated, that some of his best friends were Jews. We all struggled not to laugh. Nevertheless, Brezhnev and Kissinger developed a rapport of sorts, which in international politics is a valuable attribute.

Brezhnev showed special deference to Nixon. He had found a photo of Nixon's "kitchen debate" with Khrushchev, with himself as an onlooker. He rather plaintively produced this photo, as if to prove his legitimacy.

In my view, we never quite appreciated that Brezhnev's détente policy may have been resisted inside the Soviet Politburo. One reason for our skepticism was that we were wary of being charged with the error of dividing the Soviet leaders into the good and the bad; there had been far too much foolishness along these lines in the past—during the war even Stalin was portrayed as our ally against the dark forces in the Kremlin.

Nevertheless, there were genuine divisions in the Soviet leadership over détente, and this became evident one day during the first Nixon summit. Brezhnev was mysteriously absent for one afternoon. It turned out that he had presided over the Politburo purge of one of his major rivals, Pyotor Shelest, the Ukrainian party leader. It was thought that Shelest had opposed Brezhnev's foreign policy, and that he had adopted too much of a Ukrainian nationalist position. Shelest was then required to join in the festivities surrounding Brezhnev's summit. He appeared at Nixon's reception at Spaso

House, our ambassador's residence. When he entered the room the Soviet guests immediately scattered as if he were a leper. He stood alone, somewhat bewildered, until the Soviet minister of culture, Katerina Furtseva, had the courage to approach him and, mercifully, lead him off to the side of the room.

In 1972, the Soviet leadership was still a triumvirate: Brezhnev, Premier Alexei Kosygin and the president, Nikolai Podgorny. Brezhnev and Podgorny seemed to enjoy a friendly relationship. Brezhnev, who was trying to ration his cigarette consumption, would steal from Podgorny's pack. Yet in 1977 Brezhnev unceremoniously pushed Podgorny out of office and took over the presidency himself so he could meet other world leaders as an official head of state rather than just the party chief.

Kosygin was a major force in the Brezhnev era, but he appeared only at the formal sessions; Kissinger never held any separate meetings with him, even though he was the premier. In 1971 Dobrynin had to urge Kissinger to stop addressing Nixon's letters to Kosygin and to send them to Brezhnev. The American analysis of the Politburo was that Brezhnev and Kosygin were rivals in domestic policy. Kosygin favored economic reforms, but Brezhnev had successfully opposed them in 1965. If they did disagree, there was no way to know this from their conduct at the summits.

Kosygin had the reputation in the West of being a "liberal," mainly because he favored economic reforms, but on the occasions when he spoke at the summit sessions, he was tough, even harsh. His presentations were turgid repetitions of standard Soviet positions that could have been found any day in *Pravda*. Whether this was for the record is difficult to know. His countenance was invariably dour; Kissinger proposed to Nixon that I be allowed to tell a joke to see if it was possible to get Kosygin to laugh. I remember one particular moment. At the end of a long session with Brezhnev during one of Kissinger's trips to Moscow, as we were walking down the long staircase from Brezhnev's Kremlin office, we passed Kosygin trudging slowly up the stairs, impassive and unmindful of the gang of Americans rushing down to their motorcade. Presumably, he was on his way to learn from Brezhnev the results of his meetings. This incident established more than most Kremlinology who was in fact in charge.

The role of Andrei Gromyko was always somewhat puzzling. Occasionally Brezhnev seemed curt and rude to him, but there were times he would defer to Gromyko, leaving it to him to make long presentations. Gromyko, of course, had an awesome reputation. He had, after all, been foreign minister since 1957 (he was finally removed by Gorbachev in 1985 but was elevated to the ceremonial presidency). Over the years, Gromyko had become a thorough professional, highly competent and irritatingly painstaking in style. Negotiating a document with him was an adventure in the wily arts of diplomacy; he would shift his ground and his arguments with ease, even contradicting himself and reversing his position.

Gromyko understood one thing clearly: that the Soviet system and Soviet society were poorly equipped for a flexible policy of international maneuvering. Thus, he tried to conduct a policy of seeking out and defending prepared positions, and he was quite successful in doing so. His style seemed better suited to the conservative Brezhnev than to the free-wheeling Khrushchev, and probably was not at all tuned to the more innovative Gorbachev.

Brezhnev and Gromyko were preoccupied with the United States, and, given their wartime memories, ill-disposed toward Japan and Germany. But it was China that was the critical element in the early days of détente. Brezhnev had raised the question of China directly with Kissinger during their April meeting that preceded the summit. Brezhnev had been irritated by Nixon's speech during the China trip, asserting that the United States and China were holding the world's fate in their hands. Brezhnev claimed that the Chinese were obsessed with achieving world hegemony and suggested that he and Nixon go into the matter in more detail later. When he visited the United States in June 1973, Brezhnev told Nixon he feared a U.S.-Chinese military agreement. He also speculated that within ten years the Chinese would become a nuclear threat to both the United States and the USSR.

At the end of the 1973 meeting in San Clemente, Brezhnev urged, as diplomatically as his obviously strong feelings allowed, that the United States not enter into any military agreement with China. He said that he had refrained from raising the question in 1972, but that he was now worried about the future on the Chinese front. He asserted that the Soviets had no intention of attacking China, but that if China were to have a military agreement with the United States, that would "confuse the issue." Gromyko quietly went a good deal further, warning Kissinger that a Chinese-American military agreement would mean war.

Against this general background, the last Nixon summit took place in June 1974—a meeting in which Brezhnev was to make an all-out effort to recruit the United States into a formal alliance against China.

IV

END IN THE
CRIMEA

It was June 30, 1974, in the Crimea. Nixon's second summit in the Soviet Union was in its final days—as was his presidency. Kissinger was fuming. So was Haig, by then Nixon's chief of staff. Even the usually impassive Gromyko looked mildly upset. The source of their common concern was not far away: two men sitting in a stone grotto on the shores of the Black Sea—Richard M. Nixon and Leonid Brezhnev. The world's most powerful leaders were locked in a private conversation, accompanied only by a Soviet interpreter. And they had been there for some time.

During the Moscow phase of Nixon's visit there had been no breakthrough in SALT negotiations. The last chance for a significant accomplishment was in this gathering at Brezhnev's beach house on the Black Sea, near Oreanda and not far from the famous czarist palace at Yalta. Brezhnev had requested a private meeting with Nixon. The rest of us were sitting around Brezhnev's large swimming pool. Occasionally someone would pace nervously around the pool or through the grounds that adjoined the low ranch-style house. But after a time everyone settled down to wait on their masters.

Eventually we were summoned. Nixon looked somber. Obviously nothing had happened to revive his spirits. He made a few remarks and turned the dialogue over to Kissinger. Brezhnev asked Kissinger to sum up the strategic arms negotiations. The two leaders had apparently been talking of something else.

I learned later that the subject had been Brezhnev's obsession: China. More directly than ever before, the Soviet leader had laid out before Richard Nixon the prospect of a treaty of alliance against China. After all the prior hints and probes, there it was, straight out: the United States and the Soviet Union, the two superpowers, would join forces, ostensibly against China, but in reality to police the world—the global condominium that was the nightmare not only of the men in Peking but of America's European allies as well.

Bold as it was, the overture was not surprising. For some years the Soviets had been testing the United States on this very issue. They had approached it from almost every angle. Brezhnev first raised the issue of China during Kissinger's secret visit to Moscow in April 1972, to prepare for the summit. But Brezhnev had avoided mentioning China to Nixon at the summit. Instead, at the end of the meetings he gave Nixon a Soviet proposal for an agreement to prevent the outbreak of nuclear war. This first draft specified that the United States and the USSR would take joint action against third parties in case of a threat of war; it took no expertise to recognize which third party Brezhnev had in mind. We negotiated for a year on this document. Brezhnev was not happy with our successful efforts to dilute the anti-Chinese aspects of his proposal, but an agreement to prevent the outbreak of nuclear war was finally completed and signed at the Brezhnev summit in Washington in June 1973. Brezhnev's discontent with the outcome prompted new warnings to Nixon in San Clemente, where he launched into a long discussion privately with Nixon.

Brezhnev's exposition was almost always the same: the United States did not fully understand the danger of China; within a decade the Chinese would pose a major nuclear threat. The Chinese, he contended, were obsessed with achieving world hegemony. He said Chinese strategy was summed up in Mao's epigram that China would sit on the mountain and watch the two tigers fight. Chinese policy, according to Brezhnev, was directed at driving the United States and the USSR toward a confrontation.

In May 1974, a month before the last Nixon summit, Brezhnev revived his anti-Chinese maneuvers. Kissinger and his team had spent several days with Brezhnev in a complex of country dachas in Zavidovo. Brezhnev took Kissinger on a Soviet-style safari to hunt wild boar. While comfortably sitting in a tree house, watching as the unsuspecting creatures approached their fatal feeding ground, Brezhnev laid out for Kissinger both his worries about the Chinese menace and the prospect of joining forces to block Moscow's one-time allies in the East. "Something has to be done about China," he exclaimed. What he proposed was joint Soviet-American action, in the case of war, and even in the face of a threat of war. In the grotto on that day with Nixon in the Crimea, Brezhnev made virtually the same proposal—an unconditional treaty of nonaggression, which in actual practice was an alliance against China.

Between 1972 and 1974, Kissinger had repeatedly tried to mollify Brezhnev by promising that we would not enter into any military arrangements with China directed against Russia. Nevertheless, in dealing with specific Soviet proposals, such as the agreement to prevent the outbreak of nuclear war, Kissinger had to drain them of any anti-Chinese substance, and he also kept the Chinese informed of the state of his negotiations with Moscow. Brezhnev's concerns over China were genuine, and he was never reassured by Kissinger's explanations; indeed, it was not possible to allay Brezhnev's fears without joining his anti-Chinese strategy. Kissinger continued to argue that the problems of war and peace in the near term concerned the two superpowers primarily; but he also acknowledged that in the longer term this might change, if China and Japan were eventually to combine against Russia and the United States.

When Kissinger informed the Chinese about Brezhnev's proposals, their reaction was to brush off Soviet threats. Mao Tse-tung insisted that Russia was "pitiful" but said that the United States was not reacting firmly enough. "Shadow boxing," he called it. Mao accused the United States of trying to turn Russia eastward, much as the Western powers had done with Hitler in the 1930s. Once Russia became bogged down in

China, he said, the United States would be able to overthrow the regime from the rear. But after the October 1973 Middle East crisis, the Chinese shifted their line. They began to play up the danger of a Soviet attack, even though they continued to argue that Soviet ambitions were constrained by Soviet weaknesses.

It is a safe assumption that both Moscow and Peking gave each other their own versions of their exchanges with the United States. Thus, in 1973, the Soviets, while negotiating with the United States for an agreement to prevent nuclear war, gave the Chinese an almost identical proposal two weeks before the Nixon-Brezhnev summit in Washington. The Chinese informed the Americans, but belatedly. The Soviets never informed us.

Throughout, the United States had been politely but firmly turning away the obvious thrusts from Moscow. Thus, nothing had come of the Soviet maneuvers until June 1974, when a politically crippled president sat on the shore of the Black Sea and was tempted. Obviously, if Nixon took Brezhnev's bait on China there would be a payoff in the SALT negotiations and Nixon's third summit would be a success—a success that might just save the wounded president from his impending impeachment.

It must have been agonizing for Nixon. Probably not much more than a hint of interest would have satisfied Brezhnev at that point; Nixon could then have returned home with a triumph, a new agreement limiting strategic missiles that would head off the dreaded Soviet buildup of forces all were then predicting in Washington. He could have confronted his critics and challenged them to remove a chief executive at a moment so critical for the national security: only he could consummate the SALT negotiations with Brezhnev. His enemies would have found themselves stymied. How could they drive a president from office at such a sensitive juncture?

Whether or not these were Nixon's daydreams as he sat motionless while Brezhnev and Kissinger jousted, he decided to resist the temptation. Later, he told Kissinger of Brezhnev's offer on China. They decided nothing could be gained from confronting Brezhnev with a rejection then and there, but Kissinger subsequently made it clear to Ambassador Dobrynin that Brezhnev's proposal was not acceptable. Ever the European

historian, Kissinger alluded to the famous meeting between
the czar and the kaiser at Björkö in 1905, where the two
sovereigns concluded a secret alliance, to the astonishment of
their governments. Their ministers quickly repudiated them.

This Chinese angle of the private talks was not yet known
to us as Kissinger turned the meeting to SALT. Brezhnev
found a dozen reasons why the latest American offer was not
satisfactory. He was clearly not about to sign on to a new
strategic arms agreement without knowing where he stood in
his projected alliance against China. Kissinger laid out the
American terms for a new agreement restricting strategic arms.
The main proposal was for a special subceiling on Soviet
multiple warhead missiles (MIRVs), which would give the
United States a slight advantage to make up for the larger
overall Soviet missile and bomber forces. The limits on MIRVed
missile launchers then being negotiated were about 850 for the
Soviet Union and 1,000 for the United States—substantially
below the level of 1,200 eventually agreed to in the 1979 treaty
of Jimmy Carter. But the Kissinger exposition was almost an
academic exercise.

Brezhnev, flanked for the first time in these encounters by
two general officers, produced a stream of arguments and
statistics to prove that he needed to catch up with the United
States. His statistics were so badly skewed to show American
advantage that when we reported his presentation to American
intelligence, they used it for months to show Soviet perfidy.
The fact is that the Kissinger proposal for a ceiling on MIRVed
missiles would have blocked the Soviet effort to catch up and
would have preserved an American lead. Brezhnev was not
inclined to bargain, and after more than two hours, he and
Nixon agreed that it was time for a boat ride on the Black Sea,
a welcome relief to a dreary debate.

The summit was over. We did not fully realize it that day in
the Crimea, but we suspected that any opportunities there
might have been had come and gone. The boat ride along the
shore of the Crimea was pleasant enough but there was an air
of disappointment. Brezhnev played the host, explaining the
sights along the shore to Nixon. The president was in some
obvious discomfort since his leg was infected with phlebitis,
which was soon to prove life-threatening. We passed Yalta and
the Livadia Palace, where the Big Three—Roosevelt, Stalin and

Churchill—had met more than thirty years before. I wondered what must have been the thoughts of Richard Nixon, who had made his early career by assaulting the treachery of that very place.

Brezhnev donned his dark glasses and, clad in a sporty blue jacket, sat at the rear of the boat and conducted his sightseeing tour. It was a rather elegant yacht, with a Bokhara carpet laid over the deck and a few deck chairs arranged in a semicircle around the two leaders. After a time, the group began to unbend and stroll around the deck.

I tried to engage the two Soviet generals, who seemed baffled at being caught up in this strange gathering. But they were politely reticent. After a snack we came back on deck, and I noticed that sitting in the back of the yacht, completely alone, was Richard Nixon. I went to him and offered a few remarks about the similarity between the Crimean coast and that of southern California. The crowd moved downstairs as the boat approached the dock. Nixon made his way painfully down the stairs and onto the landing. He walked for a moment with Brezhnev and Gromyko and then summoned Kissinger, and the two of them walked alone along the seawall. It was a poignant moment as they receded in the distance.

They both knew that Nixon would not be returning triumphant as he had only two years earlier. Although the détente that the two of them had so carefully orchestrated had not yet ended—it would continue for several years—the political momentum and the intellectual vision that animated it were collapsing.

Among most defenders of détente it has become customary to blame Watergate for its failure. A weakened president could not carry out his grand design; his critics filled the vacuum and gradually undermined what had been achieved in those first years. There is much to be said for this view. Surely a healthy and vigorous Nixon would have found a way to bull through another SALT agreement with Brezhnev and to ward off assaults from the right.

There is obviously much more to Soviet-American relations than the contributions of personalities; and too much should not be attributed to the political scandals. But in my view Watergate did play a decisive role in preventing a lasting breakthrough in those relations.

Until the summer of 1973 the Soviets seemed puzzled by the affair and not inclined to take it too seriously. When Brezhnev visited the United States that June, however, the Soviets began to pay attention. Indeed, it would have been hard not to. The famous Senate hearings conducted by Senator Sam Ervin, with John Dean, Nixon's former counsel, in the witness chair, had to be postponed temporarily so as not to embarrass the White House during Brezhnev's visit. But the Soviet leader had no sooner left San Clemente than the press returned to the Watergate attack. The Soviets did not miss this, and Dobrynin began to chide Kissinger about it. Thereafter, Dobrynin performed what Kissinger called the Watergate ritual, needling the secretary of state periodically about his master's political indisposition.

Yet it is not clear that the Soviets drew any firm conclusions. Dobrynin's comments were in the nature of tactical gamesmanship. The Soviets continued to treat Kissinger and Nixon as if they were in full possession of their powers. And, occasionally, they would even reassure the Americans. Gromyko went so far with Kissinger as to express his hope that Nixon would soon overcome his "problems." Even Mao dismissed it as a meager affair.

Watergate was like a low-grade fever; it made for continuing discomfort and suddenly would burst into a new virulence. How far this penetrated foreign policy was painfully evident during the Yom Kippur war in October 1973. As the crisis mounted, the Soviets invited Kissinger to Moscow to work out a cease-fire. His arrival coincided with the "Saturday night massacre" in Washington, when Nixon fired his attorney general, Elliot Richardson, and Richardson's deputy, William Ruckleshaus. As reports of this crisis came over the wires to Moscow there was great confusion in Kissinger's party about what, in fact, had happened. The confusion led to irritation between the Kissinger group in Moscow and the White House (there is a nine-hour time lag between the two capitals). The White House could not understand that we, in far-off Moscow, did not fully comprehend the magnitude of the political crisis unfolding in Washington. (Ironically, Haig, as Nixon's chief of staff, had cited the tensions in the Middle East and Kissinger's presence in Moscow as arguments why Richardson should soldier on and not resign.) For our part, we in Moscow could not understand why the White House had not shown more sensitivity for our negotiations in the Kremlin. Clearly, ships passing in the night.

As it became apparent how much political damage Nixon had done to himself, we began to ponder whether the Soviets would try to exploit the fiasco in our negotiations for a Middle East cease-fire. Until then we had calculated that the Soviets were on the defensive because Israeli forces were about to break through across the Suez Canal and encircle Sadat's army. We calculated that Brezhnev would appeal for a quick cease-fire, and this would put us in a position to dictate the terms; a rough bargain would be struck in which Israel would be recognized for the first time as a legitimate negotiating partner by the Arabs—and, of course, we would earn some credit with Sadat. At least that was Kissinger's strategy. But with another Watergate blowup, he worried that perhaps the Soviets would now try to maneuver and play for time. They did not. Brezhnev still seemed eager to settle. Apparently he was unaware of what, exactly, was happening to Nixon that weekend. But it was a sharp lesson in the vulnerabilities imposed by the unfolding Watergate crisis.

We flew directly from Moscow to Tel Aviv, a historic first; Kissinger offered to give Dobrynin a ride, but he wisely declined. Over the Mediterranean, Navy F-4 fighters from a carrier flew alongside as we descended to Tel Aviv. The airport was alive with American C-5As, landing and unloading tanks and equipment, a reminder of Israel's total dependence on the United States. Kissinger went to meet with Golda Meir, while Sonnenfeldt and I waited at the airport. I was disappointed to learn that it was not possible to get a good hot-pastrami-on-rye sandwich in Tel Aviv.

A few days later, on October 22, Watergate flared up again when the United States alerted its military forces in reply to Brezhnev's threat of Soviet intervention in the Middle East, contained in a letter to Nixon. For the American press the American alert was simply a Nixon ploy to take the heat off Watergate. It was not. Indeed, it was a very tense period; many of us were convinced that the Soviets were prepared to land troops in Egypt. Watergate was the last thing on the minds of Kissinger, Haig and Secretary of Defense James Schlesinger on that fateful night. But, again, the episode was a lesson.

Watergate was, in John Dean's famous phrase, a cancer: it
seemed to be growing and infecting the conduct of foreign
policy.

But then it would again subside and an uneasy calm would
descend over the White House. In early 1974, I attended a
National Security Council meeting on the day I was sworn in
as chief of intelligence in the State Department (thus leaving
the NSC staff after five years and following Kissinger to the
State Department; Kissinger had become secretary of state in
September 1973 but retained his position as national security
adviser). As the NSC advisers assembled in the cabinet room
for the meeting and awaited Nixon's entrance, I chatted with
Haig and naturally asked him whether Watergate was about at
an end. He assured me that the tide was turning in Nixon's
favor. Even allowing for Haig's natural exuberance, which in
the NSC staff we knew so well, I was persuaded that he was
right. In fact, in the middle level of the White House staff
almost no one then thought Watergate would end in impeachment or resignation.

Within a few weeks, however, opinions began to waver. We
also began to detect evidence that the Soviets were pulling
back. In a memorandum to Kissinger, Sonnenfeldt and I
concluded in early 1974 that the administration's position was
becoming weaker; it was in danger of becoming a lame duck.
We noted a new Soviet ambivalence. On the one hand, they
wanted to bind Nixon's successor through bargains with Nixon,
but on the other hand, they worried that he could not deliver.
The uncertainties had grown considerably. We concluded that
"détente was in jeopardy," and that the Soviets were beginning
to reassess their relations with the United States.

By that pleasant day in June 1974, in the Crimea, Nixon's
fate had already been sealed in Washington. Sensing that the
result could be a foreign policy disaster, especially if the Soviets
became more aggressive, Kissinger, with Nixon's concurrence,
rather wisely sought a commitment from Brezhnev to attend
another summit meeting quite soon, rather than waiting for
another year, as had become the custom. But by the time the
meeting took place, in Vladivostok, in the Soviet Far East, that
November, it was Gerald Ford who was sitting opposite the
Soviet leaders.

The flight back to Moscow from the Crimea proved to be a

rare opportunity. Nixon had gone on to Byelorussia to a memorial for World War II victims. (The site was called Katin, which unfortunately was confused by some of the press with the infamous Katyn forest, where Stalin had the Polish officer corps massacred in 1939.) Confusion and plain bad luck seemed to dog Nixon. He had insisted that his meeting in the Crimea be named for Oreanda, the small seaside resort where in fact he was housed and the meetings occurred. Unfortunately, the American press filed its dispatches from Yalta, and that became the dateline. So much for advance planning.

While Nixon was headed for his ceremonial duties, Kissinger and his small staff flew back to Moscow on Brezhnev's private aircraft. This permitted more informal talks with the Soviets. I was in the outer cabin talking with Brezhnev's national security adviser, Andrei Alexandrov-Agentov, Gromyko's press aide, Leonid Zamyatin and some others. It was intriguing to listen to the small talk. They were apparently old colleagues and, much as their American counterparts might do, they began to reminisce. They had worked together in various capacities over the years, and I realized that there was something to the black art of Kremlinology—who had worked with whom and where were, in fact, important details. They had all risen in the ranks together but had taken different paths. Some, like Zamyatin, were obviously Gromyko protégés; others had worked in a group that had concentrated on German affairs. Alexandrov had been in the Soviet foreign service, working on Nordic countries, when he was assigned to Brezhnev in 1961. He wrote speeches and, as talented men often do, made himself indispensable and thus earned a permanent position on Brezhnev's staff. As Brezhnev moved up in the hierarchy, so did Alexandrov. He stayed on as a Politburo adviser after Brezhnev's death and was finally retired by Gorbachev.

No secrets were divulged in my presence, but it was a chance to observe some of the staff outside the formal confrontations over the negotiating table. Alexandrov showed me the press summary prepared for Brezhnev, which he had just retrieved from the rear cabin. The first item, ironically, was datelined Peking. It was, however, simply an innocuous report from the Soviet news agency, Tass—about as removed as it could be from the explosive offer of an anti-Chinese alliance that was the day's real news.

This brief interlude ended and soon we were back to the realities of the final days of the summit. Kissinger and Gromyko had one more session, and by normal standards the summit did achieve some results. A treaty was signed limiting underground nuclear testing to a low level—no more than 150 kilotons in size. There was an agreement to prevent the altering of environmental conditions for military purposes. Finally, Nixon and Brezhnev agreed on an important amendment to the antiballistic missile (ABM) treaty of 1972. In the original treaty, both sides had been permitted two separate ABM sites; in this amendment both sides would cut back to only one site. Brezhnev made the interesting side comment that the scientists had concluded that ABM had "little effect," but why not let "them" have their one area to do what they wanted?

Kissinger briefed a cantankerous press corps that badgered him about the failure to get a SALT agreement. The late Peter Lisagor of the *Chicago Daily News* persisted in questions that implied that the Joint Chiefs of Staff had vetoed a new SALT agreement because it would concede military superiority to the Soviets. Questions of this kind finally provoked Kissinger, and in exasperation he said, "One of the questions we have to ask ourselves as a country is: What, in the name of God, is strategic superiority? What is the significance of it, politically, militarily, operationally, at these levels of numbers? What do you do with it?"

These were remarks that he would always regret. His rhetorical outcry subjected him to endless lectures, especially from his former academic colleagues, on the meaning of superiority. Kissinger, of course, answered his own question many times. Perhaps his most concise statement came shortly after the summit and Nixon's resignation. It was made before the potentially hostile audience at an American Legion convention on August 20, 1974:

"Today, we, as well as the Soviet Union, must start from the premise that in the nuclear era an increase in certain categories of military power does not necessarily represent an increase of usable political strength. When two nations are already capable of destroying each other, an upper limit exists beyond which additional weapons lose their political significance. The overwhelming destructiveness of nuclear weapons makes it difficult to relate their use to specific political objectives and may indeed generate new political problems."

Kissinger's question about the meaning of superiority in the nuclear age is still relevant. Neither side has developed a convincing answer in the intervening thirteen years.

The summit drew to a close with a reception in the Kremlin. There was music and forced cordiality. Soviet orchestras have concluded that "Turkey in the Straw" is very popular in America. They played it over and over. The entire Politburo, minus the mysterious KGB chief, Yuri Andropov, turned out (many Americans in later years would claim to have met Andropov that evening but he was not there). It was fascinating for me to observe the men who had previously only been names in *Pravda*. I chose to converse with Fyodor Kulakov, who was widely regarded as one of the new generation that would eventually take power after Brezhnev. He was the youngest member of the Politburo at that time. Kulakov was quite personable. He spoke some English and said he was eager to visit the United States, especially the Midwest. Despite a long association with Soviet agriculture, that graveyard of Soviet political fortunes, he was indeed on his way to the very top. But a few years later, in 1978, he died suddenly and was replaced in Moscow by a protégé from his own political bailiwick in the Caucasus. His name: Mikhail Gorbachev.

As the festivities ended, President Nixon motioned me over and said, "Get me General Haig," which of course I did. They were the last words I was to hear from him while he was president. I have often thought how well that plaintive request summed up his plight.

Nixon's return to the United States was strange. In order to avoid Washington, he had arranged to land at a remote air force base in Maine. When the backup plane on which I had traveled arrived, we joined a small crowd to await the arrival of Air Force One and the president. There was a local high-school band warming up, and Vice President Gerald Ford was on hand with a small entourage.

It was a striking contrast to the grand reception in Washington two years earlier. Then Nixon was a great statesman returning with an unprecedented arms control treaty. Now the reception was almost pathetic.

The press was almost gleeful in writing off Nixon, the summit and détente with Brezhnev. An "epitaph for détente," *The Washington Post* editorialized. Liberals hated Nixon; even though they had pressured him to conciliate the Soviets in 1969, they were now gloating over his political problems. They were also beginning to realize that Nixon's foreign policy might become a casualty of Watergate.

It is still difficult to recall that period between the end of the summit in Moscow and Nixon's resignation on August 9, 1974. It seemed as if Nixon was almost a fugitive, first vacationing in Key Biscayne and then in San Clemente. I spent my time trying to pick up the pieces of the SALT negotiations and participating in what turned out to be a frustrating attempt to save our détente policy.

As concern mounted over what was perceived as Nixon's failure on SALT in Moscow, the assault on détente also continued to grow. Even before the summit, Senator Jackson had taken a few shots against the anticipated SALT agreements, revealing what he claimed was a coverup of "secret" agreements concluded during Nixon's first summit negotiation in Moscow in 1972. The charges were absurd and soon fizzled, but they were indicative of the poisoned atmosphere in Washington.

Another indication of the waning of support for détente was the shift in attitudes toward trade with the Soviet Union. In 1972, *The New York Times,* after the first Nixon-Brezhnev summit, had complained of the lack of progress in economic relations. In September 1974, after the last summit, trade was no longer the key to Soviet-American relations but a technological trap: "The danger of détente as it has been pursued therefore is that the United States may get an eloquently expressed design for interrelationships while the Russians get a new generation of computers."

The spirit of growing skepticism was best expressed by that most astute observer the late Hans Morgenthau, who wrote that détente had become a "disembodied spirit" preventing a detached examination of the "objective factors of interests and power."

In collaboration with Senator J. W. Fulbright, Kissinger agreed that it was necessary to try to establish a broad public platform for détente to rally supporters. The vehicle for this would be a major statement of policy by Kissinger, given before

Fulbright's Senate Foreign Relations Committee. For most of July we worked on drafts of the formal statement that Kissinger would present. Kissinger, of course, was preoccupied with Nixon's plight, and this simply increased his natural irritation at the imperfect drafts produced by his staff.

The date set for Kissinger's testimony (August 8) began to loom ominously. The chances that Richard Nixon would remain in office until then were dwindling. So the testimony was postponed, and some of us questioned whether the entire project should not be abandoned. It hardly seemed the most propitious time to man the ramparts in defense of détente.

Our fears were justified. When the hearing actually took place in September, after Nixon's resignation, Kissinger delivered a comprehensive statement that was almost totally ignored.

Fulbright concluded that détente was dying not of inconsistency but of indifference: "I find there seems to be an indifference to the idea of détente partly because of a feeling that it is futile and I do not know how you overcome that. . . . When the Secretary [Kissinger] advanced it there was widespread interest in it and now as you can see from the committee this morning, there is relatively little."

Fulbright's complaint was underlined when one of the illustrious members of his committee, Jacob Javits, fell asleep.

Watergate inflicted a severe wound to the development of Soviet-American relations. Critical blows to détente were delivered by the desertion of the same liberal constituency that had supported trade, SALT and the general relaxation of tensions. They gradually withdrew their mandate, in part because of disenchantment with the Soviet repression against Jews and intellectuals, in part because of disenchantment with the limited scope and slow pace of strategic arms control, but also in some measure because of their historic resentment of Richard Nixon. The disappearance of Nixon left his principal foreign policy achievements as his only monuments—the opening to China and relaxation with the Soviet Union. The latter was the more vulnerable target. Both liberals and conservatives could temporarily join forces against it: the conservatives attacking SALT and the liberals linking expanded trade with free emigration.

This was the situation inherited by the new president. Now it fell to Gerald Ford to preserve the opening to Moscow—a task that was to prove more and more difficult.

V

THE ROAD
TO VLADIVOSTOK

On November 23, 1974, Gerald Ford and his entourage flew from Tokyo to an airfield in the maritime provinces of Russia, about an hour's train ride north of the city of Vladivostok. The airfield was clearly a military base, but all the fighter aircraft had been carefully concealed in shelters. Indeed, the entire base resembled a ghost town, covered with deep white snow: almost no one was in sight—except for a small band of officials in their traditional huge fur hats. They turned out to be Leonid Brezhnev and his staff. After the customary greetings, mercifully shortened because of the frigid weather, the Ford party was whisked away by a fleet of shiny black limousines to a nearby railroad station, which was surprisingly modern, even though we were deep in the wilderness. The train was a Russian classic, with its charming interior decor right out of the nineteenth century. A pot-bellied stove at one end of the car was tended by a Russian babushka who could have been provided by central casting. I found myself thinking of scenes from *Doctor Zhivago* as the journey continued along the rail line to Vladivostok, passing occasional isolated wooden cottages that also seemed almost too picture-perfect. I also thought of Potemkin.

Ford and Brezhnev and their immediate staffs rode in the dining car, and a friendly conversation took place, but without any particular substance. It soon became apparent that Brezhnev was comfortable with Ford, who was in many ways more compatible with Brezhnev's personality than Nixon had been. Both were rugged outdoor men of action; they loved sports and good stories, and in other times or other places might have become genuinely friendly. The following year, when they met again at Helsinki, Brezhnev confided to Ford that he was hoping for his reelection—a rather unusual and risky remark for a Soviet leader. During the journey to Vladivostock the two leaders agreed to start their formal negotiations with a general review and then turn to the SALT issues.

The train's destination was the Okeanskaya Sanatorium, a primitive resort for vacationing workers and servicemen from the nearby area. It was rough but serviceable and probably had been picked to keep the visiting Americans as far away as possible from Vladivostok and the Soviet naval base. We were later given a whirlwind tour of Vladivostok. It turned out to be quite a modern city, more impressive than many in European Russia. There were many buildings under construction, a program obviously intended to reassure the population of the permanence of Russian power. Nevertheless, it had an eerie quality—a quaint city that could have been lifted out of Central Europe but set in the vastness of Siberia. And it was easy to understand the need for reassurance, as one looked out the train window and saw a low ridge of hills beyond which was China.

China was already on our minds. Kissinger was scheduled to visit Peking immediately after the Vladivostok meetings. Those few of us who knew of the previous exchanges on Brezhnev's secret project for an anti-Chinese alliance were still wondering how he would play the issue with a new president. In October, when Kissinger had made his first visit to Moscow after Nixon's resignation, Brezhnev had warned that he intended to bring up China with Ford. When he did so—in private after the Vladivostok negotiations were finished—Ford simply listened and asked some questions. Nothing further was said. But Brezhnev was sufficiently satisfied so that after the summit he decided to stop in Ulan Bator, the capital of Outer Mongolia, where he attacked the Chinese for their demands to recover territory lost to the Russians in the nineteenth century. In that speech, Brezhnev said that the Chinese were demanding the withdrawal of Soviet forces from "areas of our territory, to which the Chinese leaders decide now to lay claims, which they began to call disputed areas." Brezhnev drew a stern conclusion: "Comrades, it is absolutely clear that this position is totally untenable and we reject it."

It was notable that only a few days after meeting the new president of the United States, Brezhnev should want to stress again that there had been no thaw in Sino-Soviet relations following Nixon's resignation. We also suspected that in choosing Vladivostok for the summit, Brezhnev could not resist rubbing salt into Chinese wounds, since Vladivostok was one of the disputed areas that he mentioned in his speech. And, of course, after the meetings in Vladivostok, Kissinger went directly to Peking; and this was not lost on Brezhnev. Kissinger later admitted that agreeing to Vladivostok, a location in the areas that China claimed as lost territory, was a mistake. On reflection we decided that Brezhnev's speech was meant primarily as a signal of reassurance that despite Watergate and the resignation of Nixon, he was prepared to continue the main line of détente policies. For Brezhnev this was the real meaning of Vladivostok.

The principal issue at Vladivostok was how to move the SALT negotiations forward. Kissinger had already laid the groundwork during his October visit to Moscow. But Ford's problems were not only with Brezhnev. The new president was looking over his shoulder at his political standing at home. There had been an immediate groundswell of support when Ford took office, but this was a temporary reaction to the agonies of Watergate, and relief that, after all, Gerald Ford could restore normalcy. But his decision to pardon Nixon and thus free the former president from any threat of prosecution had badly damaged Ford's position. There was so much speculation that Ford had made a deal on the pardon that he broke precedent and testified before the Congress about his decision. A success in foreign policy would be useful to Ford because foreign affairs was the one area where he compared unfavorably with Nixon. In any case, Ford could not afford a failure abroad. So Vladivostok was a gamble: whatever was agreed to would have to pass muster in a Congress that was edgy and potentially hostile. Gerald Ford was particularly sensitive about Congress and knew it better than his advisers did.

He was also under some pressure to prove himself a tough negotiator, one who would see through the traps and snares of détente. The main requirement was that he emerge with an arms control agreement that was "equal," interpreted to mean equality in every category of weapons. This rather simple-minded view of what was at stake badly limited Ford's maneuvering room. In the end he succeeded in reaching an agreement that was, in fact, equal in all respects. But in doing so a greater opportunity was missed, the chance to bargain for limits on those Soviet weapons that concerned us most, even if the trading resulted in an outcome that was not strictly equal.

Ford probably had no choice: it was much too early in his term to start another bitter fight over SALT. His immediate aim had to be to preserve the broader policy of better relations with the USSR until he had sufficient time to examine his longer-term strategic options. This was a reasonable judgment, but, of course, we foresaw neither the fall of Saigon a few months later nor a series of other domestic and foreign policy blows that would, in the end, leave the work of Vladivostok uncompleted.

The obsession with equality in SALT was a psychological reaction to what had been developing for over a decade—the loss of unquestioned American nuclear superiority. Eventual parity with the Soviet Union had become inevitable by the end of the 1960s, but it was such an unsettling shock that many politicians simply refused to accept the prospects. Ironically, the same conservatives who excoriated the Russians for their perfidy and guile seemed to think that somehow Ford could talk them out of their nuclear programs. This was nonsense. But the political timing was wrong for the kind of complicated and nuanced agreement that would have, in fact, served American interests better than the Vladivostok accords.

The demands for simple equality in arms control also ran against the tide that had gradually been developing under Kissinger to treat arms control as part of international geo-political strategy, rather than as an exercise in bargaining over specific weapons. Under Nixon, there was strong feeling in the White House that SALT should be regarded as only the first in a series of agreements that would flow from a more basic change in relations. SALT was, therefore, of less interest for any particular technical achievements than for its strategic impact on the Soviets. Agreements were supposed to create vested interests in the process of accommodation, an argument basically accepted during Nixon's tenure. SALT I had been overwhelmingly approved. To be sure, there was criticism that it failed to meet mythical standards dreamed up either by diehard arms controllers or by the incorrigible right wing. Out of this first SALT debate had come a vague demand for an ideal agreement that would provide for strict equality. This was incorporated into the SALT ratification law passed in the Senate in 1972. Proposed by Senator Jackson, it directed that the next SALT agreement be based on equal levels of strategic arms. This meant that one of two things would have to occur: the Soviets would have to permit the United States a substantial increase in categories of weapons, which we could not develop in any case for several years, or we would have to persuade the Soviets to reduce their weapons, presumably to earn our good will.

This approach to arms control was a fatal error. It was an expression of frustration with the past rather than a valid prescription for the future. It failed to take into account that technology was moving so rapidly on both sides that the problem of equal numbers of various weapons would soon be meaningless. In a world of multiple warheads, increasing accuracy for missiles, and mutual vulnerability, defining and maintaining strategic stability between the two superpowers was taking on a new meaning. This new complexity was the cause of Kissinger's outburst on "nuclear superiority" in Moscow. Savants could supply smug answers, but no intellectual basis was being created for a new American strategy consistent with the circumstances that were sure to prevail in the late 1970s and early 1980s. This fluidity made arms control all the more important as part of a new nuclear strategy, but also all the more frustrating as a political exercise inside the United States. Kissinger believed that SALT gave us the chance to test whether Soviet policy was engaged in merely another tactical turn, or whether there was a new policy in gestation. The polarization of the American strategic debate made this test increasingly difficult and, finally, irrelevant.

The American debate over strategic arms control was, of

course, not a quixotic interlude promoted by irascible senators. It reflected a deep-seated distrust of the Soviet Union, a distrust that was fed by the relentless Soviet military buildup in the period following the defeat of Khrushchev in the Cuban missile crisis in 1962. The Soviet Union, however, owes Khrushchev more than has been admitted there or in this country. It was the much-maligned Khrushchev who created the foundation that Brezhnev was able to use to make the USSR a truly global military superpower, virtually, though not quite, the equal of the United States.

Khrushchev raised some fundamental questions about the Stalinist thesis of the inevitability of war, about the nature of a nuclear war and about its utility as an instrument of Soviet foreign policy. He appreciated, almost instinctively, the far-reaching political ramifications for the USSR of acquiring long-range nuclear rockets. He perceived the new opportunities for coercive diplomacy and psychological warfare. He recognized that strategic missiles symbolized the opening of a new era of East-West competition on a global scale. He created the Soviet strategic rocket forces as a separate branch of his armed forces and encouraged the development and production of the first three generations of Soviet ICBMs and of ballistic-missile-launching submarines.

Khrushchev, however, became obsessed with nuclear weapons as the only means of conducting modern warfare. From this conclusion he made frequent quantum leaps: denigrating the role of conventional weapons, brushing aside the Russian tradition of large standing armies and ridiculing large warships as obsolete. He tried desperately to translate his perception of a new nuclear balance into significant Soviet political gains, but this tight linkage between weapons balances and geopolitics led him into miscalculation: his imprudent attempt to exploit the perception of a missile gap, which was in fact nonexistent, led to ever more desperate moves to force Western concessions, and, finally, to his fateful Cuban adventure.

Khrushchev's removal was in itself enough to cause massive confusion. It soon became apparent, however, that military policy, along with all other major policies, was open for important revision. Brezhnev restored a balance among Soviet military components and began a laborious buildup across a broad front. Brezhnev's policies included not only a buildup of strategic missiles but also the strengthening of conventional ground forces, including substantial increases along the Chinese frontier in the Far East. The anti-Chinese program alone amounted to roughly 10 to 15 percent in the overall total of Soviet defense spending. In addition, plans were expanded for the Soviet fleet, for reequipping the Soviet army, especially in European Russia and Central Europe, and for creating new tactical air forces. Little wonder that the magnitude of such an effort would consume huge chunks of the Soviet Union's economic resources.

It is misleading, however, to read too much into the strategic buildup. The pace of Soviet ICBM deployments conformed very closely to the pace of the earlier American program. In other words, the Soviet pace was not a rapid one, since it followed more or less the production curve for U.S. ICBMs. Indeed, the similarity between the programs of the two super-powers is so striking as to suggest that the governing factors were narrow technical ones rather than the exalted strategic plans made by the various military and political staffs.

This similarity was obscured because actual Soviet ICBM deployments in the late 1960s greatly exceeded CIA intelligence projections, so that the buildup was treated as a virtual blitz-krieg. The CIA had been unwilling to make higher estimates of Soviet production, which would have been accurate, lest the agency be accused of creating an artificial missile gap, as had happened in the late 1950s.

The truly unique aspect of the Soviet buildup—the element that most worried American planners—was the existence of a huge ICBM (the SS-9 and its replacement, the SS-18). It was this missile that analysts seized on as proof of their worst-case fears, namely, that the USSR was planning a first strike against the U.S. missile silos, which would put the United States in an impossible position. If the United States retaliated with its submarine missiles, the Soviet Union could of course launch all of its remaining ICBMs against American cities. In 1969 this nightmarish scenario had been carefully analyzed in the NSC, where it was assigned marginal plausibility. But it grad-ually found great favor in the Pentagon and among political conservatives and became a major political factor influencing arms control proposals. When questions were raised about why the Soviet Union would take such a mad risk, they were never really answered, or were brushed aside as dovish quibbling.

The fact that the Pentagon's intelligence estimates of Soviet capabilities were wildly wrong did not help. If the CIA erred by estimating too low, the Pentagon more than compensated in the opposite direction. There were almost constant alarms that the Soviets were about to break through to strategic dominance—either with a new ICBM with multiple warheads or with a new ABM system. In retrospect, it is clear that the Soviets were proceeding rather prudently. The total number of Soviet ICBMs reached its peak of about 1,600 in 1971 and declined by 200 as a result of SALT I. It is also interesting that this final total of ICBMs, about 1,400, was not that much greater than the number the United States had planned to deploy in the early 1960s.

In the buildup of Soviet nuclear-missile-carrying submarines that followed, the American lead in technology was too substantial for the Soviets to copy the pace of the American production program. After resisting any limitations on submarine-launched missiles for a time in the first SALT negotiations, the Soviets finally settled for a ceiling (60 submarines) that was considerably higher than the ceiling on the U.S. submarines (44). This concession caused a huge outcry about inequality; but the fact is that the Soviets were not able to reach their prescribed limit until 1981, four years after the SALT I agreement should have expired. By then, the Soviet Union had to retire perfectly good, but older, nuclear submarines to stay under the ceiling. The United States did not have to face this dilemma until late 1985. So the United States suffered little from the infamous inequality of SALT.

But, of course, these complex realities could not have been known to President Ford as he prepared for Vladivostok. For the new president the only reality was that complaints about the Soviet military buildup, about SALT and about détente were growing.

One complaint was that the United States was ignoring the fact that, contrary to American opinion, the Soviets believed they could "fight and win" a nuclear war, and were indeed preparing to do so. The evidence for this serious charge in the mid-1970s was supposedly to be found in the esoteric writings of various Soviet military sources. Some of these articles were published in obscure Soviet journals, others appeared at book length and some were still secret; but ingenious American analysts pieced together an alarming story that the Soviets believed they could "win" a nuclear war.

This debate about Soviet doctrine was fruitless, because most of the claims concerning what the Soviets believed dissolved into a mass of ambiguities under any rigorous analysis. To be sure, the Soviets believed that they should prepare for a nuclear war or, for that matter, for any war. Given their experience of the German attack in 1941, preparedness had become almost a religion. But the idea that they held that nuclear war could be fought to some abstract concept of "victory" was much more elusive. Indeed, there seemed some grounds for concluding that their military and civilian leaders disagreed on this point. What I believed was truly worrisome was the assertion of Soviet military doctrine that the first phase of a nuclear war would be "decisive" in determining the outcome. Soviet officials repeatedly made that case, and it was not challenged from Khrushchev through Brezhnev. This could only mean that the Soviets would feel compelled to strike first in any crisis. And it followed that the Soviets would have to launch their own strategic forces on warning of an American attack.

This was truly alarming and dangerous. Arms control ought to address this situation if at all possible. Hence I believed reducing Soviet heavy missiles might reduce Soviet confidence in a first strike. This was a legitimate and worthwhile arms control objective, and the United States ought to pay a price to achieve it. True, the Soviets might still feel compelled by their history to strike first in any crisis, but their ability to do so would be diminished just enough so that they might take pause. This concern was quite different from the incredible Pentagon scenario that assumed the Soviets would launch an unprovoked surprise attack to take advantage of the so-called "window of ICBM vulnerability."

Soviet military doctrine remained a bogeyman and was the cause of unending harassment of the White House. It led to the formation of "Team B" by George Bush in 1976, when he was director of CIA. Team B was supposed to be a group of outside experts who would develop an alternative view to that of Team A, the CIA's own analysts. It was not really Eush's doing, since he understood little of the substance at that early point. The idea was proposed by the president's Foreign Intelligence Advisory Board, and I encouraged him to undertake the experiment, largely because I thought a new director ought to be receptive to new views; Bush's predecessor, William Colby, had turned it down.

The exercise turned out to be a license for an attack on Ford's own administration—a case of self-inflicted damage. Team B's report was written by Harvard Sovietologist Richard Pipes (who later served on the NSC under Reagan). The conclusion was that we had seriously underrated Soviet determination to pursue a strategy of victory in nuclear war. This judgment was especially misleading because at that very moment actual Soviet policy and doctrine were in fact changing, significantly. From 1977 on, Brezhnev began to denounce nuclear war as "suicidal." These new pronouncements also coincided with a turn-down in Soviet defense spending. As this became apparent the Carter administration was able to take a somewhat more sanguine view of Soviet intentions. Finally, in 1985, Gorbachev completed the evolution of Soviet doctrine when he dramatically abandoned the old Soviet position and agreed to Ronald Reagan's claim that a nuclear war "cannot be won and must never be fought."

When Ford went to Vladivostok, however, the debate about Soviet intentions was still open, and he had the practical problem of how to press forward on the arms control negotiations. Eliminating the Soviet heavy ICBM force was still the most desirable objective, but it was already quite obvious that it would be very, very difficult to accomplish. In fact, in October 1974, at the staff level, we could not see what Brezhnev's incentive would be to make the kind of concessions now that had been withheld from Nixon. All that we had in our favor as Ford prepared for Vladivostok was Brezhnev's general commitment to a policy of détente and perhaps some feeling in the Soviet military that they could not achieve true superiority. Thus, in a memorandum to Kissinger we wrote:

> This almost certainly is a time of considerable uncertainty in Moscow. There are probably arguments that now, with the change of Presidents, it is time to revitalize Soviet-American relations. But a Soviet leader could also argue that prudence

dictates a strategy of procrastination—at least until the outlook for the Ford Administration's survival is clear and the impact of the "crisis of capitalism" is clearer.

As best we can judge from all the evidence the decision, if there is one, is to proceed with the atmospherics of detente but to reserve on the substance. In other words, Brezhnev probably has no urgent incentive to make the concessions now that he withheld at the last summit, or that he can offer later.

Thus, a major and perhaps insurmountable problem is how to create an incentive for the Soviets to move.

That incentive was developed during the Kissinger visit to Moscow in October 1974, and it originated in a fortuitous set of circumstances. In brief, we offered to withdraw from our nuclear submarine base at Rota in Spain, which of course greatly intrigued Brezhnev.

Our offer came about because of the political changes during the last years of the Franco regime, as Prince (later King) Juan Carlos was given more power, and the movement toward democracy in Spain gained ground. The United States had to renegotiate a treaty that permitted our military bases in Spain, and we anticipated that once Franco was out of office, the left wing would mount a major effort against retaining the bases. Washington did not want to confront a new democratic government with an immediate test of its strength over U.S. bases. So we decided to abandon the nuclear submarine base, as a concession; at one stroke this would forestall a future debate over U.S. bases and especially over the presence of nuclear weapons. We could afford to give up Rota because the new Poseidon submarines did not require forward basing. We would retain our air bases, which were important for support in the Middle East. During the summer of 1974 we decided that if we intended to do this for Spain, why not present it to Brezhnev as part of a SALT bargain?

In the aftermath of Watergate we needed some bargaining power. In late August I had done a long analysis that showed the United States would not fall behind the Soviet Union if there was an unbridled "arms race," but that we would also stand to gain if we could reach an agreement around the levels that the Soviets were proposing. In fact, I thought that we might come out slightly ahead if we proceeded with our two major programs, the Trident submarine and the B-1 bomber, and also proceeded with a program to put some kind of a new mobile ICBM into active service over the next several years.

The mobile missile idea turned out not to be so simple. There was a plan in the Pentagon to place a mobile ICBM on an aircraft, thus operating an airborne ICBM rather than a land-mobile ICBM. Ten years later this idea for an airborne ICBM would be revived and called, appropriately, Big Bird. It was rudely dismissed by an incredulous Congress. In 1974, however, the Pentagon leaders were so carried away by the idea that they ordered the air force to stage a test, in which part of an old Minuteman ICBM was actually dropped out of the tail of a cargo plane and then ignited, apparently to show that it could be done. This had the immediate and unexpected effect of converting a moderately interesting idea into a major political and strategic issue. The Minuteman test was well publicized, and the Soviets naturally saw this airborne missile as a new threat and went to work to stop it. So a Soviet drive to stop a program that was little more than a Rube Goldberg experiment was to bedevil Ford at Vladivostok. At the time, however, it still seemed a novel strategic option to us, and worth protecting from Russian onslaughts. That too would eventually cost us dearly.

I believed that we would do well to make a deal in which we banned or limited this new air-mobile ICBM in return for Soviet concessions to limit multiple warheads (MIRVs) on their heavy missiles. I thought the airborne ICBM would never be built and trading it would be no sacrifice. The missile that had a promising future, in my view, was the lighter, smaller and less expensive cruise missile. Twenty or more of these cruise missiles could be fitted onto one B-52 bomber, thus turning it into the flying equivalent of a MIRV missile.

As for withdrawing from our submarine base at Rota, I felt we should make it conditional on ending debate over including French and British nuclear weapons in SALT and eliminating the Soviet demand to limit our so-called forward bases in Europe. The Soviets had driven us nearly insane with their incessant demands to include allied nuclear weapons in our negotiations. We could not and did not agree, but finding ways to save Soviet face on the issue became a strain on our ingenuity.

At Kissinger's Moscow meetings in October 1974, he proposed limiting MIRVs on Soviet heavy missiles. Since Brezhnev had previously hinted that the Soviets might impose some limits on their own, we thought that we were adopting his hint. But he seemed adamantly opposed. Indeed, the first session with Brezhnev was filled with complaints, more or less as we had expected. In particular, he was peevish about the Middle East, where he thought that Kissinger was easing him out of any negotiations. (In fact, this was quite true.) He was convinced we were reneging on the economic bargain to grant the Soviet Union credits and expand trade that he had negotiated with Kissinger in 1972 (also potentially true), and finally he thought we were raising new obstacles in the SALT negotiations (not quite true). Brezhnev also alluded cryptically to the China proposal he had made to Nixon, in a way that suggested to Kissinger that Brezhnev might be making acceptance a pre-condition to any further arms control agreements—which would have meant an end to détente under rather dramatic circumstances.

At that moment in Moscow we thought perhaps the coming Vladivostok summit was collapsing. Kissinger cabled a warn-ing to President Ford that if the stalemate in his talks with Brezhnev was not broken and he returned without any move-ment on SALT issues, the only possibility of getting the Rus-sians to move on arms control would be for Ford to insist that the Congress dramatically increase the budget for strategic weapons.

But as was so often the case in Moscow, the next morning Brezhnev shifted his ground. Gromyko told Kissinger that the Politburo had decided to proceed along the lines of the U.S. SALT position: a ten-year agreement at equal levels of about 2,400 missiles and bombers for both sides, and some sublevels to be set for MIRVed missiles, with an additional subceiling for Soviet heavy MIRVed ICBMs. They had reached a basic decision, Gromyko said, to obtain an arms control agreement by the time of the next regular summit (then scheduled for the summer of 1975). They were still having trouble with our proposals to limit their heavy ICBMs and with the problem of how to count bombers that were armed with longer-range missiles. This last issue was a ticking time bomb that we scarcely noticed at the time.

A new Soviet proposal was then unveiled; it was close to the

U.S. position, but with the usual Soviet twists that made them
such maddening negotiators. While accepting the concept of
"equality," they rigged the numbers so that a real equality
would not be reached for some time. In Brezhnev's plan, the
United States would, in fact, concede to the Soviets an overall
advantage of 200 missiles and bombers. Full equality, therefore,
at a ceiling of 2,400 missiles and bombers would be only
theoretical, because, in practice, for the years up to 1985,
Moscow would have a numerical advantage over the United
States. Moreover, Brezhnev refused our idea for a cap of 250
on Soviet heavy missiles armed with MIRVs. The full complement of these Soviet missiles (308) would not be affected. They
would be counted only in the overall ceiling of 1,320 missiles
with MIRVs for each side. The other problems in the Soviet
proposal were that the United States would be limited to no
more than 10 new Trident submarines, and our bombers could
not be armed with missiles with a range greater than 3,000
kilometers. (The clever scheme of dropping a missile out of a
cargo plane had obviously alerted the Soviets, who were now
trying to get rid of it.)

Brezhnev's new proposal, however, was within the boundaries
of what we might accept, allowing for all the negotiating fat
that the Soviets usually included in their proposal. Both sides
were agreed on an overall ceiling of 2,400 missiles and bombers;
we also agreed on a subceiling of 1,320 missiles armed with
MIRVs. Thus the summit at Vladivostok would be not merely
a get-acquainted meeting but a real bargaining session that
might permit completion of the Geneva negotiations.

There were, of course, obvious problems with the Soviet
proposal. The petty discrepancy of 200 missiles/bombers that
Brezhnev wanted would be of little strategic significance, but
because of the inequality, it would be political dynamite for
President Ford. Obviously it could not be accepted, and Brezhnev probably knew this. A second, more difficult problem was
that we still had nothing to show for our effort to limit the
Soviet heavy ICBM. We concluded that the last word had not
been said on this issue, and it might be part of a trade. Finally,
the idea of limiting the range of our missiles that might
eventually be put on American bombers was also a serious
problem. We might have to argue for the right to have an
airborne ICBM, if the Pentagon really wanted to have this

projected missile. Even if this scheme was dropped, there would still be the issue of preserving the option to put the lighter cruise missile on our bombers. This was important to the United States and could not be bargained away. We even gave some thought to linking the two ideas, agreeing to limit the missiles on our bombers, but making our agreement conditional on Soviet limits on their heavy MIRVs. In this case, we could propose that these "new" systems would each be limited to no more than about 250: the Soviets would have 250 MIRVed heavy missiles, and we could arm 250 bombers with airborne missiles. This was not much arms control, but an agreement along these lines would have pointed in the right direction.

There was one other seemingly minor problem, and that was the strange notion of counting each and every missile on a bomber if the missile had capability over a certain range. This would mean that a single B-1, for example, would have to count as 20 to 25 because each could carry that many shorter-range cruise missiles. This would turn any agreement into a farce. We assumed (not correctly) that the Soviets knew this as well, and that they were playacting. As for limiting our Trident submarines to a total of 10, we also put this down to bargaining, since the Soviets knew our Trident program was planned to go up to well beyond 10 submarines; perhaps as many as 20 were planned.

In short, we saw a possible deal: despite the probability of domestic backlash, we could concede some "inequality," as Brezhnev proposed, if in return we could get some restraint on his heavy ICBMs, perhaps limiting the number equipped with MIRVs to a level well under their full contingent of 308. We could give up the very longest-range missiles on aircraft, while keeping shorter-range ones. There would be no further limits except for those roughly agreed: a 2,400 ceiling on missiles and bombers and, within that, a ceiling of 1,320 MIRVed missiles.

When this rough outline was put before the Joint Chiefs of Staff they were "encouraged" that the Soviets were moving toward equality. In commenting on the details, however, the JCS wanted to allow for a new American ICBM (known then and thereafter as the MX) but they did not foresee it's being necessary until after 1985, though Ford had ordered it for

1984. (The first ones were in fact available in 1986.) Most important, the joint chiefs were skeptical of the so-called "window of vulnerability," the threat to American missile silos posed by the next generation of Soviet ICBMs. They saw this as a problem for after 1985, if ever. Finally, and surprisingly, the JCS accepted a limit of 10 Trident submarines. The civilians in the Pentagon, however, finally and wisely decided this was not acceptable. The truly strange turn was that the JCS wanted to preserve the option for having a "mobile" ICBM deployed on an aircraft: the air force experiment was still raising its ugly head and becoming serious. Basically, however, there was a green light from the Pentagon. If Ford could get "equality," he would win the right wing in the Congress and would have JCS support for a new SALT agreement.

The real question was whether this was the best possible outcome. Many of us thought we could do still better, but only if the new president was willing to take a considerable amount of political backlash. This was a call that only Gerald Ford could make. That was why he occupied the White House; only the president can weigh the overall balance of domestic and foreign policies and decide how to reconcile competing interests.

All this is what Gerald Ford had in mind that wintry night at the Okeanskaya Sanatorium in Vladivostok.

The first session began around six in the evening; it was scheduled to last an hour or so before adjourning for dinner. It lasted until after midnight and, as it turned out, with no dinner, which is always hard on the lowly staff members. Presidents can always rustle up some food, to say nothing of general secretaries in the USSR, but it is not so easy for the rest of us.

The first part of the meeting was predictable, beginning with obligatory small talk. This time the subject was the Congress of Vienna in 1815, where, Kissinger volunteered, the Austrians had to cut special doors through the walls of the meeting hall so that each of the monarchs, including the czar, could enter simultaneously. Brezhnev commented that at that time Gromyko had been the czar, and Gromyko countered that he had only been an observer. It may not seem very humorous, but it was contrary to the traditional image of the somber Gromyko. One always wondered whether these gibes conveyed a hidden meaning or were simply the residue of the grisly style of humor characteristic of Soviet politics under Stalin.

In any case, Brezhnev began with his customary bobbing and weaving, testing the American president—whining about inequalities and hinting that all was lost, charging the American side with hardening its SALT position and making new demands. This took the usual straightening out by Kissinger. It was notable that Brezhnev took instruction from Kissinger almost as a student, while impatiently waving away his own advisers. Ford made his case, insisting that the United States had to have full equality if he was to get the necessary support for the agreement in the United States. After a time, Brezhnev called for a break and suggested reconvening in a smaller group. Obviously he was accustomed to doing business with the smaller circle that Nixon and Kissinger had used. So the rest of us were sent to wait in an anteroom. Kissinger and General Brent Scowcroft, who had become Kissinger's deputy at the NSC, remained, along with Ford's interpreter, Alex Akalovsky, who had translated for President Kennedy at the Vienna summit with Khrushchev in 1961.

In the private talks, Brezhnev continued to test the possibility that the United States would give him a slight numerical edge of 200 within the overall ceiling of 2,400 ICBMs, submarine-launched ballistic missiles and heavy bombers. In other words, the Soviet forces would be at the full 2,400, and this would mean a very slight Soviet reduction from about 2,500. But the United States would be stopped at 2,200, which was in fact higher than the U.S. forces could reach by 1985 in any case. But the issue was politics, not arithmetic.

Kissinger warned that in the current political situation (meaning the post-Watergate climate), it would be extremely dangerous for the United States to agree to this small differential. Brezhnev then went back to a much earlier variant, which we had introduced in early 1974. In this scheme the Soviets would still have an edge of 200 in the overall ceiling, but the United States would be compensated by having a small edge in the number of MIRVed missiles. Kissinger had pressed for this in the Nixon summit. Now Kissinger replied that while this might be preferable, the times were such that it was no longer possible. Ford argued that any tinkering with the concept of equality would be turned against the agreement itself in the United

States and inevitably would be turned against détente as well. In this case, the results of such a SALT bargain could lead to the election of a new administration far less committed to détente (meaning Senator Jackson).

Finally, the wily old pro Andrei Gromyko threw out what was really behind all of this stalling. Would the United States be prepared to do something about its forward bases? he asked. This was the invitation to clarify the hints that we would withdraw from the nuclear submarine base at Rota in Spain. Ford responded that he would be willing to give a commitment to such a withdrawal in 1985, a decade hence. And Gromyko, ever the rug merchant, said "by" 1984, not "in" 1985, thus gaining a year in the bargain. This small ploy illustrated a Kissingerism about Soviet bargaining: they would knee you in the groin to pick up a nickel from the sidewalk, even though it cost them a million in good will.

All of this produced an interesting Brezhnev digression about the professional military. In his country, he said, the military could not determine policy. They could determine doctrine, but policy, including military policy, was decided at the political level. "In other words, the military decide what to shoot at, while the political leadership decides whether or not to shoot." This was supposed to be reassuring, but it was disconcerting to think of the Soviet defense minister, Marshal Andrei Grechko, arbitrarily deciding which target to hit, whereas in the United States targeting was the source of endless debates, both in theory and practice. Only the president and a very small circle of advisers could see and approve the nuclear war plan known as the Single Integrated Operational Plan (SIOP), and the president definitely had to approve it. In the USSR, apparently, Brezhnev had delegated this responsibility—at least this is what he implied, though he was trying to make a different point, emphasizing civilian control.

Then Brezhnev left the room, and as he exited, began shouting "Kozlov, Kozlov." (Colonel General Mikhail Kozlov was a first deputy chief of the general staff and head of its Main Operations Directorate; he had first appeared as part of the Soviet delegation in the Nixon summit.) They disappeared into one of the small private rooms and they stayed there for some time. Whatever Brezhnev's criticisms of the military, he was not loathe to rely on General Kozlov. It is perhaps instructive that after this session with the general, Brezhnev began to wrap up the negotiations. He obviously had sought and received advice from Kozlov.

Brezhnev returned to the meeting with Ford and promptly accepted the U.S. demands for full equality: both sides under a ceiling of 2,400 and both sides limited to no more than 1,320 MIRVs. And he pointedly noted that he would inform his "colleagues" of the information about Rota. With agreement staring them in the face, after two years of frustrating haggling, Kissinger and Ford decided they too wanted a break for one final review.

What followed was a marathon circling around and around the compound in the bitter cold while we debated the Soviet proposition. It is always a bit disconcerting when the Soviets accept your proposal. Naturally, Ford was inclined to button up the agreement then and there. We all agreed that it would be a satisfactory outcome. At that point I volunteered that it was surprising how quickly Brezhnev had agreed, and that perhaps we should probe for more; we might salvage some limit on the number of Soviet heavy ICBMs that could be converted to MIRVed missiles. Kissinger also thought this was worth trying, but others warned that we might be getting into a jungle of new issues, especially if the Soviets countered with the question of our missiles on B-52 and B-1 bombers, as Brezhnev had done in the October meeting with Kissinger. But, finally, we all agreed that if this should happen, we could easily drop it and go back and accept Brezhnev's proposal, which, after all, was our own position.

Ford did try for another concession on limiting the number of Soviet heavy missiles equipped with MIRVs. Brezhnev balked and did in fact bring up our missiles on bombers. He again took the far-out position that each missile on a bomber would count under the 2,400 ceiling. This was obvious nonsense; it would mean that we could have only ten bombers and nothing else. Ford turned it down. Both sides agreed it was getting very late, and the talks adjourned about twelve-thirty.

We trooped back to our barracks only to find—as I had feared—that the Soviet service staff, bewildered by all of the late-night activity, had simply retired. A decent meal could not be scraped together, and the American staff went to bed muttering and grumbling. I was thereupon confronted by my second great plumbing crisis in Russia. The first had been in the Kremlin itself, where Helmut Sonnenfeldt and I roomed together during the Nixon summit the previous July. One evening the insides of our toilet tank simply collapsed into a pile of rusted junk, with water running out of control. We appealed to the Soviet guard, who suddenly seemed not to understand any known language, including Russian. And so, falling back on our Yankee ingenuity and the fact that we were both old homeowners, we somehow pieced together a makeshift arrangement that worked for the remainder of the summit, but only under a very gentle touch. We left it to the next guest, a Communist functionary, we hoped.

The Vladivostok plumbing crisis was simpler, though quite startling. As I was washing my hands and face I became aware of a growing pool of water at my feet. Peering under the sink I discovered that the gooseneck that should join the pipe to the drain was not there; indeed, it was lying in the corner. It was a simple task to pound it back in place. But I still wondered what the reasoning was for its being disconnected at all and, in particular, why no one thought to put it back. Could it be an insidious psychological warfare plot by the KGB?

The next morning the Americans convened to decide where to go in the next round. Papers were prepared and talking points for Ford to use were worked out with Kissinger; and by the opening of the next session at ten, it was more or less decided that we would probe gently for a time and, if nothing transpired, take the agreement on the table.

Ford returned to the heavy-missile gambit, but it drew only a typical Russian escalation; namely, a new demand to ban all ballistic missiles on bombers. Ford had to turn down Brezhnev's proposal, whereupon Brezhnev turned down our proposal for a limit for heavy Soviet MIRVed ICBMs. Thus the two sides returned to where they had been at ten the previous evening. Both sides decided to agree, and I was summoned to draft the document of agreement, with Helmut Sonnenfeldt and Georgi Kornienko, then head of the American desk in the Soviet foreign ministry.

We decided to leave out any specific numbers and issue to the press a written "framework" explaining that the two sides had agreed on equal levels for their strategic weaponry. This was the real breakthrough: the two sides had agreed on strategic equality.

The final agreement, then, was to work for a treaty that would last through 1985. Both sides would be limited to the same overall aggregate of missiles and bombers (2,400), and both sides would be limited to equal levels of missiles equipped with MIRVs (1,320). Negotiations would begin on reductions in these forces to be made after 1985, and the whole agreement was to be completed by the end of 1975.

While this announcement was being completed, Brezhnev, reducing his group even further, finally raised the anti-Chinese treaty. Ford asked what it really meant, and Brezhnev explained that if either side were to be attacked by a nuclear power, the other would go to its aid. Ford said immediately that this could not apply to an ally (having in mind Britain and France), and Brezhnev essentially agreed. Then Ford raised the key question: what about a country that was not an ally? What would happen if such a country attacked? Would both the United States and the USSR be free to counterattack, and with nuclear weapons? Brezhnev lamely said that he could not be that precise. The conversation petered out, but in a complete shift of subject and mood, Brezhnev ended by reminding Ford that the following May would be the thirtieth anniversary of the end of the World War, and that the USSR was thinking about some celebration that the United States might join. "After all," he said, "we were allies in the last war."

On this note the conference ended, except for some further cleanup work. This included sending a long cablegram to Washington, to Schlesinger and the Joint Chiefs of Staff, explaining the outcome so that they would not immediately start to undercut it, as Kissinger feared they might. With this vital cable in hand, I commandeered a Soviet car and we set out for our communications center. After a few minutes I realized that the driver was lost. It seemed that we had reached a major highway and were heading toward Vladivostok. Finally, admitting defeat, the driver stopped and asked directions back to the Okeanskaya Sanatorium. I was getting more and more nervous, though the humor was not totally lost on me. Was this a followup to the plumbing crisis by the dreaded KGB? So, in halting Russian, I told the driver where I thought the barracks were, and we finally found them. All of this took much too long, and when I returned, Kissinger gave me a quizzical look. But by then the postconference festivities had begun, with caviar in abundance.

Kornienko and I drew up the communiqué and had it retyped and printed to hand out to the press. Kissinger gave his usual background briefing, which was later to become famous because his former staff aide, Morton Halperin, sued to have the actual text released to the public. Background briefings are supposed to be off the record, but texts are usually printed; around this period there was a small revolt against the practice of keeping such briefings secret and only quoting unnamed sources. The Halperin suit was intended to break through this gentlemen's agreement between the government and the press. The government contested the case and won it years later.

In the final communiqué, which was of course made public, Kornienko and I had once again, as we had in San Clemente, inadvertently omitted an agreed upon paragraph on the Middle East. The American press could not believe it was another mistake and saw all kinds of dark plots and secret agreements behind the omission. The real reason was that Gromyko and Kissinger always waited until the very last minute to resolve their contending texts on the Middle East. The Soviets never failed to propose some outrageous language supporting the PLO or attacking Israel, and we dutifully took it out. These delays caused no end of anguish to the staffs. At one point I suggested to Kornienko that we write our own Middle East paragraph, insert it but not tell anyone. He giggled but declined, which probably explains why he became the first deputy foreign minister of the USSR, and why I retired.

VI

THE ROAD
TO HELSINKI

The Vladivostok agreement should have been a turning point. Ford and Kissinger had, after all, salvaged a framework for an arms control agreement and preserved a relationship with Brezhnev despite Watergate. Moreover, the framework, while not perfect, met the main criticisms that had been leveled against the first SALT agreements: the charge of inequality in the first agreement would be satisfied by the equal levels that would apply to weapons on both sides; and the charge that there had been an arms race as a result of the first agreements would be countered by new ceilings and subceilings that would even require some reductions. Finally, all the major strategic weapons systems would be included, both long-range missiles and bombers.

Thus, it was something of a shock that the reaction at home turned out to be not only skeptical but hostile. Moreover, the attacks on Vladivostok blended into a more far-reaching assault on the Ford administration. Within sixty days of his return, Ford confronted the repudiation of Nixon's policy of using economic relations with the Soviets as an incentive to achieve agreements on political and strategic issues. Since 1972, the Congress had been holding up Nixon's agreement with the

Soviets that settled the old lend-lease wartime debt and granted trade concessions to the Soviets. By late 1974, Congress was considering the Jackson-Vanik amendment to the trade bill, which linked any American economic concessions with Soviet acceptance of the emigration of Jews from the Soviet Union, and this legislation was accompanied by the Stevenson amendment, which would sharply limit the amount of credits to the USSR. In addition, new attacks were launched against America's commitment to attend the Conference on Security and Cooperation in Europe, still under preparation, which was to be the culmination of Brezhnev's dream of a European security conference. The domestic backlash against détente was clearly growing. The fall of Saigon in April 1975—reviving all of the bitterness and humiliation of Vietnam—simply enhanced the sense of frustration and of despair that any American foreign policy could be effective.

The anti-Vladivostok reaction centered on Senator Henry "Scoop" Jackson. Having insisted for two years on strict equality in SALT, Jackson abruptly changed his tune after Ford's return. He began to attack the agreement for failing to reduce Soviet forces. Whereas the administration argued that the agreement had put a "cap" on the Soviet buildup, Jackson commented that the cap was put on a mountain top. He pressed the case for a reduction from the 2,400 ceiling agreed at Vladivostok to 1,700—a one-third cut. How the Soviets were to be persuaded to make these reductions three months after Watergate and with the threat of the Jackson-Vanik amendment on Jewish emigration still pending, Jackson and his fellow critics did not bother to explain.

It was an absurd situation. We were withdrawing one of the carrots that tempted the Soviets—the prospect of trade and credits—and substituting a threat against their internal order; at the same time we were being urged to discard one of the supposed benefits—restraint on Soviet nuclear forces—by abandoning the SALT negotiations. It was unfortunate that the culprit was Scoop Jackson. Many in the White House admired him. He was, after all, what many considered the ideal American combination—liberal in domestic policies but conservative in foreign affairs. Nixon had wanted him as secretary of defense in 1969. And many in the White House were in close touch with him and his staff. This was to prove an embarrassment. It was not unusual to see Richard Perle, one of Jackson's assistants, in the halls of the Old Executive Office Building, visiting one or another member of Kissinger's staff. The confrontation over both SALT and the Jackson-Vanik amendment was conducted on two levels, public and private; on the private level there were prolonged negotiations with the Jackson staff, both Richard Perle and another aide, Dorothy Fosdick. Indeed, the White House staff actually wrote the Jackson SALT amendment on equality in 1972, and Jackson talked it through with Kissinger, while continuing to attack SALT in public.

By late 1974 matters had changed. Jackson was a probable candidate for the presidency in the 1976 campaign. Indeed, many thought of him as the leading candidate. And this must have shaped his tactics and strategy in dealing with the White House. His position on Jewish emigration and SALT became implacable. No matter how hard the White House tried to appease him, he simply escalated his demands. The fact that he had access to inside information in the White House made it maddening, since he would simply pocket every concession, knowing full well that more could be squeezed from an administration that did not want to start its term in a confrontation with the Senate.

Still, the breadth of criticism of Vladivostok was a surprise. We had assumed that at least among the liberal arms control community it would be well received. But even in this quarter the general reaction was critical. The Arms Control Association commented that the agreement had "serious shortcomings." When Jan Lodal, a Kissinger staffer, and I briefed a group of experts, we were treated to an all-out attack. George Rathjens, a liberal who was one of the pioneers in arms control theory and practice, said he would rather have no agreement than Vladivostok because the ceilings were much too high. In later years, when it appeared there would be no agreement, some of the critics of Vladivostok changed their tune dramatically; saving the Vladivostok accord became a battle cry, especially after the Carter administration's debacle in their first try for an agreement calling for deep cuts rather than the "cap" approach of Vladivostok.

All of this criticism could have been weathered, but there were some additional complications arising from the summit.

A summit is a most inappropriate place to do serious business on such complex issues as arms control. No leader, even with the best will in the world, can master the intricacies. The summit should be reserved for setting general guidelines or indicating a strategy to be filled in later by subordinates. This is what happened at Vladivostok, and in an era of private diplomacy this would have been satisfactory. But not in the 1970s.

It began to leak out in the press that all the details were not fixed in writing. And, in fact, an aide-mémoire filling in the gaps was being negotiated between Kissinger and Dobrynin. The discussions proved to be a problem since the Soviets blithely returned to some of the positions we had already rejected at Vladivostok. Such tactics were not unusual; the Soviets often tried to revive old positions, out of sheer perversity or tenacity, or perhaps even in the hope that we had forgotten. Naturally Kissinger bridled at these Soviet antics and we drafted our own version of the aide-mémoire, which led to a brief standoff. This too began to leak out, and Jackson, who was informed by one of Kissinger's staff, demanded to see the written record. His request had to be rejected, all of which further strained relations with the senator. Finally, a half-baked compromise was worked out with Dobrynin. A new aide-mémoire was drafted by the staff and sent to Kissinger for his meeting with Dobrynin. To play it safe, the staff had drafted two versions, differing only slightly. Rather than choosing, Kissinger and Dobrynin signed both, leaving the staff even more bewildered. It did not matter, for the issues that were to plague the negotiations could not be settled in a few days.

The first issue was whether to include limits on the Soviet medium-range Backfire bomber, defining it as a truly inter-continental weapon. The Pentagon insisted that it was actually an intercontinental bomber because, if it was refueled, it could reach the United States (of course this could apply to any aircraft if refueled often enough). The Soviets scoffed at including this particular bomber, which they strongly insisted was designed only for medium-range operations. But this claim, in turn, only aroused American suspicions.

At one point in this debate, which continued until the end of Ford's term, Kissinger asked the famous American aircraft designer Kelly Johnson what he thought of the Soviet Backfire bomber. Johnson said that it was a second-rate aircraft and we should encourage the Soviets to put all of their resources into it. The issue was never definitively resolved; but eventually, in the SALT agreement of 1979, the Soviets agreed to a ceiling on production rates for this bomber.

American insistence raised suspicions of our motives on the Soviet side. No Soviet, civilian or military, could conceive of this weapon as a bomber for attacking the United States, since its primary mission was to strike in Asia or Europe. In one of his encounters with Kissinger after Vladivostok, Brezhnev summoned generals and marshals to prove his point, but the United States experts smugly insisted that they knew more than the Soviet air force about its own bombers—a position calculated to enrage Brezhnev, to say nothing of his generals.

An interesting sidelight occurred a decade later. American F-111 fighter-bombers flew a strike mission from England to Libya, with several refuelings: this would seem to confirm Soviet claims that our forward-based aircraft in Europe were indeed a "strategic" threat, since Libya was much farther from England than was the USSR. It also proved our point that any aircraft could be strategic if refueled often enough. The Libyan missions confirmed that our old fears, in the mid-1970s, about the Backfire were justified; for it too could reach the United States if refueled in flight.

More serious than the Backfire question was the failure to resolve all of the aspects of limiting or banning cruise missiles. This had been touched on only briefly at Vladivostok. For some time the United States had been toying with these intriguing weapons but had not been able to decide whether to move ahead with specific programs; one single version could be adapted for naval, land or air use. Putting some on bombers seemed the most effective deployment; they could be fired at some distance from the target, thus allowing the bomber to use them against defenses; and, of course, they could be used instead of bombs; about twenty such missiles could be carried on a B-52 bomber. This was a more or less agreed program in the administration, and it seemed likely that an agreement could be reached with the Soviets, thus permitting the deployment of air-launched cruise missiles; but the issues that were unresolved were how to deal with sea- and land-based cruise missiles—whether to deploy them on submarines and surface ships and perhaps even station them in Europe. The navy was torn. They did not want to dilute the missions of their submarines by adding new weapons to strike land targets. But nonetheless they were reluctant to part with the promising technology involved in cruise missiles, which might be used against other ships.

This indecision became more and more frustrating as the post-Vladivostok negotiations proceeded in 1975. It was eventually solved by a compromise under Carter in his agreement of 1979; in a separate protocol to Carter's SALT II treaty, cruise missiles on submarines were banned for two years; this protocol lapsed in 1981, and cruise missiles have been unrestrained for the past several years.

In 1975, when all of these issues were still open, the U.S. Army had no particular interest in any cruise missiles that would be based on land. It was this very system for the cruise missile, however, that was to prove most controversial; it was this version that would eventually be deployed in Europe in 1983, as a counter to the unrestrained Soviet buildup of its intermediate-range SS-20 ballistic missiles.

Kissinger had rescued the entire arsenal of different cruise missiles from a Pentagon decision to scrap them in 1973, and he was naturally frustrated with the new position of the Pentagon that suddenly insisted on saving the weapons system they had wanted to drop completely two years before. Kissinger had saved the cruise missile as a bargaining chip, but in early 1976, when he suggested playing the sea- and land-based chips, he met fierce resistance.

The effect of both of these unresolved issues—Backfire and cruise missiles—was to further divide Washington over the value of the broad agreement at Vladivostok. It was in danger of being held hostage to the resolution of two second-rate issues. An additional issue, which arose immediately after Vladivostok, concerned the timing of future reductions. The agreement had indicated reductions would come later, after the ten-year period envisioned by the Vladivostok framework. This was attacked by arms control advocates, who wanted earlier reductions, and led to an unlikely coalition: Senators Edward Kennedy and Walter Mondale joined with the Republican Charles "Mac" Mathias of Maryland to introduce a Senate resolution calling for early reductions. When tipped off in

advance by Mathias, Kissinger and Dobrynin immediately
amended the Vladivostok agreement, to the effect that negotiations on reductions could start before 1985, when the treaty
would officially expire. I was asked to work with Kennedy,
Mondale and Mathias and their staffs to see to it that their
resolution did not become a Christmas tree on which all sorts
of other amendments would be added. Thus the White House
found itself allied to Kennedy and Mondale in opposition to
Jackson—a strange commentary on Washington politics. In the
end the joint resolution proved acceptable, but not until much
agonizing had gone on in the White House over the constant
maneuvering required to keep Kennedy and Mondale at arm's
length, without losing their support for SALT.

All of this was worrisome because it seemed that Ford could
not deliver what he had agreed to at Vladivostok. To the White
House, the reaction against Vladivostok seemed perverse. The
resentment, especially at the staff level, arose largely because
to some degree the White House was isolated, as every White
House is. After Vladivostok the staff was relieved that some
agreement had been reached and that the Soviets had not tried
to exploit Ford's political weakness by demanding major concessions from a new president. Thus we tended to see a great
victory in what was a modest achievement. The new press
secretary, Ron Nessen, told the White House press corps that
Ford had achieved in a few days what Nixon had not achieved
in three years. This was duly reported by the gleeful reporters
from Air Force One, who instantly saw a potential rift with
Kissinger. Kissinger was offended, since Nessen's account made
it seem that he had failed and that Ford had rescued him. But
Kissinger had made the error of going directly from Vladivostok to China while Ford returned to Washington. I rode on
Air Force One and listened with dismay to Nessen's briefing.
Kissinger exploded when he learned of it, but there was little
he could do from China. Leaving the defense of Vladivostok
in the hands of underlings who had none of Kissinger's powers
of elucidation and persuasion, or his authority, was obviously
a major mistake. It may well be that had Kissinger returned
immediately, he could have snuffed out the anti-Vladivostok
revolt.

But another storm, far worse, was brewing over the trade
bill and the amendment sponsored by Senator Jackson and

Representative Charles Vanik. This effort was typical of classical anticommunists, who saw most aspects of relations with the Soviet Union as a means to apply pressures on the Soviet system. Thus Jackson developed a scheme that would tie granting the USSR most-favored-nation treatment to Soviet acceptance of the free emigration of Jews. It reflected his view that the United States had strong cards to play, and that the Ford administration, like the Nixon administration before it, was giving away too much for too little. It may be that in his critique of arms control Jackson had a point open to debate. On the question of Jewish emigration, however, his proposal struck at the heart of Soviet power. No Soviet leader could buckle to Jackson's demands and stay in power. It is difficult to believe that Jackson did not understand this. So one is left with the conclusion that his was simply another effort to break the momentum of détente. And indeed, this was the effect.

Both Nixon and Ford underestimated Jackson. They believed that somehow, some way, there would be a compromise, especially since there had been a consensus in the United States that economic relations were a strong incentive for the Soviets to moderate their behavior. Thus, the Nixon strategy had been to promise economic concessions once major issues such as SALT and Berlin were settled. Consequently, in late 1972, a bargain was struck: the United States would accord to Soviet imports the same tariff treatment as was granted to those of any other nation. The misnomer for this was most-favored-nation treatment; it had been denied to all Communist countries after World War II but then gradually restored, first to Yugoslavia and in 1956 to Poland. The Soviets wanted it mainly as a sign of equality, since the actual level of trade was quite low—about $100 million in 1971. The Soviets also wanted credits to buy American goods, especially grain, and this was more or less promised to them under Nixon. Brezhnev had rather expansively speculated that the Soviets might buy $20 billion in consumer goods from the United States. Most-favored-nation status (MFN) must be granted by Congress, and in 1972 Congress insisted that before any of these arrangements would be accepted, the Soviets had to settle their lend-lease debts left over from the end of the war. The lend-lease problem was settled in late 1972: in return for MFN, the Soviets agreed to pay $740 million on their lend-lease debt. (I always thought trying to collect the wartime debt was shameful.) After 1972 trade began to increase, even without the formal granting of MFN. The Soviets bought large amounts of grain at low prices, causing a scandal because they proved to be such shrewd traders in the American market. They also began buying industrial equipment, which caused new worries that they might get sophisticated American technology. The net result was that skepticism was growing over the economic dimensions of détente.

This was the situation that Jackson attacked in his amendment, making MFN conditional on free Jewish emigration. The negotiations with Jackson ran for almost two years and were primarily conducted by Helmut Sonnenfeldt for Kissinger. Sonnenfeldt was also sympathetic to Jackson, but he made a determined effort to find a way out of the impasse. Various formulas were tried: some would grant MFN, but only after a waiting period. But all variants came down to one essential point—the Soviets would have to agree to free emigration. They were not necessarily opposed to Jewish emigration, which was already rising dramatically, from almost no emigrants to over 30,000 a year, as a result of the general warming of relations—thus disproving Jackson's basic thesis, that only pressures produced results with the Soviet Union. Indeed, Kissinger had extracted from Gromyko a commitment for emigration at the rate of 45,000 a year, and this had been negotiated in early 1974. Jackson simply pocketed this figure and raised his own demands to 60,000. Even that level was not necessarily out of the question, and Kissinger had warned Gromyko that Jackson's position would be to escalate the figures.

A scheme was finally developed that would solve the problem—at least so it was hoped in late 1974. First, Kissinger (or Ford) would write to Jackson, explaining the president's understanding that the Soviets would end harassment of emigrés and place no "major obstacles" in the way of emigration, or words to that effect. Jackson would accept this assurance but his reply could be couched in whatever terms he wished. Then the White House would acknowledge the guidelines described by Jackson and the deal would be struck. The Soviets were informed of this arrangement, and they agreed. The negotiations came to a head in October 1974, just before Kissinger left for Moscow to prepare for the Vladivostok summit.

But Jackson outmaneuvered the White House. Following a meeting with Ford that included the senator from New York, Jacob Javits, and standing in front of the White House before the press, Jackson hailed the historic breakthrough, but then promptly went well beyond the agreement with Ford; he said that his "benchmark" was a figure of 60,000 emigrés, and he then speculated that the figures could go even higher. Kissinger and Ford felt tricked and betrayed. Senators Javits and Abraham Ribicoff sought to calm the waters, but the damage had been done, as Kissinger was soon to discover when he went to Moscow shortly after Jackson's remark. Brezhnev and Gromyko were seething. They too thought they had been tricked, and of course could not believe that the powerful Kissinger or the president could not control what a senator would say outside the White House itself. The upshot was that Gromyko gave Kissinger a long letter that accused Washington of distorting the Soviet position, and that decisively rejected Jackson's interpretation. This happened at a breakfast, shortly before the Kissinger party left Moscow.

At that point Kissinger made a mistake. Rather than cabling Gromyko's letter to Washington or otherwise putting it into the policy-making process for discussion, he kept it to himself. He thought that the Soviets could be accommodated after the Vladivostok summit, or that something new could be worked out with both Brezhnev and Jackson. Nothing was ever done, however. Jackson decided to push his amendment and brought the matter to a favorable vote in mid-December—placing the Soviets in the position of having to guarantee emigration rates to the United States in order to receive trading benefits. The indignant Soviets released the text of Gromyko's letter. Everything then collapsed into recriminations. In a letter to Ford Brezhnev repudiated the 1972 MFN and lend-lease agreements and added some mutterings about the bad state of Soviet-American relations. Nevertheless, his letter, dated Christmas Day, was an interesting document. It seemed to cry out for some reassurance from Ford that what was happening in the trade dispute was not a harbinger of an across-the-board deterioration of relations. Brezhnev rather plaintively asked for Ford's views on how to improve the situation. My analysis for Kissinger was that a new shift of Soviet policy was not likely, but that the ball was definitely in our court.

There was a last-ditch effort to compromise. Kissinger suggested to Dobrynin that the Soviets refrain from publicly repudiating their commitments under the 1972 settlement on lend-lease; then MFN would be granted by Ford, as allowed for in the Jackson amendment, and Jewish emigration would rise. But Brezhnev would have none of it. He dismissed the suggestion in a brusque reply to Ford in early January. Kissinger finally decided we might be better off with Brezhnev's rejection. If the Soviets had accepted the compromise, there was bound to be trouble later, since they probably could not live up to Jackson's expectations on Jewish emigration. Then Jackson would launch a new attack. If, on the other hand, the Soviets did comply, then Jackson could show what real "toughness" accomplished. The Soviets, however, were in no mood for any clever gambits. They wrote off the whole mess.

The Soviet denunciation of the 1972 trade agreements proved to be the end of the affair. It was obvious that the atmosphere in the United States had changed since the Nixon summit of 1972 and the economic negotiations that had followed. Then trade was one of several elements in moving the relationship forward. Now it was being held out as a favor that we would grant in return for changes in the Soviet system. And this turn in political opinion came at the very point when American leverage was declining because of Watergate. Jackson had a great deal of support on the question of Jewish emigration, including that of many liberals who had always insisted on pursuing détente. He exalted the achievement of his new law as a vindication of his strategy and waved away the Soviet objections as mere tactics.

But in the end Jackson was dead wrong, and tragically so. Thousands of Soviet Jews were denied exit permits and remained inside the Soviet Union. And the irony was that the United States still sold large amounts of grain to the USSR; and as it turned out, according to American intelligence, much of our advanced technology was stolen. So the Soviets got what they wanted and we got nothing in return. To this day, the Jackson-Vanik amendment remains a sensitive point of controversy. Jewish emigration was a shrewd issue to exploit, but the exploitation was too cynical. For his part, Jackson always claimed the problem for the Soviets was the separate Stevenson amendment, which denied them credits. But he had made no move to stop this crippling amendment, which he might have easily done had he sincerely wanted to test the impact of his own amendment. In fact, there was no move to change any of the legislation, even after it became apparent that there would be virtually no further emigration. Thus, another of the pillars of the Kissinger strategy was collapsing because of domestic politics.

Soviet-American relations might have suffered even greater damage had the administration not preserved a bargaining chip, in the form of a commitment to attend the Conference on Security and Cooperation in Europe, to be held in Helsinki. The preliminary negotiations for this conference were still open in early 1975, and Brezhnev was determined that it should be completed. Thus Moscow limited its reaction to the Jackson-Vanik amendment (unfortunately concealing for a time the very real damage that had been done).

Suddenly, in January 1975, Brezhnev's health became an issue. It was announced that he could not make a scheduled trip to the Middle East because of illness. This caused a wave of speculation about his political power, about his successors and about the future of Soviet policy. I was worried, not about his personal health, but about his political health. I told Kissinger—I was then in the State Department—that I thought Brezhnev might be in trouble, and I was relieved when he reappeared in early February, apparently healthy. My view then was that political uncertainties in the Soviet Union about American policy were bound to be growing, and that this would make the Soviets more difficult to deal with, and also make it less likely that they would make any concessions to the United States. I was wrong about Brezhnev's political position, but I was right in that the Soviets were having doubts about the United States. This proved to be the case during Kissinger's next meeting with Gromyko, a brief session in February, in connection with preparations for a Middle East conference in Geneva. The Soviets were still stonewalling on SALT and other issues. Obviously they wanted their pound of flesh at Helsinki. Our views were summed up for Kissinger in early March:

Our basic estimate is that collapse of the trade bill, following the unexpected backlash in the U.S. against Vladivostok, led to a reappraisal of Soviet policy and a limited shift to a less conciliatory posture in dealing with us. In the past few weeks, however, we have not detected any particular pattern in Soviet moves and statements that could point to a major change beyond that initiated at the time of the trade bill.

Our sense of present Soviet attitude is that they are watching us unusually closely and are particularly sensitive to any indications that we are not living up to past promises. Obviously they are well served in dealing with us and the Congress by taking a stance of the injured party. But the top leaders surely have a genuine concern about whether the U.S. side can sustain a policy of detente.

The ability of the United States to sustain détente was soon to be sorely tried by the fall of Saigon to North Vietnamese forces and the widespread frustration that followed.

It had been over five years since I had been involved in Vietnamese affairs. I had taken no special interest in the events since then, except as they intruded on NSC work on the Soviet Union. Thus it was a surprise that when I returned to Vietnamese affairs in a peripheral way, as head of the State Department's intelligence bureau, I was confronted with an ominous appraisal of the situation in Vietnam. In early 1974 the prediction was that there would be a new, major North Vietnamese offensive sometime in the next year. Those who had been following, or were involved in, Vietnamese affairs took this in stride, but as a relative newcomer, I thought this was alarming, if true. So I wrote a summary for Kissinger, as we routinely did on such intelligence estimates. At that time, the Defense Intelligence Agency was led by General Daniel Graham, an old friend, who had served as the deputy head of intelligence in Saigon for General Westmoreland; and CIA was led by William Colby, who had served many years in Vietnam. They seemed at ease, and there was no sense of impending doom.

That was the situation for almost a year. Of course in the intervening period, the Congress practically destroyed the aid program to South Vietnam, cutting it by one half, so that the ability of the South to withstand an offensive had changed, but still no one seemed to be sounding this particular alarm.

Suddenly, in the late winter of 1974–1975, it began to appear that the estimate was in fact accurate: the North Vietnamese were gearing up for an offensive. But again, the consensus seemed to be that it would be a limited action.

It was a genuine surprise, then, when the provincial capital of Song Be was attacked and overrun by the North Vietnamese in March 1975. I was most impressed because this was an area north of Saigon, where I had visited in 1966, when the U.S. Army's First Division had been stationed in the area and had things under control. Now, of course, the First Division had long since departed, as had all of the American forces. The South Vietnamese were alone, face to face with the North Vietnamese army. It soon became evident that they could not cope with even the limited offensive that was under way. This was the real shock. Then President Nguyen Van Thieu began to make tactical blunders: The withdrawal of his forces from the highlands at this critical moment led to the unraveling of the entire situation. Suddenly the Communist forces were able to reach the crucial road junction of Ban Me Thout, which cut the north/south axis to the highlands around Pleiku; then Pleiku fell and the North Vietnamese found themselves with a clear road to the coast; this would effectively cut South Vietnam in half.

At this point even the older hands who had dismissed the first few days of fighting began to realize that it was almost all over, unless the United States intervened. After carefully examining the situation and talking with others in State and the CIA, I concluded that the South Vietnamese would be routed. It was only a matter of time before the North Vietnamese forces wheeled and headed for Saigon. If there was no U.S. military intervention, then only a desperate political rescue could save the Republic of Vietnam. I made this clear to Kissinger and Philip Habib, who was the assistant secretary for the Far East, and they more or less agreed with my estimate. Then, suddenly, our ambassador to South Vietnam, Graham Martin, appeared in Washington, returning from North Carolina, where he had been recuperating from an illness. He was in touch with his embassy staff and heading back urgently to Saigon. In Washington he told Kissinger that the situation was under control, and that Thieu had some new strategy of holding the coast while we resupplied his forces. It was pure fantasy, and it led to a bitter quarrel and shouting match between Habib, Martin and myself—all performed in front of Kissinger and to his dismay.

Martin was a courageous if somewhat pompous figure from the old days, and he comported himself with great dignity in the crisis that was developing in Vietnam. But at the outset of this final crisis he was foolishly and stubbornly wrong, and this caused no end of trouble. It was urgent that we begin certain contingency planning for an evacuation of both Americans and Vietnamese, if the worst should happen. The same applied to Cambodia. Martin steadfastly held out against anything that smacked of an emergency, lest we create a total panic. He was right, but this was a temporary state of affairs; sooner or later we would have to start evacuating if we were to save thousands of Americans and Vietnamese. Something had to be done, and valuable time was lost debating at long distance with Martin, who was clearly losing touch with the real war.

The upshot was that a gradual evacuation began, and then accelerated rapidly as the North Vietnamese approached Saigon. I was amazed at the strong defense and valiant fighting by the South Vietnamese army. Perhaps they knew that this was the last stand and found reserves of courage in their certain fate. They bought time for many of their relatives and comrades. Indeed, the airlift was a triumph for the United States that was totally submerged by the disaster of the fall of Saigon. Over a hundred thousand people were airlifted out, and the airlift continued to the very last moment, despite pleas of many in the State and Defense departments to end it. Almost every day President Ford had to fight off demands that the airlift stop. Even the military became very nervous at flying into Ton Son Nhut, with the North Vietnamese so close by.

As the end approached, there was a momentary threat that the North Vietnamese would use antiaircraft rockets against our airlift. This infuriated Kissinger, who called in Dobrynin to warn him that we would hold the Soviets responsible if anything interfered with our aircraft. And, of course, we began to send fighters to fly a perimeter around Saigon. Kissinger also sent the Soviets a proposal that we would arrange a cease-fire and open negotiations on establishing a new government. Moscow ignored this desperate plan but replied with a virtual guarantee that the evacuation could proceed "unhindered."

It was only a footnote to the crisis, but it did demonstrate that the Soviets had not yet drawn any strategic conclusions about the United States as a result of the Vietnamese debacle.

It is possible that the Soviet attitude after the fall of Saigon may also have been sobered by an incident that occurred almost immediately, involving the American ship *Mayaguez*. In the operation to rescue the ship and crew from the Cambodians who had hijacked them, the United States intervened with marines, which led to a small battle on Koh Tang island and the death of twenty-three marines in a helicopter crash. The crew was set free by the Cambodians, in my view largely because of the political intervention of the Chinese. We had approached Peking and warned that we were about to take military action; and they passed this message to Phnom Penh. But at that time there was growing chaos in Cambodia, so the reaction was delayed and we proceeded with our attacks.

I was involved only at the outset, and my participation was something of a bureaucratic fiasco. Early every morning I would read through the various communications to the State Department in preparation for Kissinger's morning staff meeting. That morning I noticed a number of cables concerning the freighter *Mayaguez* (mistakenly identified as a Philippine ship because the office of its shipping line was in Manila). The ship had apparently been captured by the Cambodians and was being towed to port. The reporting was fuzzy and unclear and the incident had occurred many hours earlier. I assumed— erroneously—that the Far East bureau of the State Department had been alerted and involved, since they would normally read and respond to all such messages.

At Kissinger's morning staff meeting I casually mentioned that the *Mayaguez* must be in a Cambodian port by now—thus contributing to a false impression that became widespread in Washington. (The ship was anchored well off shore near Koh Tang island.) Kissinger could not believe what I was saying. He was uninformed. He asked if I had called the president, a question that startled me no end. No one had talked to the president and, as it turned out, at the White House, the deputy NSC adviser, Brent Scowcroft, was at that very moment learning in some bewilderment that an American ship had been stopped and boarded (the fate of the crew was then unknown). He informed Ford at about seven-thirty. A crisis was about to

burst, at least as far as the American government was concerned.

Fortunately, the ship was regained and the crew freed.
Despite marine casualties, the U.S. force landed on Koh Tang
island, and U.S. naval air forces struck at Cambodian ports. It
may be that this strange incident marked the end of an era
even more than did the fall of Saigon. It was symbolic of the
fact that the United States seemed to be creaking and groaning.
The American navy was headed for home, so to speak. The
carriers had to be turned around, aircraft launched to attack.
It was a strain, almost as if the ships themselves wanted out of
that dreadful war. And at home the administration earned no
public or political credit for using force to rescue the ship and
free the crew. There was bitterness; the mood was sour and
turning worse.

It was not the best atmosphere in which to take up the next
phase of Soviet relations—the conference scheduled for Helsinki—which was to involve thirty-five European, Soviet and
American leaders, assembling to sign the conference documents
after a three-year negotiation. Every country in Europe except
Albania was to be represented.

Almost from the beginning, Kissinger had viewed this project
for a European security conference with disdain. It had a long
history, dating back to 1954, when it had first been proposed
by Soviet Foreign Minister Vyacheslav Molotov. The Soviet
objective was still the same: they wanted to use the conference
to gain European and American ratification of the legitimacy
of the Soviet power position in Eastern Europe. Kissinger
would have preferred to hold the conference quickly, minimize
the damage and have done with it. But the Europeans were
intrigued by the prospect of participating more directly themselves in the process of détente, and their response, especially
that of the West Germans, was to add "cooperation" to the
conference agenda, thus creating the Conference on Security
and Cooperation in Europe, known by its initials, CSCE.

The United States yielded grudgingly and gradually to the
idea of a carefully prepared, complex conference, with a large
agenda. In sharp contrast to the accusations of the critics who
attacked the Helsinki conference as part of the hated détente,
the conference was from the outset a concession to America's

allies, not to the Kremlin. And whatever critics of NATO might think, allies cannot constantly be dismissed when they fail to agree with Washington. Indeed it had been a source of irritation and bitterness in the Nixon administration that during 1973 and 1974 the Europeans were eagerly bargaining for an East-West summit at Helsinki, but they were refusing to meet with Nixon to conclude the "Year of Europe," a project Kissinger had designed to work out a NATO-wide strategy in the era of détente. The Europeans saw it as rescue of Nixon from Watergate and dismissed it, which infuriated both Nixon and Kissinger.

Despite the European-American tensions over the Year of Europe, by early 1975 Washington had begun to warm to the idea of a Helsinki meeting, including a summit, mainly because the East European leaders, including the Yugoslav president, Marshal Tito, and the Romanian leader Nikolai Ceausescu, urged the United States to become involved and use the conference to commit the Soviets to various declarations that might tie their hands. These hardened old veterans had no illusions about Moscow, but they were shrewd practitioners of dealing with Soviet pressures. Kissinger decided that we should yield to their entreaties.

Nevertheless, the overall American tactic was to drag out the process, making the Soviets pay for each step, even though they were paying in the coin of vague promises to respect Western demands on human rights and to agree to the freer movement of people and ideas.

After the initial session of July 1973 in Helsinki the conference had passed through seemingly interminable stages, most of them conducted in Geneva rather than in the harsher climes of Helsinki. The process was a diplomat's dream: numerous committees and working groups; endless drafting and redrafting of documents; rotating chairmanships and translations into six languages. The British invented the idea of grouping related subjects into "baskets," a concept that became frozen into the terminology of the proceedings. Basket I concerned security, including a declaration of principles and certain "confidence-building measures" such as voluntary notification of military maneuvers close to European borders. Basket II covered economic cooperation. Basket III concerned human rights, and the last section concerned the holding of further meetings.

At the beginning of 1974, the conference seemed to be entering its final, agonizing stage of drafting the actual documents. As that drafting began it became apparent that the abstract debates over the purpose of the conference would now be transferred to the equally tedious debates over specifics.

For the Soviets, the centerpiece of the conference was to be a declaration of principles sufficiently broad to encompass the Soviet aim of securing a general Western acceptance of the territorial and political status quo in Europe—which was to be ratified not only by the Germans but by the United States as well. To reinforce this aim the Soviets had insisted that the final meeting be at the summit. The general Western response had been to take this broad declaration as simply a starting point for a more detailed elaboration of the specific commitments on each individual issue. In particular, the West had invented a "basket" that included "free movement" of people and ideas: i.e., magazines, newspapers, motion pictures—all with the objective of countering the notion that the conference was intended only to ratify the political and military status quo.

The Soviet proposals to endorse the territorial status quo proved especially contentious. Whereas in their bilateral treaties the West Germans had accepted all existing European boundaries as "inviolable," when it came to the broader Helsinki process, the Germans balked and tried to use the leverage of the final conference to extract further Soviet concessions: namely, that there could still be a "peaceful" change of boundaries. The Soviets resisted and a stalemate developed.

The Western powers also wanted to inject some agreements on military security into the conference, and these became known as confidence-building measures (or CBMs, in the inevitable Washington shorthand). What the West wanted was prior notification of military maneuvers of a given size, if held within a certain distance from the boundaries of any state in Europe. This meant the inclusion of parts of European Russia—a proposal not calculated to make Moscow happy.

The Talmudic nature of the process was illustrated by the following: The Soviets would not discuss any of the detailed humanitarian issues in Basket III, unless it was first agreed that the text would be preceded by a preamble. And in this preamble the Soviets intended to insert a statement that none of the measures adopted would be used to interfere with the internal affairs of any state. Thus the Soviets would be free to accept the specific Western demands at the conference but would later be free to reject any item as a violation of their preamble.

There was a somewhat similar debate over the validity of the various principles that the security declaration of Basket I would contain. The discussion had an Orwellian aura. The West argued that all principles had equal validity, while the Soviets countered that some principles were more equal than others. The French delighted in this disputation. And even the more concrete and serious issues of "peaceful change" of borders was reduced to an absurd proposition. The Soviets might accept the concept of "peaceful change" of borders, as the Germans wanted, but Moscow wanted to insert this statement in a preambular paragraph detached from the statement that borders were recognized as inviolable. Somehow the Soviets rationalized that these few inches of space between sentences would protect the sanctity of the borders. The Germans, of course, saw through this ruse and stoutly resisted. Another mind-boggling stalemate.

These esoteric debates made it virtually impossible to conduct any business above the level of the experts in each delegation. The terminology alone was baffling. There were Dutch compromises, Finnish plans, and so forth—concepts that were used with ease by the diplomats but dismayed their superiors. Gromyko seemed to be well informed when the issues were discussed with Kissinger, but he carefully limited himself to those issues of importance to the USSR, ignoring or dismissing the others. When it came to specifics, such as resisting Western pressures for freer movement of people and ideas, Brezhnev and Gromyko found a windfall in a proposal that a Dutch cabaret perform in the Soviet Union. This struck them as hilarious, and they constantly used it to ridicule demands for them to be more forthcoming. More seriously, Brezhnev once exploded that he was not going to open up the Soviet Union to Western pornography—a telling point.

Even the serious problem of limiting military maneuvers was reduced to bargaining in the bazaar. For example, the West wanted notification of maneuvers sixty days beforehand; but the Soviets countered with five days. Given Soviet negotiating practice, it would be a long process to reach the inevitable compromise of thirty days. At one point our delegation wrote, "For the moment CSCE is pushing ahead, unaffected in any visible way by external events."

The Soviets, of course, were not happy at this state of affairs and complained periodically to Kissinger. Gromyko said at one point that the diplomats were simply "beating the air." For a time it had looked as if the Helsinki summit would in fact take place in late 1974, and Kissinger's staff (including me) had predicted this. We were off by almost nine months. In part, this was because of Watergate and the disappearance of Nixon and, in part, because of the resignation of West German Chancellor Willy Brandt and the death of President Georges Pompidou of France. Kissinger warned the Soviets that it was the Europeans rather than the Americans who were beginning to have doubts about the process. European opinion was in fact starting to harden as it became increasingly obvious that there would be a final conference at the summit. Each of the European leaders suddenly began to press vigorously for pet projects in order to answer those domestic critics who opposed the conference.

The United States was comfortable taking refuge behind the Europeans, much to the irritation of the Soviets. Brezhnev complained that the United States was "far too passive." "The U.S. sits in silence," he said. Kissinger's position was that the debate was becoming ludicrous. He cited to Gromyko the dispute over the "equal validity" of principles, and said that he could take any formula if the other participants agreed. This was a fairly safe offer since agreement was hard to come by on almost anything.

In preparation for the Vladivostok meeting in November 1974, our staff briefing memo had informed Ford that the conference was "creeping along"; we recommended that he take the position that he would be ready for a meeting after the spring of 1975. At Vladivostok, Brezhnev proved reasonably well prepared, arguing about specifics and pointing to the hidden desire for German unification in the dispute over the change of European borders. Gromyko was embarrassed by this frank talk of German unification, but Brezhnev seemed unconcerned. To prove his mastery of the subject, Gromyko reeled off six points of complaint to Kissinger and Ford. Finally, it was agreed to try for a Helsinki summit in March or April

1975, but the United States continued to push away the final date.

In the spring the agreement was still not completed. Brezhnev's complaints became more strident and Ford's reassurances more curt. It may well be that this uncertainty over Brezhnev's pet project was of some help in enlisting Soviet good offices to continue the unhindered evacuation of Saigon. In any case, further haggling brought more and more Brezhnev complaints. At one point Brezhnev was upset because at a press conference President Ford had maintained—as had all of his predecessors—that he refused to say whether or not he would order the use of nuclear weapons to defend Western Europe. On another occasion Brezhnev was bitter over remarks by Schlesinger on the same subject. Apparently Brezhnev sensed a trend toward a harsher American position.

One small episode particularly underscored the peculiar dynamics of the CSCE deliberations. When Kissinger and Gromyko were in Geneva there was a moment when everything seemed to fall into place and a final agreement could be announced. But one participant, the tiny island of Malta, refused to go along. A consensus of all thirty-five countries was required. Kissinger and Gromyko joined forces to instruct their ambassadors to approach the Maltese prime minister, Dom Mintoff, and persuade him to agree to the final text. But he was horseback riding along the beach and would not return for some hours. The ambassadors were urged to find him, but all efforts failed. Both Kissinger and Gromyko, upon learning of this at dinner, saw the humor in the two superpowers being held up by an obscure European potentate blithely riding along the water's edge.

Brezhnev finally proposed a specific date: July 22, 1975. Somewhat peevishly, we urged Ford to turn it down, on the principle that Brezhnev had been a pain in the neck. So Ford replied that that week was unacceptable and proposed the following week. At long last a date was agreed upon.

Our views at the staff level reflected the deeper uncertainty behind all of this maneuvering. Obviously relations were declining:

> In the six months since Vladivostok, there is no doubt that
> relations with the U.S.S.R. have deteriorated. The tone, at least

as reflected in Gromyko's last speech criticizing you [Kissinger]
personally, is more querulous. The substance has narrowed to a
few issues where there are still mutual interests, particularly
Strategic Arms Control. But the prospect of a deepening detente
seems to be fading.

This was to prove accurate. Helsinki may well have been the
high point of détente, at least symbolically. But in practice the
relationship was indeed deteriorating, as our briefing memo
had warned.

Nevertheless, we were on our way to Helsinki, and for Gerald
Ford it was a fateful moment. He realized that he had a political
problem, and his speech writers had drafted a departure
statement attacking the conference. Brent Scowcroft substituted
a more neutral statement. One can only wonder how Ford
would have behaved in Helsinki had he known what was in
store for him as Air Force One took off for the Helsinki
conference in July 1975. A chain of events began that would
contribute to his defeat in the election. The Helsinki conference
was controversial and put the administration on the defensive.
East European groups in the United States, as well as conservatives, were very critical of Ford for going. To explain our
position, Kissinger gave a long background briefing to American diplomats in London. Helmut Sonnenfeldt also gave a
briefing, and his presentation, converted into a State Department telegram, was leaked in a bowdlerized version to the
press a few months later, at the beginning of the presidential
primary campaigns. It became infamous as the "Sonnenfeldt
doctrine," which supposedly urged the United States to consign
the East Europeans to the Soviet sphere, indeed, to assist in
forming an "organic" link between Moscow and its satellites.
This interpretation was deeply unfair to Sonnenfeldt, who had
for years ardently defended exactly the opposite position—that
we should work to loosen the ties between the Soviets and
Eastern Europe. His real argument was clear from the actual
text of his briefing when it was finally released, but by then it
was too late. This allegation of writing off Eastern Europe
dogged Ford, and in the television debate with Carter, Ford
compounded the problem by insisting that Poland was not
under Soviet domination. The gaffe caused his campaign to
take an irreversible turn for the worse.

Helsinki is one of those antiseptic, bright, airy, modern and, to me, thoroughly uninteresting Scandinavian cities. The conference was a quick affair, over in two days. The official purpose was to sign a Final Act—a phrase that I thought almost obscene. Naturally there had to be speeches, and by the time the conference opened every statesman had determined to speak for at least fifteen minutes, and sometimes more. This meant a truly grueling marathon.

The hall was spacious enough and, appropriately, was called Finlandia. It had a huge anteroom, and that was where most of the real action occurred. The conference organizers would occasionally take pity on the thirty-five heads of state and permit an intermission. The leaders of great powers would head for their waiting rooms, but the leaders of average middle-class powers had to be content with milling about in the large anteroom. This led to some amusing moments, when mortal enemies would encounter each other—the Greeks and Turks, for example. (The Turks solved this by walking out of the entire conference, though only briefly.)

The most intriguing spectacle was the band of East European Communist leaders: they did not rate a private room, so they would huddle together for the entire intermission as if there was protection in numbers. Remember, they were Kádár, Husák, Ceausescu, Honecker, Zhivkov and Gierek; it would have been almost comical had it not been so pathetic. They could not mingle without raising political eyebrows and perhaps even arousing the suspicions of their Soviet comrades. So they stuck close to one another. Finally, Gierek, whom Ford had just visited in Warsaw, began to stray from the pack. And then Erich Honecker, from East Germany, found his fellow countryman from West Germany, Helmut Schmidt—this was the greatest of ironies: the two Germans banding together at a conference called to ratify the division of that unfortunate country. In microcosm, this was the essence of Helsinki: the gradual thaw between Eastern and Western Europe.

The speeches were mundane, but after hearing Prime Minister Harold Wilson of Britain give a rather good speech, Kissinger summoned me and instructed me to go to Ford's speech writers and help them to "improve" Ford's address— strengthen it, was his instruction. This was not calculated to endear me or Kissinger to the speech writers, who are a somewhat strange breed in any case. They were already irritated because they had failed to get a highly critical text accepted by the president. With some effort we agreed to change a few things, but they were inordinately proud of Ford's text. They were particularly fond of the last phrase, to the effect that history would judge "not by what we say today, but by what we do tomorrow—not by promises we make but by the promises we keep." This struck me as felicitous, but I could not resist asking why we should spend time working on a speech that ended by saying we would not be judged by what we said.

This phrase was quite in keeping with what had become a major Western theme. Feeling somewhat sheepish about making so much of the conference, most of the Western statesmen had decided to warn the Soviets to abide by the agreement. This was more than a little irritating to Brezhnev. Even the Soviets had not yet had time for major violations.

The seating in the hall was such that the baggage train of the American delegation sat near the back of the hall, in a sort of peanut gallery. But somehow this put us exactly across the aisle from the main Soviet delegation, including Brezhnev. One could therefore watch him and observe his reactions. He was, in fact, fighting sleep for most of this grand conclave. But occasionally he would become animated and send the Soviet delegation into a flurry of activity. One could not help noticing that as the conference progressed his mood changed from pleased to irritated.

One historical footnote: Seated among the Soviet delegates was an unfamiliar gray-haired man, rather older, who obviously commanded a great deal of deference from the other members of the delegation. He was not recognizable to any of the Americans and we asked who he was. At first, in typical Soviet style, the Soviet officials we knew only muttered that he was in charge of administration. But finally it emerged that he was Konstantin Chernenko, who at that time was Brezhnev's chief of staff but was rising rapidly to become a high-level Politburo member. And, of course, he was to become one of Brezhnev's successors, following the death of Andropov in 1984. None of this was foreseen then, and his presence drew no attention from the press or other delegations. This shows how little we know about the intricacies of the Politburo bureaucracy.

The routine of the conference was punctuated by a party

given by the Soviets—a highlight of the whole event. The Soviet hosts outdid themselves in caviar and vodka, but Brezhnev made only a token appearance. Thus we were left to enjoy his hospitality—one of the few genuinely pleasant social occasions with the Soviet staff. After about twenty meetings at various places, the Kissinger and Brezhnev staffs had come to know each other rather well. I knew one official particularly well because we had worked together on various documents in many meetings over five years. A year or so after I had left the government, I discovered that he had been posted to Washington but had never called me. When I met him by accident, he was friendly enough but reserved. It is an insight into the inhibitions to the Soviet system that there can be no real Soviet-American friendships, whether at the highest levels or among the spearbearers. Presidents who engage in summitry would do well to remember this. Ford and Brezhnev got along reasonably well, but that did not prevent Brezhnev from intervening a short time later in Angola, or Ford from prohibiting the word "détente." Jimmy Carter also was friendly enough with Brezhnev, holding him warmly by the arm at their meeting in Vienna. But that did not forestall Brezhnev from ordering the invasion of Afghanistan.

The conviviality of the Soviet party in Helsinki did not, in any case, carry over to the private meetings between Ford and Brezhnev. Almost nine months had passed since Vladivostok, and the worst had happened, as it often does after a summit. The bureaucrats had taken over and done their best to wreck the Ford-Brezhnev agreements. The endless debating about the Backfire bomber was an example. American experts—at least some in the Pentagon—still insisted that it was a genuine intercontinental bomber and could reach the United States on a one-way mission, landing thereafter in Cuba.

The issue might have been brushed aside had it not been for the technical complications. The Backfire was capable of flying at supersonic speeds, but when it did, it would use huge amounts of fuel, cutting back its range significantly. On the other hand, it could save fuel by flying very high at subsonic speeds—cruising, that is. So it developed that the optimum flight profile was called high-low, as opposed to, say, high-low-high, and so forth. This was confusing and irritating enough, but when it became the subject of a conversation at the summit level, between Ford and Brezhnev, it was bound to lead to trouble.

No matter how diligently the leaders do their homework, they cannot possibly master the details of these arcane subjects. But they are forced to address them by ruthless staffs that insist on resolving everything. Ford thus insisted to Brezhnev that the Backfire could reach the United States, having in mind a high-low flight profile. Brezhnev denied it, probably having in mind its supersonic capabilities. And never the twain would meet. Ford virtually challenged Brezhnev's integrity; Brezhnev reddened visibly and called on his favorite, General Kozlov, to explain. He made matters impossible, however, by saying that the Backfire had one half the capability of the older Soviet bomber, the Myasishchev. This confused the issue no end. Before things got too far out of hand, Brezhnev asked for a short break.

Ford thereupon asked me how many Backfires the Soviets had, and I said about forty; he was surprised and miffed. Somehow he had gotten the notion that we were worried about several hundred (which, in fact, was the target for production over the next several years). When he realized that nine months of haggling had been spent on fewer than fifty bombers he was exasperated and quickly closed off the discussion.

But some damage had been done, not just in those private conversations, but in the entire course of the Helsinki conference. Brezhnev was beginning to realize that he was not likely to visit the United States without settling the strategic arms negotiations, and that this would mean some Soviet concessions. He was not prepared to do that.

In retrospect, I think that his illness, the death of his mother and some political rumblings while he was ill had slowed down Brezhnev. In any case, he began to talk about deferring his visit, and setting up some further meetings with Kissinger. It was rather poignant to see how this old man, hardened by the rough-and-tumble of Soviet politics, known as an anti-Semite, would reach out to the German-Jewish refugee who had become secretary of state in circumstances that could never be replicated in the Soviet Union, and plead for help. So it was that Brezhnev proposed that Kissinger come to Moscow or meet with Gromyko at the U.N. to try to put the talks back on track. Ford naturally agreed.

At this point the room was cleared except for Brezhnev, Gromyko, their interpreter, Ford, Kissinger and myself, as a notetaker. We discussed the Kissinger brainstorm of trading American grain for Soviet oil (this was in 1975, eighteen months after the infamous oil embargo). Kissinger reasoned that we could accomplish two objectives: create another link with the Soviets and teach the Arab oil producers a lesson. Soviet oil would be instantly competitive and there would be the added symbolism of the two superpowers combining to deal with the oil crisis. Brezhnev was intrigued but, as always, the suspicious bargainer. He acknowledged that they wanted to buy a lot of grain—an additional fifteen million tons. And he offered to sell twenty-five million tons of oil over a five-year period (not much by American standards, but not insignificant either). Ford had to be cautious about committing more sales of grain; the Soviets had already forced up prices, and this was causing a political backlash. But we wanted the oil, if we could get it at discount prices; otherwise we could buy on the open market. Brezhnev asked what discount we wanted, and Ford said about 20 to 25 percent. Brezhnev was not pleased but proposed that this too be taken up privately with Kissinger—"Kissinger the farmer," Gromyko chimed in. Ford warned against taking these kinds of deals into the marketplace, because speculators would take advantage of them, whereupon Gromyko acidly remarked that Kissinger wanted 25 percent, but the speculators wanted only 2 percent.

The meeting nevertheless broke up in good humor. Brezhnev had maintained a link to further discussions. Indeed, it was fascinating to observe both sides, like two drowning men reaching out for each other's hand, lest they sink separately. So it was agreed that Gromyko would see Kissinger in New York in September, and then perhaps go to Moscow. Meanwhile the Brezhnev visit to the United States was put on hold.

Ford and Brezhnev walked out of the Soviet embassy together, and it was at that point that Brezhnev pulled Ford aside and told him that he hoped Ford would run for reelection and would win. Ford was surprised by this unsolicited endorsement, which he wisely kept to himself.

The meetings were over, as was the Helsinki conference. Within hours, Ford and his party were in flight to Romania and Brezhnev to Moscow. The trip to independent-minded

Romania was another gibe not lost on Brezhnev (Ford had already been to Poland on his way to Helsinki).

Left behind to clean up odds and ends, I strolled around Helsinki. It was almost totally deserted. Our hotel had suddenly become a mausoleum. The streets were bare; the hustle and bustle of international diplomacy was completely gone. That evening the hotel dining room was literally empty. I ate a quick meal, while an army of black-tied waiters stood guard along the walls.

One could not help thinking of other great gatherings—the Congress of Vienna, or the treaty of Versailles—where great conflicts had ended. Now, here in Helsinki, World War II had ended, as much as that was possible without formal peace treaties. The victors and vanquished, indeed all of Europe, had for two days gathered, spoken, negotiated, wined and dined. But that long evening, when the sun refused to go down in the Northern Hemisphere, the past few days seemed a dream.

Helsinki did not end with a whimper, as it seemed that evening. There was a growing chorus of protest, and only a few glimmers of understanding. Chalmers Roberts of *The Washington Post* understood that Helsinki had to be seen against the background of what had occurred in America: the danger he noted was that we would retreat into a semi-isolation; beset by internal problems we were tempted to withdraw from world affairs. So Helsinki engaged us at a time when we were searching for a new role in world affairs, after Vietnam. We were no longer the world's policeman. "The Helsinki venture is but a step on the road to the new American role. And that is all to the good," Roberts wrote.

The syndicated columnist Joseph Kraft also saw the other side: for the first time, Ford had to face the limitations on détente. The starting point, Kraft wrote, was the sudden rise in anticommunist feeling in the United States, spurred by the arrival in America of the author Aleksander Solzhenitsyn, plus the increase in food prices because of Soviet wheat purchases, as well as a lack of progress in arms control. Kraft concluded, "This country needs to be looking about for an alternative to détente."

Unfortunately this was precisely the point. Détente was eroding, bit by bit, meeting by meeting, and no one, not even Kissinger, knew quite what to do. Indeed, Kissinger complained that we had made foreign policy look too easy. The public thought that all that had to be done was to rush off to Vladivostok and sign some agreement, and then everything would work out. Few understood how precarious the process really was and how much work was involved to move a few steps forward. Brezhnev had gotten little for détente; the economic incentive had been taken away by a capricious Congress. At Vladivostok he had settled for the status quo, and the United States had then raised the ante. We were in for tough times, Kissinger concluded in post-Helsinki conversations.

Helsinki had a different impact in Europe than in the United States. It contributed to the process of European détente, breaking down the East-West political divisions on the continent. This is what our allies had hoped for, and what the East Europeans wanted. It gave the East Europeans a legitimate means to widen contacts with Western Europe, and a framework to expand contacts at future meetings. In those terms the Helsinki conference was and remains a clear success. Indeed, it provided the soil in which the Solidarity movement in Poland could flourish; it allowed the two German states to move closer; it gave the Romanians, Hungarians and Yugoslavs more freedom of action. And it made Western Europe feel that it was participating in, indeed contributing to, the détente of the superpowers. In this sense it was psychologically important.

Yet because America was still haunted by the ghost of Yalta, Helsinki added to the strains in the Western alliance after the failure of Kissinger's idea for a Year of Europe. The gathering in Helsinki reflected less of a Western consensus and more of an accommodation between American reluctance and European enthusiasm. Yet no serious rifts developed until the Polish crisis in 1981, which revealed what Kissinger had suspected in 1973 when he advocated using the Year of Europe for rebuilding a new Atlantic relationship: that there was no common appraisal of the requirements for an Eastern policy, nor was there a strategy of détente that was shared inside the Atlantic alliance. On balance, however, Helsinki was worthwhile. It advanced the process of differentiating among the East European regimes and loosened their bonds to Moscow, which is all that could be achieved, given the realities of Soviet power.

If it can be said that there was one point when the Soviet empire finally began to crack, it was at Helsinki.

In our briefing memorandum to Ford on the eve of the Helsinki meetings, we had written that the conference was crucial for two reasons:

> . . . first it will largely determine the future course of the SALT talks, and, therefore, the prospects for Brezhnev's visit; second, and equally important, it will be the opportunity to reestablish a mutual commitment at the highest level to improve Soviet-American relations as the basic policy of both sides. The latter is not a question of atmospherics, but a substantive problem in light of growing criticism of detente on both sides.

Evaluating the Soviet meetings in light of this preconference memorandum, Helsinki had failed, whatever else might be said of the process initiated by the larger conference. Summits, as already noted, are not good places for hammering out detailed agreements, but we forgot this simple rule of summitry and pressed Ford into debates about second-rate weapons. This was a squandering of the capital of the presidency. Yet it was brought on, in part, by the realization that in Washington, indeed within the White House staff, there was a growing desire for Ford to shift course to a harder line and thus preempt the right-wing challenge that was looming within the Republican party. At this point, in the summer of 1975, the politicians were sensitive to these undercurrents, but perhaps we diplomats were not sensitive enough. One consequence, however, was a rising criticism of Henry Kissinger, and for the first time since Watergate, there were some rumblings that he ought to move on, or give up his White House position as security adviser and concentrate on being secretary of state.

Brezhnev must have sensed this change of mood. With the right moves he could have guaranteed his second visit to the United States that fall of 1975 and signed a SALT agreement not too different from the one he signed four years later with Jimmy Carter. But Brezhnev had not survived in the Kremlin by taking risks. His forte was to be a steady long-distance runner. Perhaps, also, he knew what we did not yet quite realize—that he was exploiting a major American weakness in the jungles of Africa, in Angola, to be precise, where Cuban troops would soon intervene in a civil war.

It is incredible, in retrospect, that the name Angola never crossed the lips of any participant in those talks in Helsinki. A major crisis was brewing there, and neither superpower could (or would) raise the question. The United States and the Soviet Union have actually done rather well in crisis management, but they have been terrible at crisis prevention.

This is why memories of 1914 always send a shudder down the spines of Soviet and American diplomats.

VII

DEFEAT
IN ANGOLA

One of the myths about the American government is that it can cope with multiple events. It cannot, at least not very well. One reason for the difficulty of managing foreign policy is that a few major issues dominate the time and attention of those who are the so-called policymakers. There is a small circle of two or three principal actors who monopolize the power of decision. The secretary of state can shape policy through his control over daily operations. The president, of course, has even greater power, but more so on broad policy issues than in controlling operations. Only a few other key advisers can have a continuing impact, provided that they are strategically placed. But this small group does not have limitless energy, nor the time to give every important issue adequate attention.

The paradox is that much of foreign policy is managed not from the top but from below, by armies of bureaucrats in the various departments. By their action or inaction, they, more than the exalted cabinet officers, are capable of starting new policies or blocking old ones, ignoring or disseminating information, concealing reports or magnifying their importance. The public has little notion of the power of the bureaucracy.

But all presidents end up complaining about "the Bureaucracy," as if it were an enemy almost on a par with the Soviet Union. (This explains the attempt to put "reliable" political appointees into American embassies, in a futile endeavor to guarantee loyalty to the president's policy.) The bureaucracy, of course, suffers from the same limitations as its leaders do: bureaucrats, too, must have priorities; not everything can be given equal weight and attention.

In the spring of 1974 the American government was surprised by a military coup in Lisbon, Portugal, that overthrew the government of Marcello Caetano. No expert had predicted it, and even the second-guessers could not find the usual intelligence report that turns out to have been totally ignored. Portugal was on the back, back burner, of no special concern, watched over by a sleepy American embassy. The Caetano regime was, after all, the successor to the reliable dictatorship of Salazar, and was thought to be reasonably sound and secure.

It was actually rotting beneath the surface. As a result of prolonged colonial wars in Africa, the Portuguese officer corps had become disillusioned, disenchanted and disloyal. The junior officers in particular were moving to the left politically, and in league with some of the moderate senior officers, they began to plan a coup (much like the right-wing French officers, politically radicalized by their experiences in Indochina, who tried to overthrow the French government from Algeria). One sign that something was afoot in Portugal was the publication of a highly critical book by one of the most senior officers, António Spínola. It was this retired general who emerged on April 25, 1974, as the leader of the coup and, for a while at least, the new leader of Portugal. This was at once reassuring and misleading.

Spínola was a cartoon caricature of a Prussian officer, complete with monocle. Indeed, he had been an observer at the battle of Stalingrad—on the German side. So it was not thought in Washington that left-wing radicals had taken power. But that was not far from the truth. One of the key leaders of the coup was a fifty-three-year-old former professor at the Portuguese military academy, Vasco Gonçalves. He had served in both Mozambique and Angola and, as it turned out, was as

close as possible to being a Communist without being a registered member of the party. This, however, was not known in
Washington at the time.

Even as the new government was installed, the Armed Forces
Movement, a group of several hundred officers, began to exert
itself as the real power; its membership was too large and
varied to be described with a single political label, but its leftist
leanings were obvious in the various proclamations and statements issued in its name. A far more disturbing development
was the sudden prominence of the orthodox Communist party
led by an old Stalinist, Alvaró Cunhal. The collaboration
between the left-wing officers and the Communist party became
one of the distinguishing features of the revolution. Also
worrisome was the fact that the democratic parties were relatively new and disorganized. They were no competition for the
Communists, who had the tacit support of key elements in the
armed forces and had been clandestinely organized for decades.

Much of this is obvious in retrospect. At that time it was not
at all clear. Indeed, the new Lisbon administration seemed to
be under the control of moderates: the new prime minister,
Adelino da Palma Carlos, was a respected law professor, and
the nominal leader of the military was General Costa Gomez,
a former chief of the general staff, and supposedly a moderate.

Whatever the internal Portuguese maneuverings, the external policy of the new government was clear: to disengage as
rapidly as possible from the centuries-old colonial rule in Africa.
This meant independence for Mozambique and Angola. The
prospect was not particularly disturbing to the United States.
While every administration had supported Portugal and even
Portuguese rule in Africa, American support had become more
or less pro forma and was linked to the desire to retain the
American air bases in the Azores. The Portuguese regimes had
successfully used the Azores as blackmail against Washington
time after time.

But in 1974, the United States was preoccupied with Watergate, and no special attention was paid to the disengagement
in Africa. It was cautiously welcomed, and President Nixon
met with General Spínola briefly during a stopover on the
president's return from the Middle East. The State Department
bureaucracy was also rather pleased with the new Portuguese

policy in Africa. Portuguese colonial policy had been unusually enlightened by colonialist standards; Portuguese settlers did not play the role of the British raj; rather, there was more integration and far less racism. Nevertheless, the Portuguese colonies had followed the trend toward "national liberation," and as a result, the movements for independence had tended to be led by left-wing radicals. The new policy of independence announced in Lisbon was welcomed in Washington because it gave the United States a chance to side with the black majorities in the Portuguese colonies and thus shore up American policy in Africa generally. So, for a time, it seemed that an embarrassing right-wing dictatorship had been removed and a more viable policy adopted without the United States' having had to intervene.

Within six months, however, Washington had a different appreciation of the Portuguese revolution. Kissinger had come to the conclusion that the moderates, including General Costa Gomez, would be the Kerenskys of Portugal; they would become the the victims of the real revolutionaries—the Portuguese Communists. When Kissinger said so in an indiscreet moment at a luncheon, with reporters present, he was attacked for being too pessimistic. Even when his views later turned out to be essentially correct, many in the United States were loathe to recognize the trends in Portugal. Unfortunately, it appeared that the noncommunist politicians in Lisbon were either too bewildered or too weak to take decisive action to counter the Communists. It seemed that the revolution would move inexorably to the left.

But deciding what to do about it was not easy. Watergate and Vietnam still cast their shadows. The use of the CIA to provide clandestine support was not a possibility; this was the very time when the intelligence scandals about assassination attempts in Cuba and interference in Chile were surfacing. Select committees of the Senate and House were beginning their investigations into CIA involvement in the Chilean elections in 1970 and the overthrow of Allende. The CIA was in danger of paralysis, and the atmosphere in Washington created a general caution toward any American intervention.

The overall American strategy was to encourage European intervention in Portugal through the ties between political

parties, such as the European Socialists or Christian Democrats
and their counterparts in Portugal. In addition, after the
resignation of Palma Carlos and the appointment by President
Spínola of the leftist Vasco Gonçalves as premier, the Ford
administration began working within NATO to isolate the
regime in Lisbon in order to demonstrate to the moderate
Portuguese officers that the leftward drive would mean the
ostracism of Portugal from the North Atlantic alliance. What
was not adopted, or even seriously considered, for that matter,
was any plan to overthrow the leftist government of Gonçalves
by a right-wing coup. Unfortunately, this was in fact attempted
in the spring of 1975, and it played directly into the hands of
the Portuguese left. The United States was blamed for an
aborted coup in March 1975, organized around the person of
General Spínola, who had been forced out the previous September. The failed coup gave the Communists a new cause for
mass rallies and demonstrations. A crisis of the first order was
taking shape, not only for Portugal but for Europe. A Communist coup was in the making.

By the summer of 1975, Washington was in a position to act
more directly. A new American ambassador had taken over:
Frank Carlucci, a highly capable foreign service officer with
experience in various executive-branch positions. (He later
became deputy director of the CIA, deputy secretary of Defense, and national security adviser.) Carlucci's presence gave
the moderate Portuguese officers an important channel directly
to the highest levels in Washington and also gave Washington
a valuable means of operating within Portuguese politics. The
crisis began to build toward a climax that summer: the White
House gave strong assurances to the moderate officers that if
they resisted the onslaught of the Communists they would have
American support.

Whether these assurances were decisive will never be fully
known. The moderates began to rally in July and August and
to counterattack against Gonçalves. For the United States, a
key figure, and a heroic one, was Melo Antunes, then an army
major and Soares's replacement as foreign minister. In August
he rallied the moderates with the founding of the Group of
Nine, which included several key officers and had links to the
Portuguese Socialists; it was the cutting edge against the
Communists in the high-level struggles in Lisbon. It was this

group that led the way to the anticommunist coup of November 1975. The crisis ended when the army routed a left-wing and Communist counterattack. General Ramhlo Eanes, the critical figure in this action, eventually became the real leader of Portugal for the next decade.

American actions in this crisis constitute one of the un-heralded successes of U.S. foreign policy. This is seldom recognized, however, and perhaps the depth of American involvement behind the scenes cannot be fully known or properly evaluated while many of the participants are still active in Portuguese political life. Many have come forward to claim credit, both in Washington and Lisbon. And critics, noting the successful outcome, smugly attacked Kissinger for his earlier pessimism. But had it not been for his intervention, the outcome might have been different. For an administration under attack for its pursuit of détente, the decision on Portugal was vastly more important than the details of secondary stra-tegic arms issues that so preoccupied the critics. A solidly entrenched Communist regime in Lisbon would have been a disaster for NATO; it is difficult to imagine what impact it would have had on post-Franco Spain.

Indeed it is worth emphasizing that in this period, when critics were attacking the Helsinki conference for softness on communism, a truly significant turn had taken place in Western Europe. Three dictatorships, in Greece, Portugal and Spain, were replaced by democratic governments. In the Iberian peninsula these changes were helped by American policy, though other factors were equally important. In any case, the mid-1970s were a watershed for Western democracy.

The growing Portuguese crisis—July–August 1975—weighed heavily in the consideration in Washington of another crisis, the civil war in Angola. It was at this moment that the United States made the decision to intervene in Angola through the CIA, and a powerful reason was the situation in Portugal. The interaction of the two crises—in Lisbon, where a Communist success appeared imminent, and in Angola, where the indige-nous Communists also seemed about to prevail—was decisive. It is puzzling why so many postmortems by experts fail to appreciate and understand this simple linkage.

It is one of the ironies of the Angolan crisis of 1975 that the first timid U.S. steps were intended to strengthen the chances of a reasonably fair outcome. The Portuguese authorities had set November 11, 1975, as the date for Angolan independence. Facing this deadline, the various factions in Angola had started maneuvering and, in some instances, fighting with each other. But eventually a coalition of the three major factions emerged; it was supposed to govern while the Portuguese forces withdrew. The three factions were the Popular Movement for the Liberation of Angola (MPLA), a Communist group led by Angostinho Neto and based mainly in the capital of Luanda; the National Front for the Liberation of Angola (FNLA), operating in the northern provinces near the Zairian border, and led by Holden Roberto, who was a longtime client of the United States; and the National Union for the Total Independence of Angola (UNITA), led by Jonas Savimbi, a European-educated politician and tribal leader, operating mainly in the southern provinces, where his Ovimbundu tribe was dominant. These were not strongly ideological movements, or even well-structured political forces, except perhaps for the MPLA in Luanda. They had cooperated at different times.

The United States had no particular stake in Angola; even the left-wing MPLA did not seem especially threatening, and the whole situation was quite murky: Savimbi, for example, was being supported by the Chinese Communists, who were active in opposing the Moscow-oriented MPLA faction. The United States had old political ties to Holden Roberto, who lived in Zaire (the president of Zaire, Joseph Mobutu, was his brother-in-law). His ties to the United States dated back to the Kennedy administration and were formed during the Congo crises of the early 1960s. Thereafter a low-key relationship continued with the United States, but it was sustained more because of loyalty to an old retainer than for his use as a political force; he was not supported by the CIA in operations against Portuguese armed forces, for example. But looking toward an eventual Angolan election, or a period of political negotiations before or after independence, Washington had to consider which faction, if any, should be supported.

It was clear that the Portuguese left wing would support the MPLA and that the Portuguese Communists would secure Soviet political support for the MPLA, even though Soviet relations with the MPLA had cooled. Thus the CIA decided that the FNLA and Roberto could use some financial assistance for political organization. Accordingly, the CIA proposed a payment of $300,000 to buy a small printing press, some broadcasting equipment, party badges, uniforms and so forth. Although the request was anodyne, it was considered by the 40 Committee, the small interagency group chaired by Kissinger that had to approve any clandestine or covert operation. Some CIA officials later claimed they were pushed into Angola because of Kissinger's obsession with "global politics." This was not the case. Kissinger's involvement was late and hesitant. Critics have also pointed to the initial approval of funds for Roberto in January 1975 as a fatal step, provoking Soviet counteractions and causing a major crisis. This is nonsense. The funding was a small amount of money, which scarcely caused a ripple in Angola; no one reported to Washington that it was leading to a crisis. The only crisis was inside the State Department, where the very fact that the CIA had taken this minor step caused the usual nervousness that arises whenever the United States takes any action that makes waves.

The State Department was in the process of appointing a new assistant secretary for African affairs. Donald Easum was leaving, to be replaced by Nathaniel Davis, who had the unfortunate history of having been in Chile when Salvador Allende was overthrown. Though he was innocent of any complicity in the Allende affair, he was widely blamed for it. He was later unfairly and wrongly portrayed in the popular movie *Missing* as colluding with the anti-Allende coup. Davis's faults were in the other direction: still smarting from the trauma of Chile, he was terrified of having anything to do with another crisis. His appointment became a controversial public issue when the Organization of African Unity (OAU) denounced him for his alleged role in Chile. All of this colored his outlook and made him a particularly inappropriate choice to monitor the difficult situation that was developing inside Angola. His whole approach was the standard State Department solution to any problem: negotiate. It was Vietnam all over again, though in microcosm—warring parties that were struggling for power and killing each other would somehow be brought together and would magically settle their differences.

In Angola a war was indeed developing. The MPLA in effect

overthrew the carefully worked-out compromise of the three factions, known as the Alvor accords for the Portuguese city where they were signed. The MPLA's aim was to grab as much territory as possible so that on independence day in November it could proclaim itself the effective government of Angola; it could then appeal for recognition by the OAU. To this end the MPLA eventually drove Holden Roberto's forces out of Luanda and tried to neutralize Savimbi by offering him a deal while threatening to attack his bases. The coalition government naturally collapsed. Two factors helped the Communists: First the Portuguese military was sympathetic to the MPLA and was turning over weapons to them as Portuguese military units withdrew. Second, the Communist bloc countries, including the USSR, began sending in weapons by ship in the first months of 1975, in addition to opening an airlift through Congo-Brazzaville.

The American response was uncertain, contrary to the popular myth that Washington plunged into Angola. Kissinger repeatedly asked for an assessment from the State Department's African bureau, especially after Kenneth Kaunda, the president of Zambia, during a visit to Washington in April 1975, urged President Ford to become involved in Angola. The State Department was determined to drag its feet, lest Kissinger use any pessimistic assessment to raise the question of American intervention. The African bureau waited until mid-June to prepare what turned out to be a bland and ineffectual report. This delay proved to be too clever, because all that the State Department accomplished was to leave the field to the CIA. But the truly ironic aspect was that the CIA had begun to have doubts: having agitated for assistance to Roberto, the agency procrastinated when asked for a specific recommendation. In part, the problem was that the director of the CIA, William Colby, was still shell-shocked by Vietnam. He had been a major figure in supervising the Phoenix program for identifying and neutralizing Communist cadres in the countryside, which was alleged to have been an assassination program. Colby suffered some vicious attacks because of his role. Moreover, in the much ballyhooed congressional investigations of intelligence, Colby adopted a strategy of conciliation, volunteering a great deal of information. Perhaps it was the only strategy possible: a weakened White House was loathe to fight the CIA's old battles for

misdeeds that had occurred years before. But the CIA cooperation alienated Vice President Nelson Rockefeller, who thought
the agency was wrong to be so accommodating, and this dispute
sowed the seeds for Colby's later dismissal by President Ford,
in November 1975. As for Angola, Colby dreaded having to
go to the congressional committees that he was trying to placate
and explain yet another intervention. The CIA did finally
propose to the interagency committee a financial package in
two parts: first, weapons and assistance for the FNLA to stave
off its defeat (this would not be handled directly, but would
be funneled through Roberto's brother-in-law in Zaire); and
second, a similar though smaller package for Savimbi's
UNITA.

The proposal was considered in mid-July, against the background of the threat of a Communist takeover in Lisbon. The
State Department was wringing its hands, as usual. But it did
have one valid point, namely, that there still was no special
rationale for supporting Savimbi (aid for his group had been
turned down in January). He had been a client of the Chinese
Communists, and his ties to South Africa were also suspect.
On the other hand, there was a risk that he would join with
the MPLA in some new coalition, so winning him over had
become important.

The decision was to support Roberto and the FNLA, as
proposed by the CIA, and to open a limited relationship with
Savimbi. As is typical of such clandestine operations, however,
the policy discussion was cryptic and had to remain tightly
controlled, even within the executive branch. Thus a political
strategy for Angola was never thoroughly debated. The CIA
assumed that what was intended was only a holding operation,
playing for a stalemate in the fighting, and the eventual
resumption of negotiations to restore a coalition in Luanda.
Their entire approach was shaded by this view. John Stockwell,
one of the CIA officers responsible for Angola, later wrote a
controversial memoir of this period in which he said the CIA
staff was told "no win." Kissinger had not clarified American
objectives; perhaps he was uncertain whether a limited commitment could turn the tide. But the CIA had never pressed
the issue of American aims and tactics. Obviously it preferred
to run its own operations; but it did so with a notable lack of
enthusiasm.

Moreover, the operation suffered badly from the Vietnam syndrome. There were firm promises from the CIA that it would be a strictly local operation with no American mercenaries or aides inside the country. This aspect involved endless vows to the press that no Americans were in fact in Angola. Colby regularly reassured the White House also, and he was telling what he believed to be the truth. But without Colby's knowledge, the CIA did send some people into Angola, and at several different times, at least according to the revelations in Stockwell's book.

Stockwell claims that he violated or disregarded his instructions to stay out of Angola, thus jeopardizing the operation. But when he returned to inform CIA headquarters that a "win" by the noncommunist forces would be quite easy, provided the United States moved quickly, the agency wanted to hear none of it. Their position was that the objective was only a stalemate. Stockwell's supervisors decided to suppress his evaluation—an unconscionable action, if Stockwell's account is accurate. Thus, the CIA sabotaged its own plan and operation. None of this was known at the White House, where it might have made a major difference. Neither Kissinger nor Ford would have been content with the CIA slow-drag operations had they known how easy a military coup would have been.

In July 1975, having authorized the limited intervention in Angolan politics, Ford proceeded to the Helsinki conference, where he met with Brezhnev, in the face of criticism from his right wing and from the press for his concessions to the Communists. He was already under attack for not receiving Solzhenitsyn at the White House. This hapless affair incensed the right wing; in one of his most biting—and sillier—exaggerations, George Will later wrote that "not even Watergate was as fundamentally degrading to the Presidency." This, of course, was before Solzhenitsyn revealed some of his more unpalatable views about democracy and the United States.

I had not been informed of the Solzhenitsyn affair beforehand. My guess is that it was not taken very seriously at first. He was in Washington to address the American Federation of Labor, not exactly a strong supporter of the White House. I doubt that anyone involved thought that this rejection would be given so much publicity. But the blunder blew up, and Kissinger accepted the blame. I am still not convinced that the visit was turned down for fear of offending Brezhnev. It was a classic internal foul-up. Much later Brezhnev needled us that Solzhenitsyn had become our problem.

In any case, the right-wing attack on Ford seemed particularly unfair to him, coming as it did at a time when he had just ordered U.S. intervention in Luanda to defeat the Communist challenge. Indeed, it was typical of the American right wing that they could become agitated about Soviet dissidents but could not rouse themselves when two entire countries were in danger of going under.

Kissinger had argued that if we were intent on intervening in Angola, we should go in quickly. But the actual program was the opposite: slow and incremental. It was maddening how inept the CIA was in finding and dispatching military equipment. It reached the point that some equipment was borrowed directly from Zaire. This was a mistake; it gave Mobuto an excuse to confiscate CIA supplies that were coming in for Roberto. In effect, he stocked his own larder at the expense of his brother-in-law. However, it may not have mattered; the FNLA forces were pitiful fighters, but so was the opposition MPLA. Therefore, Mobuto began to send in some of his own paratroopers, and they began to make progress toward recapturing Luanda. The big change, however, was in Savimbi's forces; they suddenly became ferocious fighters, for reasons that later became apparent—the involvement of South Africans. Thus it seemed that the noncommunist forces might, in fact, win rather than merely force a stalemate. So it became necessary to reconsider our tentative relationship to Savimbi. The fight over aid to Savimbi broke out again in Washington, between the State Department and the CIA, but this time it was more muted. Ambassador Davis had resigned in protest over the clandestine program for Angola and had accepted another assignment, as ambassador to Switzerland. Out of loyalty to Davis or disloyalty to Kissinger, the African bureau of the department eventually saw to it that the fact of a U.S. operation in Angola was leaked to the press, but without the details, the leak provoked little public interest.

Indeed, shortly before leaving for Helsinki I briefed a Senate Foreign Relations subcommittee, including Democratic Senator Dick Clark of Iowa, who later attacked the whole operation, and Clifford Case, the subcommittee chairman. This was still a highly secret clandestine operation, despite one leak to the press. The briefing was mainly about the current situation—how each side was faring, and what our program involved. There was little or no discussion of contingencies in the future. No one objected, and if there were any reservations, they were not voiced, which of course is one of the reasons why the Senate's assault, six months later, on the Ford administration seemed so hypocritical.

What was otherwise a serious briefing session was marked by one lighter moment. Sitting in on my classified briefing was a first-term senator, Joseph Biden of Delaware, who was the youngest senator in many a year. I recognized him, of course, but in my briefing I must have given an impression of unease over his presence. Finally he interrupted and said that he wanted to reassure me that he had a right to be there, that he was in fact a U.S. senator. This provoked some polite laughter, and the briefing continued on its dreary course.

The senators who later became strong critics may have had a point. If they had been informed by the White House or the State Department that we were determined to wring a military victory out of the mess in Angola, they might have registered reservations and objections much earlier. They accepted the idea of playing for time and forcing a standoff. On the other hand, there was still no objection, even as the U.S. intervention escalated, both in its scope and in the money and equipment involved. In the late autumn we had committed in the neighborhood of $28 million. By mid-October all of this began to look like a success: the FNLA and UNITA were beginning to close in on the capitol—Roberto from the north and Savimbi from the south.

However, two disastrous events had not been reckoned with: first, the intervention of Cuban forces in increasing numbers; and, second, the blatant appearance of South African forces with Savimbi. These two factors combined to upset the fleeting prospect of a noncommunist victory. But in the end it was the U.S. Congress's refusal to stay the course that was decisive.

The Cuban intervention—or, more accurately, the Soviet-sponsored Cuban intervention—is still somewhat puzzling. It was a gross violation of the so-called rules of superpower engagement that were reflected in the "principles" signed at the Nixon summit of May 1972. Neither the United States nor the Soviet Union had used such direct intervention through proxy armed forces. Indeed, the United States had scrupulously avoided direct involvement in Angola, to the point that the actual clandestine operations were hampered. So even a small Cuban intervention seemed to go beyond the implicit rules, and its eventual size made a mockery of any such superpower rules not to seek "unilateral advantage."

The Soviets later justified their intervention on the grounds that it was to counter South African involvement. But the facts refute this: Cuban forces were already in Angola, or on their way by air and sea in large numbers, well before the first South African started fighting. A more plausible rationale is that Moscow was mindful of the disaster in Chile and had determined not to let another Communist regime go down without a fight. There is a problem with this explanation also: the Cuban involvement preceded the U.S. decision in mid-July to support an intervention in Angola, but it was not truly effective until much later. In other words, the Cuban intervention began when their allies, the MPLA forces, were winning.

Some argue that Angola was the beginning of a worldwide offensive by the USSR, which ended in the invasion of Afghanistan four years later. There is something to this. No doubt the Soviets were feeling more and more confident of their strategic position, compared with that of the United States; we were still suffering from Watergate and Vietnam, especially the fall of Saigon. The United States was subjected to blow after blow. At the time of the Cuban involvement, the Soviet defector Arkady Shevchenko, who was then a Soviet employee of the United Nations Secretariat, inquired of one Soviet official in Moscow the reasons for the Soviet-Cuba intervention; his colleague "laughed" and said it was Castro's idea originally, but that the Soviets had supported it because they believed the United States was too tied up by internal politics to do anything about it. This explanation may well have been correct, at least so it seems in retrospect. In addition, however, the United States, with the Jackson-Vanik amendment, had withdrawn the proposed economic incentive; the Helsinki conference had an anti-Soviet edge, with its emphasis on human rights; Brezhnev's health had faltered, and the United States was pressing for new concessions in SALT, while trying to exclude the USSR from serious bargaining in the

Middle East. All of these events could have persuaded Brezhnev
that it was necessary to take some action to reverse the adverse
trends implied in these developments, even at the risk of a
deterioration in relations with Ford.

The size of the Cuban military intervention caught Washington by surprise. A race was developing between the forces
of Savimbi, attacking toward Luanda and led by South Africa,
and the Cubans pouring into Luanda and onto the battlefield
to support the MPLA. In the only real battle, the South Africans
badly beat a small Cuban force. Luanda was within sight of
Savimbi's forces. On Angolan Independence Day, November
11, 1975, victory for the anti-MPLA forces seemed a matter of
days. Then the situation exploded on the battlefield and in
Washington.

The Cubans began to drive back the FNLA on the northern
front. The U.S. clandestine involvement became public in the
United States through a report in *The New York Times* by
investigative reporter Seymour Hersh. His revelations, apparently based on information given to him by a congressman,
brought the whole affair into the open and immediately produced anguished cries of "no more Vietnams." It was in part
the administration's own fault, because as the situation intensified in Angola, the CIA, in a peculiar initiative, decided to
ask Congress for the reprogramming of some additional Defense Department funds against the contingency of running
out of money for Angola in early 1976. The White House was
told by the CIA that it was essential that new funds be acquired,
and immediately. The projection of spending proved to be
wrong; it was not yet urgent, but the request for more money,
even though secret, nevertheless aroused the Congress.

Suddenly questions were being asked and pressures exerted
to hold off transferring more funds. It was a strange affair: the
CIA was pressing for money it did not yet need, but was
causing a crisis that jeopardized the entire operation. The
behavior of the CIA in this instance is inexplicable; there were
strong suspicions in the White House that the agency simply
wanted out of Angola. And once the public crisis broke, the
CIA did want to abandon the whole operation. This attitude
in itself made it almost impossible to sustain the operation on
the ground in Angola; and even if the CIA had been enthu-

siastic, it was clear that the congressional attack would be difficult to counter, since the congressional critics were citing Vietnam and claiming that we were about to engage in yet another fatal intervention.

The public crisis broke at the very moment when the administration, in its dealings with the Soviet Union, was negotiating for an end to the fighting and the restoration of a coalition government. In late October, Kissinger had exploited the temporary successes in the fighting to persuade the Soviets (through Dobrynin) that their case was lost. A direct correspondence was opened to Brezhnev, and even after the first Cuban intervention by mid-November, it appeared that we might score a real coup. The Soviet airlift of Cuban troops was temporarily suspended and there seemed to be a political pause. In early December Ford pressed Dobrynin hard for a cease-fire and offered to arrange a political settlement. It was at this very crucial moment that the American Congress intervened, and the Cubans were beginning to gain an edge.

The opponents of the Angolan operation, led by Senators John Tunney of California and Dick Clark of Iowa, pushed through a law that prohibited any "new" CIA funding of factions in Angola. This virtually guaranteed a Communist victory. And the odd fact is that this law had broad support from conservatives, many of whom voted for the "Clark amendment," as it became known after its passage on December 19, 1975. They were determined to punish Gerald Ford and Henry Kissinger.

The administration fought a brief but losing battle. It seemed to be arguing for another Vietnam. No matter how many assurances were given that no Americans were involved, or would be involved, the assurances were simply not credible to the Congress. The situation in Angola was also too complicated to be easily explained, with three different Angolan factions— MPLA, UNITA and FNLA—as well as Cubans and South Africans all involved. Warnings of the consequences of a Communist victory were no longer impressive in the wake of the humiliation of Saigon. If the Congress denied funds to South Vietnam, why would it turn around and approve funds for Angola? The vote on the Clark amendment also occurred as the Senate rushed to a Christmas recess. The Senate, in an act of total irresponsibility, passed a law forbidding new CIA actions, and left the final outcome in abeyance until the House returned and could consider the Senate action.

This put the administration in an impossible position. It had to continue its operations in Angola against the possibility that the House would not follow the Senate. (We had $5 million still not spent.) But it had to do so against the background of the Senate's signal to the world that we would not in fact persevere. In early January, I told the interagency working group on Angola, which I then chaired, that the aim was to "win," but no one really believed it, nor did I.

An immediate result was that the South Africans, facing tough fighting with the Cubans, decided to pause, and then began to retreat and withdraw. They wanted firm assurances from Washington that they would be assisted if the fighting escalated. These requests came from Ambassador Roelf "Pik" Botha, who was later to become foreign minister—Brent Scowcroft and I were the recipients of his increasingly urgent pleas to the White House. He was cordial enough, but increasingly upset. We were politically powerless to give even a nod of encouragement to South Africa, and this was difficult for Botha to accept. One wonders what view of the United States he formed in those crucial days and how it affected him in later years as a leader of his party and government.

Without greater South African efforts, the Cubans began to prevail, since they had heavy equipment by Angolan standards. The noncommunist forces collapsed. For the first time since the Truman Doctrine and American intervention in Greece in 1947, the United States had formally refused to contest a Communist offensive campaign. Critics argued that it was the Ford administration—in particular, Kissinger—that had produced the Angolan crisis; they insisted that the Cubans would soon withdraw. Ten years later the Cubans were still in Angola and had advanced to Ethiopia as well.

To be sure, major mistakes were made by the administration. The original decision to intervene was unclear. The Congress was ignored for too long. The actual operation was slow and fumbling; the CIA was unsure or inept; and in the end we were allied with South Africa—the kiss of death in Africa.

Nevertheless, in retrospect, the situation could have been salvaged. The Soviets were clearly becoming nervous in November when they halted their airlift to Angola. They seemed to be signaling that they would settle for a draw, not a military victory. A few more weeks might have turned the tide for the United States–backed forces, despite the political burden of being associated with South Africa; indeed, the drubbing of Cuban forces by the South Africans might also have given the Soviets pause.

There were larger messages in this affair. One was that the United States and the Soviet Union had yet to reach any firm understanding on the conduct of the contest in the Third World. Despite the statement of principles of 1972 that neither side would seek unilateral advantage, both sides regarded the Third World as an arena for a continuing struggle. On the other hand, between 1972 and 1975 there were no new clashes. The Angolan crisis was the product of unforeseen circumstances in Portugal, not the result of some clever Soviet master plan. Having won an important round in Angola, however, the Soviets must have begun to contemplate whether there was a major shift in the "correlation of forces" that would provide more opportunities that they could exploit without fear of a major American reaction. This was the doleful lesson of Angola.

Thus, another of the underpinnings of détente was crumbling. It was a basic part of the Kissinger strategy that the USSR had to be resisted wherever it became necessary, but that it should also be rewarded where it showed restraint. The stick and the carrot. The Congress had acted to deprive the United States of both: in the Jackson-Vanik amendment the carrot was withdrawn, and in the Clark amendment the stick was thrown away. It is little wonder that Soviet-American relations were deteriorating. This was a particularly poor backdrop for what proved to be Kissinger's last trip to Moscow. Two months later President Ford would make his statement expurgating the word "détente" from his administration's vocabulary, as he desperately tried to fend off the right-wing challenge of Ronald Reagan.

VIII

THE END
IN MOSCOW

The Angolan crisis came between two other disasters—the so-called Halloween massacre and Henry Kissinger's last and least successful trip to the USSR.

The Halloween massacre was actually announced on November 1, 1975, All Saints' Day, but it had been brewing for some time. That day President Ford fired his secretary of defense, James Schlesinger; his director of the CIA, William Colby; and, in effect, his vice president, Nelson Rockefeller, who announced his withdrawal from consideration as vice president on the ticket in 1976. In the process, Ford also relieved Kissinger of his White House position as national security adviser, while leaving him as secretary of state. Elliot Richardson returned from London, where he had been our ambassador, to replace Rogers Morton as secretary of commerce, and Morton temporarily assumed the leadership of Ford's election campaign. Donald Rumsfeld, who had been White House chief of staff, replaced Schlesinger as secretary of defense, turning over his position as White House chief of staff to his assistant, Richard Cheney. George Bush, then ambassador to Peking, eventually became Colby's replacement as director of CIA. At the White House, Brent Scowcroft, who had been Kissinger's deputy,

moved up to Kissinger's position, and I became Scowcroft's
deputy.

I learned of all this a few minutes before Kissinger's 8:oo
A.M. staff meeting at the State Department. As was my habit
when the secretary was in Washington, I arrived early at the
State Department and read through the previous evening's
intelligence. That morning I received a telephone call asking
me to report immediately to the secretary's office on the seventh
floor. I encountered Kissinger in his large, formal office, pacing
like the proverbial caged tiger. He opened by saying: "You
have to go back to the White House. I've been fired. Schlesinger
too, and Colby." I could not believe it, and for a moment I was
confused, believing that he had been fired as secretary of state.
He quickly explained, and then added that Rockefeller was
"out" as well—all to be announced that day. There had been
a hot Washington rumor about Schlesinger, but the other news
was a shock.

Anticipating my protest, Kissinger insisted that I return to
the NSC, because I understood intelligence and arms control.
(This was the period of the congressional investigations of the
intelligence agencies.) He told me that Brent Scowcroft also
wanted me as his deputy, and that he had to tell the president
of my decision that morning. I agreed, of course. I later learned
that Don Rumsfeld had argued for someone else for my
position, and that President Ford was hesitant about having a
former CIA officer in a high position in the White House.
Kissinger and I had no time for any real discussion, though it
was clear that he was deeply troubled and thinking about
quitting. He and I walked into the morning State Department
staff meeting, where his staff had been waiting for some time.
My friend Helmut Sonnenfeldt understood immediately when
he saw me walk in with Kissinger. I was also probably still in
deep shock. Later that day I went over to the White House to
talk briefly with Brent Scowcroft, who was already a very close
friend.

By the end of the week I was ensconced in the small White
House office that had been occupied previously by Scowcroft,
and before him by Alexander Haig. Haig had left behind a
pewter ashtray adorned with an American eagle, and I promptly
appropriated it and proceeded to fill it with thousands of
cigarette stubs over the next fourteen months. About ten feet

away in another minioffice was Robert "Bud" McFarlane, who would eventually occupy Scowcroft's office and position under President Reagan.

Working at the White House this time was quite different. Previously, I had had the protection of being in a lower-level staff position and under the wing of Henry Kissinger. Now I was far more politically exposed, known as Kissinger's man and so treated in the White House. It took about six months to establish a rapport with the others on the domestic and political staffs, but that was not the case with Gerald Ford, who was gracious and supportive from the beginning. He earned my undying gratitude that first week when I was delayed driving to work from Virginia and was late for a small meeting, which had already begun. I had to decide whether to make a dramatic entrance into the Oval Office or not go at all. I would hardly be missed, I thought, but then I was told by Scowcroft's secretary that the president's office had already called for me to come as soon as I arrived. Ford eased my problem by offering a pleasant greeting without the slightest sign of irritation. Scowcroft never let me forget it. He insisted that all my problems with my automobile, of which there were an unbelievable number, were designed to get me a limousine and driver.

While personally rewarding for me, these shifts in personnel turned out to be a blow to Ford's election prospects. Rather than displaying strength and independence, which was Ford's intention, the changes made him look disorganized and confused. The press naturally went wild and concluded rather quickly that it was all Kissinger's doing, in order to dump James Schlesinger; or it was Don Rumsfeld, who had engineered himself into a cabinet post and into the leading position for vice president (the two other possible candidates had been Rockefeller and George Bush). The fate of George Bush was the ultimate irony. The Congress, still caught up in the spirit of Watergate and influenced by the intelligence investigations, decided that George Bush should renounce any claim to the vice presidency, on the theory that this made his directorship of CIA politically pure—this despite the fact that he had already been chairman of the Republican National Committee. Bush eagerly agreed; the result was to assure that he was not on the losing ticket in 1976—which he could not foresee, of course.

The rest is history. Thus he eventually held the very job denied to him by the Congress for two terms and put himself in a position to become president. After the elections Rumsfeld faded into the privacy of the Chicago business community, where he was quite successful, however.

I came to know George Bush fairly well while he was director of CIA, because I had some responsibilities for intelligence at the White House. We put together a quick reorganization plan for the intelligence community, and it served to placate the administration's congressional critics. It did not survive the change to a Democratic administration in 1977. At first, Bush had some trouble finding a deputy director, and he asked me to take the job; but Ford and Scowcroft vetoed it. It seemed of no great importance at the time. Later, after the presidential elections of 1976, Bush left his position, and his deputy, Eno Knoche, served for a time as acting director of CIA when Carter's original nominee for director, Ted Sorenson, decided to withdraw from consideration in the face of congressional criticism. Thus, for a brief moment, I could have been director of CIA—at least I fantasize about it that way. Shortly after, of course, I would have been unemployed.

The withdrawal of Rockefeller from the 1976 ticket was the most important change at that moment. Ford thought he could appease the growing challenge from the Republican right wing, which identified Rockefeller as its prime target. But the right wing was not to be placated. Ronald Reagan called Ford two weeks later to inform him that he would be a candidate for president. Without Rockefeller to fight the right, Ford was, in effect, partially disarmed until the convention that summer. Had Ford waited, he could have used Rockefeller, a spirited campaigner, to hold the right wing at bay, and then, in a gesture of reconciliation, Rockefeller could have offered to stand aside. Rockefeller would have understood such a strategy. But his exclusion in late 1975 left him without much leverage at a critical moment for the Ford campaign.

The removal of Schlesinger from Defense and the division of Kissinger's duties hurt Ford in the operation of foreign policy. Schlesinger was a brilliant secretary of defense. The country already owed him a debt. He had begun to break out of the strategic straitjacket of the 1960s, which had dictated the strategy of threatening to retaliate against the Soviet population and cities. In 1973 and 1974 Schlesinger introduced some important modifications, shifting targeting away from cities and population to cover some Soviet military installations; this would give any future president the chance to avoid the agonizing decision of whether to retaliate against the people of the Soviet Union, killing perhaps a hundred million and ensuring a similar retaliation against the United States. Schlesinger's second contribution was that he began to enunciate publicly the ideas underlying these modifications, and he began to gain some political and intellectual support for a new strategic doctrine, inevitably named for him. On a practical level, he began to have these ideas of discrete targeting built into the actual operation of our strategic forces, especially by improvements in command and control.

A man of his ability naturally could not be excluded from arms control planning and negotiations. This brought him into a collision with Kissinger. Both behaved badly, as Kissinger has admitted, and their conduct fed the rumors of bitter feuds and battles. It was unfortunate, because in the main they agreed on the direction of American policy. At times Schlesinger could be an eloquent defender of détente and a persuasive supporter of the imperatives of American political and military strategy in the 1970s. He was certainly not the hawk that the right wing sought to portray him as after he was fired. Schlesinger was a difficult man to deal with. He did not suffer fools gladly, and his demeanor was such that he seemed in a perpetual state of condescension. This irritated Ford, and in any case, Ford was being fed unfavorable reports about Schlesinger's conduct on Capitol Hill, where he had trouble taking seriously the mutterings of the Senate's would-be strategists.

At first it was believed that Kissinger had orchestrated Schlesinger's dismissal. This was not true; but at the same time he did nothing to stop Ford's drift in that direction, even though at the last minute he tried to talk Ford out of it. A second rumor that started to circulate was that Kissinger had arranged all the personnel shifts, including, as a cover, his own relief as national security adviser, in order to facilitate a SALT deal with Brezhnev during the trip to Moscow that Kissinger was scheduled to take in December. Schlesinger was widely portrayed in the press as the major obstacle to a SALT agreement. This was also not true, though the Pentagon was not averse to letting the press believe in the Defense Department's toughness. Schlesinger generally agreed that a new treaty was necessary for political purposes, that something might even be achieved of strategic value and that the differences within the U.S. government were quite manageable. He had actually gone along with several compromise proposals made to the Russians over the course of 1975.

The result of his dismissal was the opposite of the speculation. The new secretary of defense, Rumsfeld, was not about to jeopardize his political career—including, potentially, the presidency—by agreeing to a controversial SALT compromise while he was in the Pentagon. But he could not (and did not) suddenly adopt this position, since only recently, as Ford's chief of staff, he had made no objection to SALT. His new tactic was simply to stall and harass, and this first became evident during the weeks preceding the Kissinger trip to the USSR (before the Angolan crisis broke). Rumsfeld began to reopen old issues and, in general, to raise questions about the agreements that had already been concluded. He formed a strange alliance with the head of the Arms Control and Disarmament Agency, Fred Ikle, supported by Ikle's deputy, John Lehman. (Lehman became secretary of the navy under Reagan, and Ikle became under secretary of the Defense Department in the Reagan administration.) This odd coalition introduced a complicated set of new proposals: one linked future American deployment of cruise missiles to a U.S. assessment of the effectiveness of Soviet air defense. They argued that if the Soviet air defense against cruise missiles was restrained, then American cruise missiles might not be needed. Moreover, their approach was to impose various abstract conditions on the Soviet Backfire bomber, limiting, for instance, where it could be based and how it could be flown in Soviet training. How all of these vague conditions could have been written into a treaty was never explained.

The outcome was that to keep peace in his cabinet, Ford agreed that Kissinger would take two different positions to Moscow—one, the supposed tough line, and the second, a softer, fallback position. It took no genius to guess that Brezhnev would reject the "tough" position and then explore for the second. Kissinger was furious at this hectoring and began to reconsider his trip to Moscow. The Soviet trip was scheduled at a time when Rumsfeld would also be traveling. Rumsfeld proposed several scenarios in which Kissinger would stop somewhere to meet him before flying into Moscow, which further irritated Kissinger. All of this was being negotiated at long distance because Ford and Kissinger were then in China, along with Brent Scowcroft; this left me alone to deal with Rumsfeld and the Defense bureaucracy.

I had been given the assignment of chairing the SALT working groups, where the second level of the various departments would try to put together positions for the NSC and the president. The results of these first few meetings were leaked by John Lehman to the columnists Roland Evans and Robert Novak, who would periodically warn of impending appeasement. Monitoring our clandestine program in Angola was also one of my responsibilities under Scowcroft. Thus two fiascos fell under my authority—not exactly a good omen.

Meanwhile, I was trying to negotiate with the House Select Committee on Intelligence, under the chairmanship of Otis Pike of New York, whose interest in intelligence was incidental to his use of his committee to test the grounds for running for the Senate from New York. The conduct of the committee's investigations of the CIA's operations was haphazard. The Senate committee had already conducted its investigation, and Pike was shrewd enough to realize that his target should be not the hapless CIA but Kissinger. That was where the headlines would be, he believed, and he was right. Consequently, he turned every issue into a Kissinger issue. He issued subpoenas for some policy documents, including presidential decisions on clandestine activities. He also demanded State Department documents, especially one memorandum, written by a junior officer, dissenting from official policy. Kissinger took the position that he had to protect the integrity of the policy process, and with Ford's agreement invoked executive privilege. This is what Nixon had done to protect the Watergate tapes, and thus Ford's invocation of the same legal principle created a poor impression, even though the courts had upheld the legitimacy of the defense in policy matters. This gave Pike the opportunity to cite Kissinger for contempt of Congress, which wounded him more than most realized. Citing a secretary of state for contempt was not an everyday occurrence; Kissinger was concerned that the public would not understand the legal complications or the political gamesmanship.

I was given the assignment of finding a way out of this mess. Only the full Congress could actually cite Kissinger for contempt, and no one believed that would ever happen. But the committee had to be given some way to back down and save face. One congressman proposed that we cut up the various documents and hand over the pieces. They could be patched together, but we would preserve our principles. We eventually compromised; I briefed the committee on the contents of the documents, which I brought to the table but would not show to the committee members. Pike absented himself, but this silly farce placated the rest of the committee, which then repudiated Pike and voted to withdraw the contempt citation.

Pike finally outsmarted himself by having his entire report leaked to Daniel Schorr, the television correspondent, who had it published in the *Village Voice*. In doing so, Pike outraged the committee, the Congress, and the White House. Pike was politically finished, and to a large extent so were the intelligence investigations. The Senate committee issued a number of studies but could not prove Senator Frank Church's original thesis that the CIA was a "rogue elephant." It was embarrassing to Church that some of the worst CIA transgressions, such as assassination plots against Castro, occurred during the Kennedy-Johnson years. In my view these investigations did a great deal of damage to American intelligence and accomplished little. The CIA still has not fully recovered.

This, then, was the atmosphere of early 1976. It was scarcely conducive to a rough negotiating session with Brezhnev. Kissinger had decided to postpone his trip, to the irritation of Brezhnev, who would shortly appear before his party congress, in March 1976. We had assumed that the party congress would work in our favor, and that Brezhnev might wish to announce a SALT breakthrough. So the Kissinger trip was not intended to be simply another round of bickering. It might be decisive.

For a time it appeared that the Pentagon might actually prove helpful, especially the Joint Chiefs of Staff. Within a few days after Schlesinger's firing, both William Clements, then acting secretary of defense and a foe of Schlesinger's, and Air Force general George Brown, then chairman of the JCS, came to see Kissinger one evening at the State Department. It turned out that they wanted to cooperate with Kissinger to help his Soviet negotiations. They blamed previous problems on Schlesinger (a very dubious claim, in my view), and offered a new SALT variant for Kissinger's consideration. I do not recall the details but remember the offer as mildly interesting, though still too complex for real negotiations. The spirit seemed to be changing, and this was encouraging, but misleading, as it turned out. The more Rumsfeld took hold, the more he turned hard right.

One result of Rumsfeld's tactics, however, was to create considerable confusion over the JCS's real position. This was important because the key issues concerned the JCS more directly than usual. Since the Vladivostok summit, little progress had been made on the two key disputes with the Soviets. The first was the status of the Backfire bomber, which we still wanted to limit in some fashion, but which the Soviets insisted time and again was completely outside the consideration of the negotiations. The second issue was the uncertain state of the various types of cruise missiles. We were undecided about which to adopt for the armed forces, and which to offer away in arms control bargaining. The Soviets wanted all of the longer-range missiles on aircraft banned outright. Kissinger had saved these missiles from oblivion in 1973, when the Pentagon wanted to junk the program, and now he wanted to use them as bargaining chips. The military had wanted a cruise missile only for its long-range bombers (the B-52 and the B-1). We thought we could convince the Soviets to go along with this. But the use of the cruise missile for the navy was more uncertain. Putting such a missile on a surface ship had no particular attraction for the navy, but they did want to have a short-range cruise missile to use against enemy ships. Similarly, the navy was not enthusiastic about putting cruise missiles on attack submarines because they would displace torpedoes. They feared that their attack-submarine force would be turned into a sort of offshore bombardment force if armed with cruise missiles. Thus the navy was ambivalent. And the army had almost no interest in a land version of a cruise missile because they feared it would compete with the older Pershing medium-range missile, which had the great advantage of being a ballistic missile.

It appeared that we had some bargaining room with the Soviets—that it would be easy to persuade the Soviets to permit a limited number of cruise missiles on naval surface ships if we offered to give them up on land and on submarines. This outcome seemed acceptable to the factions in Washington, despite some haggling about details.

As for that old favorite the Backfire—the Americans still insisted it was a long-range aircraft, while Brezhnev stuck by his statement to Ford in Helsinki that it was a medium-range bomber and thus not to be counted under the agreed SALT rules. In the fall of 1975 our position was to count the bombers in a separate category, under a separate ceiling—for example, permitting the Soviets to keep but not count those Backfire bombers already produced. The rationale was that the Soviets might legitimately claim that they would have produced a different version had they known that the Backfire would be counted under SALT, and so the previous production, about 120 bombers, would be set aside. But however clever our various formulas, the effect of counting the Backfire as a strategic bomber in any SALT agreement was to force the Soviets to reduce the other categories of their missiles and bombers from the overall ceiling that had been agreed at Vladivostok. There was a long list of variant proposals that we were contemplating in Washington. Most of this would probably be much too complicated for Brezhnev, and all that we wanted at this point was to demonstrate movement, and to break one of the stalemates.

I was given the unenviable job of turning this mishmash into two discrete packages that could be presented to the Soviets. The first option was to be a tough one: to count Backfires produced after October 1977 (the expiration date of the SALT I agreement); this would mean including a total of about 300 bombers, based on Soviet production plans. It was sure to be rejected. Moreover, this plan allowed the United States a free hand in cruise missiles. This package had almost no chance of being accepted.

Our main interest, however, was to gain an agreement that allowed some defined number of cruise missiles on U.S. heavy bombers as well as on surface ships. To achieve this we wanted to have the authority to make a second offer: to give up cruise missiles altogether on submarines, while leaving their status on land bases to be determined later. In this option, the production of Backfires would be limited to no more than 30 per year for five years. Ford endorsed both packages, and Kissinger gave the first one to Dobrynin in advance so that Brezhnev could be well briefed on it before we arrived.

Thus Kissinger left for Moscow in mid-January, probably in his weakest negotiating position since he took office, but with one of his most complicated negotiating tasks. We had suffered a bad defeat in Angola; Ford's election prospects had been damaged—he was already under a challenge from Reagan; the national security apparatus was in some disarray; the CIA was still under attack; the Defense Department was under new leadership; and Kissinger's own personal position was being questioned, not only by the Ford reshuffling but by the growing attacks from the Republican right, including Reagan. All of these aspects were being aired almost daily in the press. The hemorrhaging of leaks on SALT negotiations was appallingly high, even for Washington. We thought that Brezhnev might be in a mood to bargain, despite Washington's problems, but we had a very difficult case to explain with all the variant proposals on cruise missiles and Backfires.

The meetings with Brezhnev started badly and never recovered. As usual in these sessions, the reporters and cameramen were allowed into the room for a brief picture-taking session as the two men met and shook hands. It was also the practice for reporters to shout out questions during the picture-taking, in the vain hope that one of the leaders would answer. The shrewd American reporters were the ones who could and did shout their questions in Russian. Nicholas Daniloff (who later gained international fame when detained by the KGB in Moscow in 1986) shouted a question about Angola. Brezhnev replied that he was not going to talk about it, which prompted Kissinger to say that we were—and then Brezhnev said, "Well, Kissinger can talk about it to Sonnenfeldt." This was not only rude, it set the tone for the real negotiations. Kissinger did, in fact, attack the Soviets on Angola, but Brezhnev simply shrugged it off. And then we turned to SALT. But the atmosphere did not improve.

Brezhnev was still rigid on excluding Backfire bombers from the main treaty; he simply could not understand how we could doubt his word that it was not a long-range bomber. We were still paying for his sharp clash with Ford on this issue at Helsinki. So he again summoned General Kozlov to give us some data on the Backfire's performance. This was in some respects a mark of how far we had progressed in four years: the general secretary of the Communist Party of the Soviet Union instructed his chief of operations for strategic forces to brief Americans on the performance of an aircraft that our intelligence was dying to learn about. Kozlov gave us some statistics on the Backfire's performance capabilities, and we cabled his data to Washington, where the information caused a flurry since it obviously did not track with the far-out estimates that were being peddled by the Pentagon. However, our analysts in Moscow—for the first time we had two Defense experts in the delegation—indicated that General Kozlov was probably giving us accurate information, though he was describing a performance under circumstances that he did not clearly spell out (and that we did not make clear in our telegram). He was not lying, but in Washington the acting secretary of defense, William Clements, was using our report to show Soviet perfidy and to attack the negotiations in general. Donald Rumsfeld was still out of town, but he also contributed a telegram raising doubts about Soviet veracity. A storm was brewing, but we were ignorant of it in Moscow.

On the other hand, Brezhnev accepted some compromises: for example, that our bombers with cruise missiles would count the same as an ICBM with MIRV warheads, under the ceiling of 1,320, as agreed at Vladivostok. This eased life greatly and ended a long wrangle to our clear advantage. But he insisted on banning all other long-range missiles on bombers. This left us about where we thought we would be.

Brezhnev was also getting nervous and weary. At one point he began pacing the room, going back and forth to look at a map on the wall, because we had been arguing that from various takeoff points inside the USSR the Backfire bomber could reach the United States. He threw up his hands and exclaimed, "Backfire, Backfire, I wish I had never heard of it." It was mildly amusing, because he had fallen into the habit of using our name for the plane, rather than the Soviet's own— Tupolev-22. He pronounced it "Bach-fear." Once he complained about our use of code names, ratherly bitterly accusing us of denigrating Soviet weapons: for example, calling

their ABM the Galosh, an old shoe. We satisfied him by pointing out that we called his bombers Bisons and Bears; this
pleased him.

Another light moment, in an otherwise serious and discouraging session, occurred over the Soviet proposal to count our
new B-1 bomber as three bombers, whereas the older B-52
would count as one (as would Soviet bombers, of course).
Kissinger inquired, "Why this weighting of the B-1?" And
Gromyko, obviously rather pleased with himself, said, "Because
it is faster and will arrive on the target first." Kissinger reflected
for a moment and then replied, "Not if it takes off later." This
ended the conversation; the Soviets quietly withdrew their
proposal.

The problem that evening in Moscow was whether to put
the approved fallback proposal to Brezhnev, in a manner that
would engage his attention and appeal to his sensitivity about
equality. We decided to make a new offer, based on a theory
that would link our cruise missiles to the Soviet Backfire, on
the grounds that both were "gray" systems, not truly strategic
in their range and capability, compared with, say, the ICBM,
but also not short-range tactical weapons. This seemed to be a
bargain in which both sides would gain and lose equally. The
idea was that if the Soviets could have about 300 Backfires
without being penalized under SALT, then we could have the
same number of cruise missiles on surface ships. Thus, we
suggested that the United States have the right to deploy cruise
missiles on 25 ships, with 15 missiles per ship (giving us 375
such cruise missiles to offset their Backfires). If this was agreed,
we would then give up longer-range cruise missiles on submarines. We thought this package might open the door to an
eventual bargain, especially because Brezhnev would recognize
that it was trading one of his systems against one of ours, the
kind of negotiating that he understood.

And then we would add to the Backfire/cruise missiles
package a proposal for a slight reduction in all categories, from
the 2,400 ceiling agreed to at Vladivostok for all strategic
weapons to 2,200. Thus, we would please those who wanted
some early sign of reductions. We were all rather content with
this variant. It was proposed to Brezhnev, who seemed to sense
what we were trying to do and responded favorably, without
accepting it outright. He indicated that he could agree to an

overall reduction to 2,300, or "even less." The Backfire/cruise missile trade bothered him but he said he would think it over. We thought we had a breakthrough, and that the entire agreement could be worked out within a few months. Then, a bombshell arrived from Washington.

It seems that at the urging of the Defense Department, an NSC meeting had been convened by the president. During the meeting the chief of naval operations claimed the navy had no interest in our plan to protect their right to put some cruise missiles on surface ships; on the other hand, they might have such an interest for submarines—in other words, the exact opposite of what we had proposed to Brezhnev. Scowcroft later told me that Ford was furious at this turnabout. Moreover, there were complaints at the meeting that we had gone too far in Moscow. We were stunned when this news was received in a private message from Scowcroft. To hold a high policy meeting in the midst of negotiations with Brezhnev was in itself unprecedented. It seemed to us that we were close to being repudiated, though this turned out not to be the case. Ford was outraged at the confusion in the Pentagon.

At first Kissinger exploded, but then he became strangely resigned. I think he realized that this was the beginning of the end for him; his role would never be the same as in the old days. Despite all of the disclaimers, his position had been damaged by the changes under Ford. Even without the changes in personnel, the outcome in Moscow would have been about the same; but it is possible that had Schlesinger remained at the Pentagon, he would have been more of an ally in the last stages of bargaining. Sonnenfeldt and I took it upon ourselves to write Scowcroft, expressing our distress at the procedures followed in Washington, and he forwarded the message to the president.

In any case, we were finished—in practice and in theory. The talks were over. Brezhnev promised to study our ideas and to exchange views in the interim. We would have to get back to Washington to find out what was happening. SALT was on its last legs, staggering for a few more weeks before collapsing altogether.

The next several weeks were confused. Once Kissinger returned to Washington, the revolt that had been brewing in his absence evaporated. There were no head-to-head collisions or dramatic confrontations. What happened was far more insidious and damaging. The entire story of the Kissinger trip to Moscow, of the "secret" NSC meeting in the middle of his negotiations and of his "unauthorized" proposal was leaked to the press. By early February the version circulating was that Kissinger had violated his instructions and had been reprimanded.

I think at this point Kissinger concluded that he could no longer force the pace on SALT without building up an insurmountable opposition that would rebound against Ford in the election campaign. So he lost interest in the fight over the SALT details. When Ford offered to go ahead along the lines that Kissinger had proposed to Brezhnev in Moscow, Kissinger turned the idea down in favor of trying another Pentagon scheme. He reasoned that the president could not go through the primaries against Reagan's irresponsible attacks if he had the secretary of defense and the joint chiefs against him on a critical national security issue.

Thus we sent to Brezhnev a proposal known as deferral: it would set aside the issues that could not be agreed—both the Backfire and the cruise missile controversy—but finish a treaty on the other issues. The Soviets would show "restraint" on the deployment of the Backfire (where it would be based and so forth), and we would not test cruise missiles at longer ranges (over 2,500 km) for two years, until January 1979, if the Soviets did not accelerate their production of Backfires. This was a particularly galling outcome; we were passing up Brezhnev's offer to reduce his forces from 2,500 to 2,300 "or less," which he had offered to Kissinger; we were simply deferring the political fight over Backfire, and meanwhile its deployment would be unconstrained; and our cruise missile programs would be difficult to fund in Congress once the critics learned of the restrictions on testing. My view was that it was simply a clever way of killing the negotiations, and this was the outcome. Brezhnev replied to Ford that this proposal was a "step backward." This was in early March, and Ford concluded that SALT was finished, at least for that year.

It was, of course, the end of the SALT negotiations for the Ford administration and for Kissinger. He later seemed to have some regrets that we did not pursue the small opening that had been created in his last meeting with Brezhnev. And others have speculated that a SALT agreement concluded, say, in September would have upstaged Carter and won the election for Ford. I am not so sure. It would have been controversial. Carter could have attacked it as a desperation ploy arising from secret negotiations and so forth. Nevertheless, Zbigniew Brzezinski told me after the election that the Carter campaign's greatest fear was the announcement of a SALT agreement in the fall.

But Ford's thoughts were running almost completely contrary to this speculation. On March 2, without any warning or preparation that I can recall, he expunged the word "détente" from his political vocabulary in an interview in Florida. It was a complete surprise to the White House staff and there was an embarrassed moment at the State Department, where it was explained as only a change in nomenclature, not in the essence of policy. But policy was in fact shifting. Kissinger himself had given one of his best speeches on Soviet relations in early February, in San Francisco, where he spelled out a policy that had strong echoes of the classic policy of containment. He was still rankled by Angola, much more so than by the faltering in SALT. He knew that a SALT agreement could be revived after the elections, if we could keep the Soviets quiet for a time. But the situation in Angola was irreparable and could cast a long shadow over any other Third World conflicts. If the United States could not contain the Soviets and their proxies in Angola, what would happen in the next crisis? And, with this in mind, he laid down a tough line in this speech:

"The policies pursued by this administration have been designed to prevent Soviet expansion, but also to build a pattern of relations in which the Soviet Union will always confront penalties for aggression and also acquire growing incentives for restraint. It is our responsibility to contain Soviet power without global war, to avoid abdication as well as unnecessary confrontation. . . .

"So let us understand the scope and limits of a realistic policy. We cannot prevent the growth of Soviet power, but we can prevent its use of unilateral advantage and political expansions. We cannot prevent a buildup of Soviet forces, but we have the capacity, together with our allies, to maintain an equilibrium. We cannot neglect this task and then blame the Soviet Union if the military balance shifts against us. We have the diplomatic, economic and military capacity to resist expansionism, but we cannot engage in a rhetoric of confrontation while depriving ourselves of the means to confront."

This was more or less classic Kissinger, but with a new emphasis on the requirements of containing Soviet expansion, intended for those conservatives who had opposed Angola as a foreign entanglement. This speech, though meant to explain Angola, was also an interesting forerunner of the debate that would break out later over Afghanistan. In addressing the question of sanctions in retaliation for Soviet actions in Angola—for example, dropping SALT—Kissinger explained that this was not really the central issue; arms control was part of long-term strategy for dealing with the Soviet Union. His point was a different one:

"History has proved time and again that expansion can be checked only when there is a local balance of forces, indirect means can succeed only if rapid local victories are foreclosed."

But it was impossible to move far enough to the right. Reagan's stump speech on foreign policy was a collection of right-wing clichés that seemed unanswerable. Détente was a one-way street. We should be more aware of our bargaining strength; the balance of forces was shifting to the Soviets. Even the Chinese had lost confidence in us, because, while warning the Soviets in Angola, Kissinger was "packing his bags for Moscow."

And, of course, there was also the Panama Canal. This issue was like a long foul ball that curved into fair territory at the last minute and became a home run. Suddenly Reagan had his issue: "We bought it, we paid for it and we are going to keep it," he repeated endlessly. This caught Ford by surprise and left him defensive on the one issue that the public could easily understand and resent: giving away the canal. Ford could have spoken out against attacks on SALT or Helsinki or any number of other foreign policy issues, but Reagan's use of the Panama Canal issue was a stroke of genius. There was no real answer that did not take a long explanation of the situation in Central America. In retrospect, one can only shudder to think what would have happened if Ford had been so weak as to repudiate the negotiations with Panama. If we had been forced to defend the canal against harassment, terrorism and guerrillas, and the Somoza regime had fallen, as it did in 1979, the Sandinistas in

Nicaragua would have had the canal as an issue and rallying cry against the United States.

In any case, the political atmosphere for foreign policy was clearly turning sour. The press began to take notice of the new hard line coming out of the Ford White House. Rumors that Kissinger would be fired or would resign began to reappear. The *Washington Post* correspondent Murrey Marder summed it up in mid-March: "A serious stiffening in the United States' attitude toward the Soviet Union is under way."

This was true, but I still had some hope. I thought that once the Republican primaries were over, perhaps we could resume negotiations with Brezhnev. But even my lingering optimism was shattered in May 1976. We had completed negotiations in Moscow on a new treaty that would regulate "peaceful" nuclear explosions, such as using nuclear devices to dig a canal or create a massive excavation for underground storage. This treaty had been an American condition to the earlier treaty of 1974, in which the two sides agreed to apply a ceiling on the size of underground nuclear weapons tests.

Lest there be a loophole for testing under the guise of a "peaceful" explosion, we insisted on having this second treaty, and in the process we gained some major concessions: the Soviets agreed to the emplacement of U.S. equipment at the site of any such "peaceful" explosions in the USSR, and even agreed to various other monitoring devices. We saw these concessions as a very good omen for future arms control. They were close to the famous on-site inspection that we were always demanding in arms control. So the treaty seemed a landmark, and a signing ceremony was scheduled for the White House Rose Garden. Suddenly, the day before the event, the White House political staff panicked. They decided that Ford would be playing directly into Reagan's hand, with key primaries coming within days. The ceremony had to be cancelled and some plausible excuse offered. I was appalled; it would be completely transparent to the press. But Ford agreed, and by this time I think Kissinger did not care.

I devised the rationalization that we would not sign the treaty until it had actually been delivered from Moscow and had been carefully scrutinized. When I told this to a number of reporters, they shrugged it off. They knew the score. Some time later the treaty was signed without ceremony. Both treaties have remained unratified by the Congress, casualties of the 1976 election campaign. Even some of the hard-liners in the Pentagon were chagrined, because they too recognized the concessions that the Soviets had made. If the Ford White House could not stand the heat of a simple signing ceremony for a treaty clearly in our interest, then SALT probably would have been political death.

Not long after, Brezhnev sent the president another long appeal. It was a rather pathetic plea for maintaining the semblance of good relations. If one read between the lines, it seemed to be an offer to pick up relations later, or even to help Ford during the campaign. But by then Ford was in a desperate fight for his political life. It even seemed that he might not be nominated at the convention in Kansas City. Four years earlier, foreign policy had been a shining star in the Republican firmament. Now it seemed an embarrassment. This was not really Ford's fault. His instinct was to fight back, to take Reagan on frontally. But his advisers wanted him to dodge and weave and pull out the nomination at the convention. It came out all right in the end; but the price became higher and higher.

A particularly bad passage came in May, because of a trip that Kissinger took to Africa. He had belatedly, after the Angolan crisis, come to the conclusion that the United States had to become actively involved in the Rhodesian crisis, where the danger of a racial war was rapidly growing because the white regime of Ian Smith refused to compromise with the black majority. Moreover, among the blacks, the more radical elements were gaining ground. Rhodesia was still largely a British affair, but the United States could no longer afford to stand aside without facing serious consequences throughout central and southern Africa. The high point of Kissinger's trip was a stopover in Lusaka, where he made a significant policy statement, calling for a settlement in Rhodesia and, in effect, abandoning any lingering support for white rule and Ian Smith.

It was an international bombshell. In retrospect, it seems clear that it saved U.S. policy from a series of major disasters in Africa. But the speech coincided with the defeat of Ford in the Texas primary. Before leaving, Kissinger had talked through the implications for domestic politics of his planned anti-Rhodesian declaration. Ford did not blink; he recognized that it might cost him votes in the Deep South, but he accepted it.

Ford's political advisers, however, were upset and angry, and they blamed Kissinger for inept timing, if not for the substance of his policy. I attended the annual White House correspondents dinner at the Washington Hilton the night of the Texas primary, when the political disaster became known: Ford had lost all of the Texas counties. He salvaged something that night and got a great laugh when, during his remarks, he put on a Panama hat and said, "I bought it, I paid for it and I'm going to keep it."

But the defeat in Texas set a gloomy mood in the White House while Kissinger and his traveling staff were basking in the considerable praise given his Lusaka speech. This led to a testy exchange of telegrams between me and my good friend, Winston Lord, who was then chief of Kissinger's policy planning staff. I informed him that we were not forwarding Kissinger's flowery trip reports, written by Winston, to the president; he was miffed by my curt explanation, but after he returned to the United States, he understood our anguish.

In the aftermath of his African trip, the speculation about Kissinger's dismissal or resignation revived. The Ford political staff was leaking to reporters that Kissinger's timing could not have been worse, and that it was an example of the cost of Kissinger's domination of foreign policy. They claimed that Ford should and could have stopped the whole African trip, but that he did not want to offend Kissinger. Typical of the tone was the comment of the former Nixon speech writer Pat Buchanan (who later went to the White House to work for Reagan). Then a journalist, Buchannan wrote: "It is too early to determine if Secretary of State Henry Kissinger's safari through black Africa did greater damage to U.S. policy interests or to President Ford's hopes in the remaining primaries."

One of my favorite reporters in those days was John Osborne of the *New Republic*, whose avuncular manner concealed a sharp intelligence and a fine analytical mind. He had covered the White House for some years and had become the regular recipient of background stories and leaks. The Ford staff, about this time, in mid-May 1976, told him that what the president really feared was a "lacerating contest" before and during the convention in Kansas City, which would effectively destroy what was left of the Ford presidency and, in the process, destroy the Republican party. Osborne concluded his report: "As one who prefers Presidents and presidencies to do well, I'd hate to see such a nincompoop as Ronald Reagan bring about either." Finally, *The Wall Street Journal* editorial page, strongly pro-Reagan, concluded that when Kissinger's job had been to extricate us from Vietnam, his pragmatic style was suited to the task, but Reagan sensed that the "public doesn't want continued retreat just because the alternative is said to be unrealistic."

One effort to avoid a fight at the Republican convention was the attempt to draft a party platform that would bridge the Reagan-Ford differences. This seemed difficult, if not impossible, in light of Reagan's continuing attacks on Ford. I was asked to write a first draft of the foreign policy planks. Brent Scowcroft also asked me for the name of someone not in the administration who could serve as a mediator and help to push our draft through the various committees in Kansas City. I suggested Richard V. Allen, who had worked on the Kissinger NSC staff for a time in 1969, and who was thought to be close to Reagan (in 1981 he became President Reagan's first national security adviser). Allen agreed, and we eventually worked out what we considered an acceptable draft. I thought this was a waffle large enough to cover every faction, but that proved to be wishful thinking, though Allen made a sincere effort to avoid a fight in Kansas City.

At the convention the Republican party finally approved a plank of the platform mentioning Solzhenitsyn in a way that was a clear repudiation of Kissinger and, only slightly more subtly, a repudiation of Ford as well. To the disgust of Kissinger, Ford's advisers decided not to fight against this effort, in order to save their strength for the struggle over the nomination. That evening I went over to the State Department, to Kissinger's office, for a drink before he took off for the convention in Kansas City. He was angry and hurt by the events in Kansas City. He thought that Ford was damaging his campaign against Carter by not fighting off the Reagan attacks; obviously Carter would pick them up and turn them back. But at that time we were still distracted by a North Korean crisis, provoked by the killing of two American officers a day earlier. Since I would be in charge at the NSC during the convention, Kissinger wanted to make sure that the game plan that he had orchestrated for a show of force would not be undermined by the bureaucracy.

The Korean incident had broken on August 18, 1976, after Ford and Scowcroft had gone to the convention in Kansas City. When Washington learned of the incident, Kissinger called me and asked for an immediate meeting of a special interagency crisis group that afternoon. At the meeting, we all agreed that the United States had to respond, and quickly. The Koreans had bludgeoned to death two American army officers in the neutral area of the demilitarized zone; an American work party had been preparing to trim a tree that prevented a clear view of the zone. The Koreans entered the zone and attacked the American group, and beat two Americans to death. All of this had been filmed by a U.S. Army monitoring unit. So there was none of the initial doubt or confusion that is often present in the early stage of a crisis. The film made it clear that it was premeditated murder.

The outrage we all felt after watching the film produced some wild suggestions for retaliation, such as sinking a North Korean ship or mining harbors. But in the end, the commanding general in Korea, Richard Stillwell, offered a simple and ingenious plan: to reenter the zone and cut down the tree. Kissinger agreed, but proposed that if the Koreans interfered, the U.S. Army would than unleash an artillery attack against the barracks of the North Koreans, located a few hundred yards away from the demilitarized zone. Cutting down the tree would cause the Koreans to lose face; and, of course, we would also demand an apology for the murders. Moreover, we agreed that behind this simple act we would stage an awesome display of power, for the benefit of Moscow and China as well as North Korea. Kissinger had told both the Soviets and Chinese of our determination to punish the Koreans. It was interesting that neither the Chinese nor the Soviets supported the North Koreans.

The display of force included: flying some F-111 fighter-bombers from their base in the United States to Korea; flying B-52s over South Korea and northward to the DMZ, turning them away only a few miles before they reached the boundary line at the very moment that the tree-cutting took place; and mobilizing and deploying an armored unit on the edge of the zone. All of this, of course, was monitored by the Chinese and the Soviets. The plan was sent to Kansas City, where it was approved by Ford, with the provision that the artillery retaliation was not to be automatic; it would require presidential approval.

At the last moment, late in the evening, the acting secretary of defense, William Clements, called me to express his worries about the whole affair. He came over to the White House and brought Admiral James Holloway, the chief of naval operations, who was then acting chairman of the Joint Chiefs of Staff. Clements had a memorandum written by a colonel who had served in Korea, and who was predicting World War III if we went ahead with our plan. This officer had impressed Clements because of his firsthand experience in a previous Korean crisis. Clements wanted to make absolutely sure that no artillery battle would be started unless the president had had a chance to approve it; he feared that the president, in Kansas City, accompanied by Scowcroft and Kissinger, would be under pressure to show his toughness, especially in the acrid atmosphere of the convention. But Clements would not make a formal recommendation to call the action off; what he wanted was for me to intervene and persuade Scowcroft and Kissinger to hold off with any order for retaliation.

I sensed that Holloway was embarrassed, but he had been uneasy with the operation in earlier discussions. I asked him directly whether the JCS was making a formal request for a change in orders. He quickly denied any such idea and said that they would support the commander in the field, General Stillwell. So we agreed that the operation would proceed, but I would report their concerns to the president through Scowcroft. I telephoned to Kansas City, and Scowcroft was appalled. He refused to disturb the president, who had just delivered his acceptance speech to the convention and had said, "Not a single American is at war anywhere on the face of this earth tonight." Scowcroft told me to summarize the meeting in a cable, that he would show it to Ford in the morning; nevertheless, that morning Ford approved the operation and it began that afternoon. It came off without any problems; indeed, the Koreans offered a lame apology—"regretful that an incident occurred"—and agreed to negotiate new rules of conduct for the zone, which we had wanted for years.

It was a small classic in the combination of power and diplomacy, worthy of Palmerston, I thought. All of this had happened over the very days when the Republicans were attacking Ford for his softness and rebuking Kissinger for his realpolitik.

IX

GERALD FORD'S DEFEAT

One rule of thumb in politics is that foreign policy issues are not as important as domestic questions in presidential elections. A particularly unsuccessful or unpopular foreign policy hurts, of course, but even a steady, effective one cannot rescue failing domestic programs. Political professionals prefer a foreign policy that is nondescript, gray and more or less benign. What they fear is that a foreign problem will suddenly complicate or disrupt carefully constructed strategies to win some region or state, usually in the South, or will otherwise interfere with good old-fashioned campaigning.

Nevertheless, foreign policy has figured prominently in most of the postwar presidential elections. In 1960 John F. Kennedy campaigned against Nixon on the alleged missile gap; four years later Lyndon Johnson attacked Barry Goldwater as the man who would start a nuclear war (this campaign featured the famous television scene showing a small girl counting flower petals until she reached zero, and then a huge nuclear mushroom cloud filled the screen). Hubert Humphrey was saddled with the Vietnam War in 1968, and four years later Nixon exploited his trips to China and Russia for maximum benefit in his reelection campaign in 1972.

It is not surprising that foreign policy played its role in the Ford-Carter campaign of 1976. Ford's blunder in the second television debate over Soviet influence in Poland was a significant negative (about which more below). Perhaps he never could have overcome the legacy of Watergate, his pardon of Nixon and eight years of Republican rule. But he was beginning to close the gap as the campaign progressed, and the Polish gaffe interrupted his momentum for several weeks. After the election was over, the opinion-poll leader, George Gallup, said that Ford's mistake was the "most decisive moment in the campaign." He explained that the foreign policy debate had "fatally stalled President Ford's comeback, which until that time was the greatest in [polling] history."

In addition to this special prominence of the Polish incident, Ford's general foreign policy played an odd role in the campaign. Here was a candidate burdened with a political scandal not of his own making and valiantly trying to overcome a 30-point deficit in the popular opinion polls (as compared with Carter after the Democratic convention in July). One would have thought that any advantages would have seemed worth exploiting. But his campaign advisers were still shell-shocked by the Reagan attacks on détente and on Ford's "soft" foreign policy during the primaries. They assumed that the enemy was still on the right and that foreign policy was still a liability. Actually, it was an asset: the Nixon legacy in foreign policy had not been discredited, and Ford had added to it in the Middle East, in China and in the arms control talks at Vladivostok. Even his trip to the Helsinki conference had advantages: an active president trying to make peace is always worth votes. And Carter had no foreign policy experience, which should have been a liability.

Carter's use of foreign policy was a typical populist strategy. He had little to say on complex substantive issues. His approach was to combine the usual glittering generalities of any campaign with a high moral tone, packaged in a series of sermonettes. Thus, his stump speech featured his "principles" of foreign policy:

"Our policies should be as open and honest and decent and compassionate as the American people themselves. . . .

"Our policies should treat the people of other nations as individuals. . . .

"It must be the responsibility of the President to restore the moral authority of this country in its conduct of foreign policy. We should work for peace and the control of arms in everything we do."

This was a fairly shrewd approach for an election campaign held two years after Watergate. Of course, what he described bore little resemblance to American foreign policy as practiced since the founding of the Republic, but it had an appeal that played not only on Watergate but also on the way Kissinger operated. There was a campaign theme that linked foreign policy to Watergate: Carter suggested that because Kissinger was conducting a secret policy, he was violating a true American principle, and worse, was substituting the balance of power for a just world order. This too had an appealing, Wilsonian ring. And Carter began to bear down on Ford for his deference to Kissinger. Carter's call for replacing the balance-of-power politics with "world-order" politics was a favorite thesis of Zbigniew Brzezinski, the prominent Sovietologist from Columbia University who was emerging as a key aide to Carter. Brzezinski's criticism of Kissinger was reflected in his insistence on a new foreign policy of "architecture" to replace the high-wire balancing act—"acrobatics." In a long article entitled "America in a Hostile World," he had written a sharp critique of the administration's foreign policy:

> A gap in values and perceptions has opened between America and major parts of the world. The attendant danger of a philosophical isolation is without precedent in American history and has been accentuated by the new style and substance of U.S. foreign policy, especially as pursued by the Nixon Administration that came into power in 1969. Covert, manipulative, and deceptive in style, it seemed committed to a largely static view of the world, based on a traditional balance of power, seeking accommodation among the major powers on the basis of spheres of influence, and more generally oriented toward preserving the status quo than reforming it.

It was easy for Carter to pick up Reagan's attacks on Ford. Indeed, the Carter and Reagan campaigns of 1976 on foreign policy issues were remarkably similar. In the Republican primaries Reagan had attacked détente as a "one-way street";

Carter, in turn, said that Ford was "giving up too much and asking for too little." The Helsinki accords received due attention; Reagan had attacked Helsinki for legitimizing the boundaries of Eastern Europe and legally acquiescing in the loss of freedom of millions of Eastern Europeans. Carter echoed this: for the Soviet Union détente was our "acquiescence in Europe within boundaries defined to their benefit, and without the requirement of living up to the human rights provisions of the Helsinki agreement." Reagan attacked "sudden surprises" in arms control negotiations; Carter criticized the Nixon shocks and Kissinger surprises (I later learned that this theme was adopted because the Carter staff feared that Ford would, at the last minute, sign a SALT agreement). Carter constantly insisted that the American people "themselves" should make foreign policy; Reagan had foreshadowed this theme by saying that the "individual citizen can be trusted to make an intelligent decision if he is armed with the facts." Both campaigned as "outsiders," attacking the Washington establishment, and, in short, both campaigned for a foreign policy worthy of William Jennings Bryan.

Despite their attack on secrecy and their emphasis on an "open" policy, soon after the election both Carter and Brzezinski, in their briefing sessions with the Ford staff, were intrigued to learn they would be able to send messages to foreign leaders without the State Department's finding out. We dutifully explained the operation of the so-called back channel, a communication facility that all presidents have used for their own messages to foreign leaders. So much for "open" diplomacy. Moreover, once in office, Carter conducted his foreign policies without extensive popular debate and relied heavily on his White House advisers. Carter revealed little about the status of the Panama Canal treaty negotiations, until the agreement was ready for signature. The Carter administration tried to keep the SALT negotiations from the public, though because of the incessant leaks, this was not easy. He negotiated the entire Camp David accord in 1978 in complete secrecy. The new administration continued to participate in the Helsinki accords and sent representatives to the follow-on meetings and did not challenge the European boundaries approved at Helsinki. In many important respects the Carter—and Reagan— foreign policies were similar to those of Nixon and Ford. There were differences, to be sure, especially in public style and in political ideology. But on the essentials of the Atlantic alliance, the opening to China, and even in arms control, both Carter and Reagan ended about where the Nixon and Ford policies had settled—close to the middle of the road.

The Ford campaign, however, was obsessed with one thing: he was behind in the polls. It became almost a ritual to begin every conversation in the White House with the phrase "when we are this far behind. . . ." The campaign was organized on the proposition that Ford desperately needed to catch up, and his campaign advisers never wavered from this strategy. Even in the last weeks, when Ford was running even, his campaign was a frenetic thrashing-about. What may have been a necessary strategy to overcome a huge Carter lead was no longer a good strategy when running dead even. Yet in the last weeks Ford was on the hustings, acting like a precinct politician trying to eke out a few more votes. Had he taken the high road at the end, acting presidentially in Washington instead of haranguing crowds at shopping malls, he would have been far better off. What was not realized at the end of the campaign was that Carter was slipping badly: it was dawning on voters that Jimmy Carter might in fact become president. This was a far different proposition from being indifferent toward Ford. In those final days Ford had every chance to drive home the contrast between a sitting president and an untried aspirant.

The depressing atmosphere of the campaign added to the tensions between Kissinger and the Ford election campaign staff, led by James Baker, later White House chief of staff, and secretary of the treasury under Reagan. It was widely rumored that Baker considered Kissinger a liability and wanted to drop him. The previous spring, Rogers Morton, then campaign manager, had publicly speculated that Kissinger would leave. Other advisers wanted to scuttle the whole foreign policy, especially the Panama Canal negotiations. As far as I know, Ford never entertained any such far-out schemes, but he had already moved away from the Soviet dimension by dropping "détente" in favor of "peace through strength." As far as one can tell, this did him little good.

It was on a related question, however, that he got himself into trouble, and partly because of his staff, including me. Here is how the Polish gaffe came about. We recognized that Carter would pick up on the idea that at Helsinki there had been a "sellout" of human rights and of Eastern Europe. By the time of the second television debate, which would focus on foreign policy, we thought we had a golden opportunity to strike back on these Helsinki/East European issues and to show Carter to be uninformed. But it was necessary to be ready. In preparing for that debate we assumed that the questions would more or less center on the "Sonnenfeldt doctrine." We planned that Ford should immediately deny that there was any such doctrine and stress that indeed we had not abandoned Eastern Europe to the Soviets. Ford had already done this, but a television debate was a major opportunity to make the point again. Ford had, in fact, read the telegram reporting the Sonnenfeldt briefing, and we had written a memorandum pointing out the distortions in the press versions.

He was thus familiar with the issue when we began practicing for the debates in the White House theater, where a stage was set up and members of the staff would quiz the president. I was the foreign policy questioner, and I bore down on the Sonnenfeldt doctrine so hard that Ford got angry, and I had to remind him that I was on his side. In any case, we had the issue mastered, or at least we thought we did. In fact, Ford was probably overtrained.

When Max Frankel of *The New York Times* sprang the fateful question in the debate, it sounded like a soft ball. Popular memory is that Frankel asked if the Soviets dominated Poland and Ford answered no, whereupon Carter guffawed. In fact, Frankel began with a meandering speech of his own about relations with the Russians, in which he asserted that, "we virtually signed, in Helsinki, an agreement that the Russians have dominance in Eastern Europe." Frankel went on to mention loans to the USSR, huge grain sales and the prospect that even larger loans would have been made if the Jackson amendment had not been passed. He concluded by asking, "Is that what you call a two-way street of traffic in Europe?"—a strangely disconnected question, I thought.

Watching in the Roosevelt room in the White House, I could see Ford beginning to lean forward, anticipating and eager to answer—too eager, as it turned out. It was a long answer, starting with a claim that he was negotiating from a position of strength; he then mentioned Vladivostok, justified the grain sales to the Soviet Union and, turning to Helsinki, noted that the Vatican had attended the conference and had signed the final document. Ford always thought this reference to the Vatican was an impressive rebuttal, though the rest of us were never as impressed. He ended with a reference to the agreement at Helsinki to provide advance notification of each nation's military maneuvers, and then, almost as an afterthought, he added the fatal sentence: "There is no Soviet domination of Eastern Europe, and there never will be under a Ford administration."

Frankel magnanimously gave him a second chance, asking, ". . . did I understand you to say that the Russians are not using Eastern Europe as their own sphere of influence and occupying most of the countries there and making sure with their troops that it's a communist zone . . . ?"

I doubt that Ford realized what Frankel was doing; perhaps he was not really listening because he was so intent on repudiating the "Sonnenfeldt doctrine." He came back with a reasonable answer: that the Yugoslavs did not consider themselves dominated, that the Romanians did not, and, finally, "I don't believe that the Poles consider themselves dominated by the Soviet Union. Each of these countries is independent, autonomous, [has] territorial integrity. And the United States does not concede that these countries are under the dominance of the Soviet Union."

This was a perfectly valid reply. It made the key point that the United States did not concede Eastern Europe to the Soviet sphere; this had indeed been the burden of the Western position at Helsinki. And the great irony is that four years later, uniting under Solidarity, the Poles obviously did not consider themselves under Soviet domination. But the damage was done. Ford had made a major political mistake and, worse, had not immediately clarified his answer.

I had let out a moan at the end of the first answer, and John Marsh, an assistant to Ford, asked me if the president was in trouble. I honestly could not say, because I thought he had rescued his first answer with his second explanation. But soon after, on the telephone with Brent Scowcroft in San Francisco, I realized that we were in trouble. The press was beginning to smell blood. In an informal briefing, Scowcroft tried to put an acceptable gloss on the Ford statement, but the press was implying that Ford was in fact ignorant of the presence of Soviet troops in Poland. That he had visited there in 1975 was quickly dismissed. The perfectly acceptable interpretation that he meant the Polish people would not give up their spiritual independence and accept a permanent Soviet dominance did not work. The result was a period of ten days during which Ford was dogged by the Polish question. At first he was so irritated and angry that he refused to rectify his mistake. By the time he did, it was too late.

The London *Economist,* an ostensibly neutral observer, concluded that "this time Mr. Carter looked and sounded the more assured. . . . He called for moral foreign policies that Congress could support and the American people could respect. And first reactions suggested his audience this time gave him a narrow victory on points for it."

There were two practical results of this fiasco. The first was that thereafter every conceivable East European group was invited to the White House, and there were countless meetings and ceremonies with Hungarians, Poles, Czechs, and so forth. These were tedious but occasionally colorful; old grizzled veterans of lost wars would appear in the remnants of uniforms and wearing campaign hats adorned with various decorations. The press was merciful: had they looked more closely into the backgrounds of some of the participants they would probably have discovered a few odd persons who had fought on the wrong side in the two world wars.

These gatherings revealed a side of Ford that was not widely known. In 1956, during the Hungarian revolution, he had been on the Austrian-Hungarian border receiving refugees as a congressional observer. This was a human touch that would have helped in the debate, but staffs are often the last to learn of these sidelights. For example, in 1969 we prepared a lengthy briefing book on Romania for Nixon, only to discover that he had visited there when out of office.

The second result of the debate was that Ford began to pay more attention to foreign policy, trying to make up for his mistake, but also, finally, trying to use foreign policy as an asset. This involved drafting some more thoughtful remarks than the usual stump speech. And it is a frustrating reflection of American politics that as the campaign moved into the last weeks, these speeches were largely dismissed by the reporters.

To relieve Brent Scowcroft for the last two weeks, I joined the traveling campaign. I had been working on a major foreign policy address for the president to give in Pittsburgh, at the Economic Club, on October 27. I arrived the night before and went over a few final touches with Scowcroft. I could tell that he was discouraged by the campaign, but we had some forlorn hopes that a serious foreign policy speech might have an impact. It dealt with the principles of American foreign policy (of course), and Ford accused Carter of proposing a "fundamental change in the direction and the conduct of U.S. foreign policy." We thought that this theme would also have an impact. Ford warned against "venturing into the unknown with a doctrine that is untested, untried and, in my view, potentially dangerous." As one of the authors of these warnings, I often thought about the speech in later years, especially during the Iranian hostage crisis and the proclamation of the Carter Doctrine. But at the time, it turned out to be simply another last-minute speech. The White House reporter for the *New Republic,* the late John Osborne, commented that the speech was a "dissertation . . . well conceived, well delivered and singularly inappropriate."

Campaign reporters are a hardened lot. To relieve the boredom they engaged in some highjinks: a favorite was for one of them to dress up in a chicken costume and suddenly appear in a large crowd, hoping to provoke a laugh from the candidate. But when it came to the substance of the campaign, they were all business, looking for truly significant developments, not warmed-over speeches. Only once did I see a few of them moved. In a small theater (in Pennsylvania), Ford gave an ad-lib speech on a round stage—a particularly difficult setting, even for a professional actor. Ford became eloquent, holding his audience and creating a beautiful mood. Those few reporters who had decided to stay for the speech were stunned, as were we all. It was a great performance, known only to a few people.

The low point for me was in Houston, Texas, where it was already quite cold and a fairly heavy rain was falling. It was evening, and Ford was scheduled to attend a high school football game. I recall that the two teams were Jefferson Davis and Robert E. Lee, but that may be my memory playing tricks. In any case the staff was invited to attend, and one by one most of us begged off; no one was eager to sit in the cold rain, even with the president of the United States. Ford had to attend, of course, and this undoubtedly contributed to his growing laryngitis (which got so bad that on election morning he could scarcely speak). It was a shock to read a day or so after the game that the Ford campaign was at last becoming "coherent," that his attendance at the high school football game was a master stroke by his campaign manager, Texan James Baker, who said Friday-night football was "religion" in Texas. But it was a total waste for Ford. Neither Baker nor John Connally, who was leading the Ford campaign in Texas, was able to deliver the state.

There was not much to do in these final days except present the classified morning briefing to Ford. Otherwise, I rarely talked with the president. I received a few calls from Kissinger, complaining about one thing or the other, and at one point Ford discussed with me his plan to go to Egypt after the election. Occasionally, at some convenient stopover, I would call Washington. Ron Nessen, Ford's press secretary, would always watch me apprehensively, fearing I was about to report some disaster. But the campaign wound down without any foreign incident. Haunting echoes of the Polish TV affair would appear from time to time. In a Czech meeting hall in Cleveland, Ford roused the audience with pledges of loyalty to Eastern Europe. The titles of those speeches tell the story of a typical American election campaign: "We Share the Same Great Hope," in Cleveland; "We Must Stay Strong," in Milwaukee; "A Strong and Free America," in Langhorne, Pennsylvania (a speech given, I think, in a shopping center). One reporter described the "well-oiled" Ford machine rolling through the Midwest, but it certainly did not seem so from the inside. A better insight was provided by the reports of Osborne in the *New Republic;* he had the advantage of writing only once a week, so he could observe with a greater detachment. He called the trip a phony, saying its real purpose was to create a roadshow for Ford on local TV, where he appeared with the baseball announcer and former player Joe Garagiola.

The routine of the trip was indeed livened by the presence of Garagiola. He had played for the St. Louis Cardinals when I was a student at Washington University in St. Louis, and we would play sports trivia during the long rides back and forth from airports. He developed an interesting television spot in which he interviewed Ford; this would appear on local stations and seemed to be effective. According to Osborne's evaluation, in these TV advertisements the "true Jerry Ford came across as he'd never come across from interviews with orthodox and certified journalists." Of course, Garagiola was recognized everywhere he went. He and Ford became quite close, and he spent election evening with the Ford family.

In the last few days of the campaign the polls began to show a truly close race (the final Gallup Poll showed Ford one point ahead), and spirits began to pick up. Until then there had been an atmosphere of resignation, as if the gap was too great to close. On a subconscious level, however, the campaign was still conducted as if nothing had changed since the convention, when Ford was in fact trailing behind Carter.

An interesting vignette occurred one Sunday late in the campaign when the message was flashed to New York, where Ford was making a television commercial, that Jimmy Carter's church in Plains, Georgia, had barred four black men from attending services. Supposedly, there was a membership rule preventing blacks from admission; and on that Sunday the services had been cancelled rather than waive the rule. These stories electrified the Ford campaign staff; here, it seemed, was that last-minute development that would weigh heavily with the voters. But, in fact, it was turned to Carter's advantage when his staff implied the incident had been something of a setup, perhaps even a "dirty trick," and that Carter had opposed the membership rule. By Sunday evening the gloom was returning.

Ford's defeat provoked surprisingly little bitterness in the White House. On the morning after, there was still some vain speculation that the returns in some state would be challenged, and that a last-minute miracle would thereby occur. But it passed quickly. Ford called the staff together to thank them for their efforts; because of his laryngitis he could barely speak above a whisper, and that made it a poignant moment. In the period that followed the elections, Ford did all the right things, ordering immediate briefings and liaison contacts. I was the transition officer for foreign policy at the White House. As for the rest of the staff, many quickly made their own arrangements and began to leave. There were no recriminations about

Kissinger, or his foreign policy. After the fact, most of us recognized that it would have taken a titanic effort to overcome Watergate.

Gerald Ford's position in history is firmly fixed and needs little embellishment. He rescued the country from a constitutional and psychological catastrophe, and had he done nothing else, this would have secured his historical niche. But he did more than just that. The *New York Times* editorial of January 13, 1977, paid him a fine tribute, shortly before he departed: "His political comeback was both a testament to America's innate conservatism and a tribute to his own durable personal qualities. Mr. Ford today enjoys the respect and affection of his fellow citizens. Moreover, he leaves the country in better shape than he found it. Those two achievements may seem modest, but they eluded several of his more brilliant predecessors. Mr. Ford has a right to take satisfaction from them."

The transition from one administration to another is an awkward period. The new team is excited, straining to get started, but barred by law from doing too much. The old team is worldly-wise but jaded and weary, willing to give some advice, but not too much. After the initial shock wears off there is a period when the outgoing government, which has no real authority, must make some decisions, such as sending a budget to Congress. What happens is, there is a sudden burst of determination in the White House to take everything very seriously. Thus, we drafted a long national security directive on defense policy; it was quite an eloquent document that Ford signed shortly before Carter's inauguration. It was immediately cancelled by Brzezinski, who was puzzled by its very existence. Even the budget becomes a phony process. The outgoing administration, which is required by law to submit a budget, loads everything into its proposed budget, especially a huge increase in defense spending, accompanied by a fantastic projection of increased defense spending over the coming five years. This leaves the incoming administration with the distasteful task of having to cut defense and thus appearing "soft." Ford did it to Carter and then, four years later, Carter did it to Reagan. In fact, the final Carter defense projection for five years came out about the same as the actual Reagan budget.

Carter's aide Hamilton Jordan had warned during the campaign that if Zbigniew Brzezinski and Cyrus Vance were appointed to lead foreign policy, then the Carter campaign would have failed. They were appointed, of course—Vance as secretary of state and Brzezinski as head of the NSC—but in a sense Jordan may have been right. Neither Vance nor Brzezinski planned a radically different foreign policy, at least not the populist foreign policy Carter had espoused during the campaign. Both Vance and Brzezinski were liberal establishment figures, much more so than Kissinger had been in 1969. Indeed, if there is any truth to the charge that American policy is secretly conducted by the dreaded "eastern establishment," it could be found in the staffing of Carter's national security and foreign policy teams. Many of them had served under Republicans, and most had some ties to Johnson or Kennedy. A few genuine Carterites appeared in the State Department and the NSC, but they were not in prominent positions.

Brzezinski had all the right tickets—Harvard, Columbia, Council on Foreign Relations, Trilateral Commission, and a brief stint in the State Department's policy-planning staff. He even benefited from being foreign-born and retaining a slight accent. Kissinger had turned these attributes into an advantage, because the popular view is that foreigners somehow understand foreign policy better than the native-born. Brzezinski and Kissinger began to be compared immediately, of course. It gave the press a few juicy stories and irritated Kissinger no end.

I found that the similarlites in outlook between Kissinger and Brzezinski were far greater than either of them would admit. They were both conservative anticommunists. The chief differences were in their approaches to international politics. Kissinger, as a historian, was conscious of nuances and the vagaries of policy; he appreciated that strategy was a patient, sometimes elusive affair that could not be adjusted to every passing issue; thus he tended to stick to his plan, and in Vietnam, perhaps he did so too rigidly for too long. He had a sense of irony and humor that comforted him when history played its inevitable and outrageous tricks, as it always does on great statesmen. Brzezinski's claim that American foreign policy lacked "architecture" reflected his training as a political scientist; he was intrigued by the structure of policy, and this led him into intricate analyses: for example, the danger of a conjuncture of East-West with North-South crises. At the same time, both were truly power politicians: both manipulated the triangular relationship with China and Russia, both had an almost instinctive suspicion of European weaknesses, both appreciated and worried about the power of Japan. A real difference was in their public relations: Kissinger had become a world figure, and his stature did not diminish after he left office, as was the case even with Secretaries Acheson and Rusk. Brzezinski wanted to become a world figure, and this meant that he was haunted by Kissinger, and in my view he was too determined to demonstrate a difference in style and substance. Kissinger served for eight years, Brzezinski for only four. The Kissinger period was one of great tumult, peace in Vietnam, disengagement in the Middle East, détente with the Soviet Union, the opening to China, Watergate. The Carter years seemed more an interlude and ended in the humiliation of Iran. Kissinger enjoyed the support of his presidents, which gave his conduct of policy a strong sense of assurance, even in the last year of difficulties. Brzezinski found himself at the outset struggling for the mind of his president.

During the transition Kissinger thought of his successor not as Brzezinski but as Cyrus Vance, who was to be secretary of state. Kissinger's relations with Brzezinski were cool in any case; Brzezinski had made a number of acid remarks about Kissinger during the campaign, while Vance had remained aloof.

Vance had served in various high-level jobs and, ironically, had been a classmate of Jerry Ford at Yale Law School. I scarcely knew Vance, but the new secretary of defense, Harold Brown, had served in a part-time capacity on the SALT delegation under Nixon and Ford. When it was rumored, well before the election, that Brown would become the Democratic secretary of defense, John Lehman wanted to have him fired as a member of the SALT delegation. I refused even to forward the proposal to Ford. Brzezinski's deputy, David Aaron, had also served on the SALT delegation, during the Nixon period, and later had joined Kissinger's NSC staff, before departing to work for Walter Mondale. One deputy assistant secretary of defense, Walter Slocombe, had also worked for Kissinger, as had the director of policy planning at the State Department, Anthony Lake (who had resigned in protest over Cambodia in 1970).

This is not to say there were no differences between Carter and Ford, but rather to underline the point that it is far more difficult to change the conduct of foreign policy than domestic policy. At first, many on Carter's domestic staff resented this dependence on the establishment. But when they sought the support of Ford and Kissinger on the Panama Canal treaty, for example, they began to appreciate that a certain continuity is inevitable and desirable.

Nevertheless, a new administration does have considerable freedom of action. And after eight years, the opposition party develops a new set of priorities, some, of course, inherited from the campaign, but most the result of staff work, debate and discussions among the new members of the administration. That old, settled policies are being reviewed always comes as something of a shock to the departing administration. Thus I was surprised to come upon a small group of familiar faces meeting in the Old Executive Office Building; Aaron, Slocombe and his deputy, Lynn Davis—all of whom had worked with me—and some others were going through a huge black briefing book we had prepared on the status of the SALT negotiations. Somehow I had assumed that they would pick up where we had left those negotiations, but it began to dawn on me that this was not likely.

Brzezinski had asked me to stay on the staff at the White House temporarily. Kissinger and Scowcroft urged me to do so, and I had agreed. This put me in the uneasy position of being the Ford transition officer, as well as a prospective Brzezinski staff member. I gradually realized that it would be particularly difficult to give advice because my inclination was to defend past policies. But on the issue of SALT, I thought I knew the new players well enough to argue for finishing the old negotiations, which were about complete. I had not reckoned sufficiently with the momentum of election politics. Carter clearly wanted something new and different in arms control and wanted it quickly. And this was to become the source of the first of several minor disasters in dealing with the Soviets.

For their part, the Soviets had waited out the campaign without attempting to influence it very much. They genuinely seemed to prefer Ford, but it took no great effort for them to shift gears, and soon they were in private discussions with the new White House staff. One of the subjects was an early Vance trip to Moscow. I was appalled at this eagerness, but it was part of a rapid-fire strategy that also sent Walter Mondale to Europe within a few days after inauguration. The planning for this trip produced an interesting episode. Mondale was upset that on his first trip as vice president he would have to be received in Brussels at NATO headquarters by General Alexander Haig, who was then the Supreme Allied Commander in Europe. Mondale of course identified Haig with Watergate, and wanted him fired, but David Aaron and I convinced him that this would politicize the job of NATO commander. So Mondale relented but insisted that all of Ford's political ambassadors be quietly told to absent themselves.

The Mondale trip took David Aaron away from his desk as Brzezinski's deputy and, to my great surprise, Brzezinski asked me to fill in for the week. So there I was, back in my old office in the White House, under a totally different administration, but dealing with some very familiar issues. The situation had the enormous advantage of allowing me to retain my parking place.

KISSINGER APPRAISAL

As the Ford administration prepared to leave office, it suddenly dawned on many in Washington that for the first time in eight years American foreign policy would not be conducted by Henry A. Kissinger. This naturally provoked a rush to judgment about the "Kissinger era." In many of the commentaries the difference between style and substance was blurred. There was a natural interest in how Kissinger did it, sometimes at the expense of what he did. This curiosity is to be expected in Washington, but in Kissinger's case it was magnified. He, of course, contributed to the fascination with his style. His secret diplomacy added immeasurably to his aura of mystery, which in turn made him an even more compelling figure for the media. And Kissinger's own comments—especially his celebrated description of himself to Oriana Fallaci as the Lone Ranger—encouraged a focus on style rather than substance.

Style is important in politics, as well as in diplomacy. In a vast bureaucracy, a distinct style guarantees a hearing for one's policy preferences, and in Washington the struggle for power is greatly influenced by the press. Watergate demonstrated the power of a single newspaper—*The Washington Post;* and almost everyone at the upper levels of Washington bureaucracy reads

The New York Times, however briskly. State Department and White House staff meetings are often dominated by a discussion of what appears that morning in the *Post* and the *Times.* Where a reporter got a story is a question that echoes throughout the halls of most government agencies; usually the source is obvious, at least to insiders, who suspect those superiors who complain the loudest. This preoccupation with the press reflects the determination of an administration to manage the news. Each administration has its own strategy, but in general there is a consistent effort to influence the media's perception of policy by the use of leaks from the vast amount of information available to officials. The Washington press corps is far too savvy for any obvious effort of this kind to work for long. But some administrations and some individuals are more successful at it than others. Kissinger was very successful indeed, and for a long time.

Kissinger believed that even in the era of television, power in Washington still rested on the printed word, not only because the bureaucracy was a captive audience but also because the most powerful print journalists lived and worked in Washington (none of the TV anchormen lived in Washington). What the Washington journalists were thinking and saying within the narrow social and political circles of the capital was perhaps even more important than the columns and news stories they wrote. Nixon hated what he always called the Georgetown cocktail crowd, in which he included most of the Washington journalists. Kissinger, however, understood the role of the journalists, as well as that of Washington society, and he profited thereby.

Every high official enjoys a honeymoon with the press, but usually it is a brief one. As he took office, Kissinger became a natural magnet for political commentators, and he managed to charm both the reporters and columnists for some years. He provided them with elegant background briefings that were easily translated into lead articles; he was meticulous in cultivating reporters, columnists and editors. His predecessors had done the same, of course, but Kissinger provided a refreshing break from the acrimony of the last days of the Johnson administration. Kissinger's successor as national security adviser, Zbigniew Brzezinski, tried to emulate Kissinger's performance, but Brzezinski lacked Kissinger's flair, especially his sardonic humor. Analyzing Kissinger became something of a cottage industry in the early years of the Nixon administration. The odd contrast between the rumpled German professor and the "secret swinger," as he described himself to a society reporter, made him all the more fascinating in a dull capital where the most colorful event was a visit from any member of the British royal family.

Yet a gap gradually developed between what was said and what was actually happening. His early briefings were erudite analyses of the nature of international politics, but they could not go into what he was trying to do in private diplomacy. No manipulation of China and Russia, let alone negotiations about Vietnam, could have withstood the scrutiny of open diplomacy openly reported. Of course, Kissinger's successes reinforced the tendency to conduct a closed policy. Had he failed, had he returned from China rebuffed in July 1971, then his style would have been the first casualty; the failure would have been attributed to his mania for secrecy. As it was, the secrecy made the genuine breakthroughs even more dramatic. Revealing only so much at any given time was Nixon's clear preference, and it suited Kissinger's temperament. Kissinger and Nixon's success through 1973 encouraged them to believe that they could continue without change.

In the end, Kissinger became a prisoner of his own style. At first, when he was in the White House, Kissinger could use anonymity to his advantage; he did not have to testify or speak on the record unless he wished to, as he did in the "peace is at hand" press conference on Vietnam in October 1972. It is sometimes forgotten that it was not until 1971 that he began to receive public attention as "Super K." Moreover, he had a free hand because he enjoyed Nixon's confidence. The press soon understood that he was indeed speaking for Nixon, and Nixon gave him considerable latitude to interpret his instructions.

After he became secretary of state, and especially after Nixon's resignation in August 1974, Kissinger had to operate far more openly, and in the aftermath of Watergate, he could no longer count on the almost instinctive support of the president. Ford was supportive, but the intimate relationship with Nixon had given Kissinger greater autonomy. Kissinger found that he had to explain, persuade and occasionally cajole

Ford's staff for support. This was especially true of the new chief of staff in the White House, Donald Rumsfeld. Some others on the White House staff were openly hostile to Kissinger. For example, during the fall of Saigon the White House staff conspired to have Ford publicly proclaim in New Orleans the end of the Vietnam war—"a war that is finished" for the United States—without advising Kissinger.

Moreover, as secretary of state Kissinger could no longer afford the luxury of concentrating on one or two of the most dramatic and rewarding areas; he was charged with the full range of foreign affairs, including the onerous task of testifying before Congress. And the Congress in those final years was increasingly pugnacious and belligerent. Kissinger became embroiled in the stupid contest described earlier with Otis Pike's House Intelligence Committee, which led to a committee citation for contempt of Congress. Kissinger understood better than some of his subordinates the symbolism of a contempt citation. He was periodically involved in other controversies, particularly over his role in the FBI wiretapping of his own staff at the White House. His threats to resign became more frequent and more dramatic.

This guerrilla warfare took its toll, and in a broad sense Kissinger too was a victim of Watergate, that is, of the climate of bitterness and distrust that it generated. One of the most astute of Washington observers, Meg Greenfield of the editorial page of *The Washington Post,* conceded Kissinger's achievements were of "historic value and importance." But she ended her final appraisal of his tenure by noting that "Kissinger's particular method of doing his job seems to require a degree of freedom, privacy and license that people who make these complaints are no longer willing to grant him."

Thus, Kissinger eventually paid a high price for the press's love affair with him. No one in Washington can rise so far so fast without becoming an inviting target. In Kissinger's case this inevitable turn of the tide was deferred by Watergate. For a time, as Nixon fell, Kissinger rose. In a nation increasingly ashamed of its government, Kissinger's foreign policy was a redeeming virtue. It could not save Nixon, but Kissinger came to be protected by Nixon's most bitter political opponents. This too would not last beyond the winter of 1975. By then, there was little news in yet another feature story about Kissinger's brilliant tactics; the news was whether he was failing, or falling out with the new president. And his departure from the White House position of national security adviser in November 1975 marked a sharp shift in his fortunes.

Yet it is substance, not style or official titles, that counts. Scarcely anyone but historians can recall the particular manner of our great statesmen. Was Secretary of State John Quincy Adams humble or pompous, difficult or accommodating? He is remembered as the author of the Monroe Doctrine. Few would care whether his relations with President Monroe were cordial or tense, whether he "coordinated" his famous draft declaration or prepared it in secret. History judges only the results. The Kissinger era also needs a historical perspective. The contemporary judgments tended to be too narrow. The *Washington Post*'s valedictory editorial summed up Kissinger thus: "With the European intellectual's bent for conceptuali- zation and the European survivor's knack for maneuver, Henry Kissinger was precisely the man to elaborate and execute the Nixon design. It consisted, quite simply, of playing China against Russia."

This was not wrong, but it was too simple. It reduced policy to a crude manipulation of Russia and China. For Nixon, perhaps, this was the case. He did see playing China against Russia as an end in itself. He often talked of an "even balance" of five power centers. This phrase—an "even balance"—irri- tated Kissinger because it ignored the dynamism inherent in the balance of power and failed to emphasize America's role as holder of the balance. Nixon had a long and intense interest in foreign policy. His instincts were finely honed, and he had steeped himself in the background of key regions and new issues. He understood that the role of the presidency was to supply strategic guidance, not tactical management. His interest tended toward the manipulative aspects; indeed, his feel for manipulation, which proved disastrous in Watergate, was an asset in dealing with foreign affairs. Moreover, he had the wit to appreciate that Kissinger provided the intellectual rationale for his instincts. Even more important to Nixon the political leader, Kissinger provided a convincing philosophy and some protection against the left wing. But I doubt that Nixon had much appreciation of the historical mission that Kissinger sensed.

That historical mission was no great secret, though it was never clearly understood. In 1969, when a professional historian from Harvard came to the White House as security adviser, the pundits went scurrying for Kissinger's writings to detect what he would do, not just about Vietnam but about America's global predicament. They quickly discovered Kissinger's first book, *A World Restored,* a political and diplomatic history and analysis of the end of the Napoleonic wars and the peace settlement that followed. A reading of that volume led to the conclusion that Kissinger was an advocate of the balance of power; hence, it followed that American foreign policy would follow the politics of power-balancing. The German word *Realpolitik* kept popping up in news analyses.

Kissinger was always uneasy with this close identification with the balance of power, not because he did not accept the validity of the concept but because he knew that it could not be mechanically applied in the 1970s. The balance of power presupposed a limited number of participants of roughly equal weight; each had to have the ability to affect the other, and there had to be a broad agreement on the purpose of the system and the legitimacy of domestic claims on foreign policy. World War I destroyed this intricate mechanism and resulted in the rise of three truly revolutionary powers, the Soviet Union, Germany, for a brief period, and, finally, China. The old balance was invoked to defeat Hitler, but even if the old order could have been restored after Hitler's war, the appearance of nuclear weapons made a simple return to the old system impossible. The new system inevitably had to revolve around two superpowers.

Yet Kissinger did not entirely abandon the idea of a balance of power; what he did was redesign it to accommodate the coexistence of two military superpowers with several important regional power centers. Kissinger had concluded that there was still a need to reestablish some accepted measure of what constituted legitimacy. In this sense he was still a nineteenth-century politician, since he also concluded that diplomacy, or the adjustment of conflicts and differences, had no chance, except in an international order based on a common notion of legitimacy. He wanted to give the Soviet Union and China a sense of belonging to that order—hence his willingness to concede to Russia a sense of parity and equality with the United

States. This was the theoretical basis for the strategy of the carrot and the stick.

Kissinger also understood that the idea of a balance of power did not resonate well in the country. Americans were by and large legalists and moralists in foreign policy, not balancers of power. After leaving office, when he was freer to speak out, Kissinger said: "The peace we seek must rest on something more tangible than a hope or a fear of holocaust. It must also reflect a military and geopolitical equilibrium. The notion of balance of power has always been unfashionable in America. But it is the precondition of security, and even of progress. If the mere avoidance of conflict becomes our overriding objective, and if our military power is disparaged, the international system will be at the mercy of the most ruthless."

Unofficial Washington would have been well advised to read Kissinger's essay "The White Revolutionary: Reflections on Bismarck," published in *Daedalus* a year before he came to Washington. It was Bismarck, not Metternich, who intrigued him most. What Kissinger admired was that Bismarck managed to change the orientation of German society as well as the international order: "the new order was tailored to a genius who proposed to restrain the contending forces, both domestic and foreign, by manipulating their antagonism." Surely this was Kissinger's approach. He wanted to change American attitudes: to persuade the public to accept America's permanent engagement in world affairs, to end the longing for a neo-isolationism and to temper emotional interventionism. But he understood that Bismarck's system depended overwhelmingly on the Iron Chancellor's genius. How could a policy survive if every generation had to produce another genius. Kissinger's answer was that a new international order had to be institutionalized. This explains a great deal about Kissinger's dealings with the Soviet Union. He sought, whether in written principles, arms control agreements or summit meetings, to build a foundation for a permanent change in relations. He succeeded in laying that foundation. His successors' conduct of Soviet policy still rests on the Kissinger foundation.

But he could not institutionalize Soviet-American relations, nor could his successors. The permanency of his accomplishment is therefore still open to history's judgment. The failure to create stable Soviet-American institutions is one aspect of the great tragedy of Watergate. It wrecked Kissinger's strategy and threw him back on his own resources to limit the damage.

In sum, events conspired to create a divide between two Kissinger periods. In the first, he had a strong position and was relatively free to try to construct a new policy out of the wreckage of Vietnam. In the second period, his objective had to change: he was forced to try to salvage something of what he had helped to create in the Nixon presidency. Some observers believe that this latter period, under Ford, was a more masterly performance, given the growing odds against him and his policies. In my view history will judge his initial period as the more significant and durable, because it was creative. There are not many such periods in foreign affairs. His last years were defensive and tactically admirable but of less historical importance.

The historical significance of the Kissinger years of American foreign policy is relatively clear: he managed the transition from the period dominated by the cold war and its residue to a new phase in which elements of the cold war were brought into balance with the new elements of détente, not simply with Russia but with other Communist powers. The 1970s brought to a close the era of virulent anticommunism begun in the late 1940s and marked the end of the policy of pure containment.

On his last day in public office, Kissinger was interviewed by *The New York Times* and was asked the inevitable question: what legacy he was leaving. He mentioned in passing the trip to China, Middle East shuttle diplomacy and the SALT agreements, but his first answer is worth quoting, for it gives a flavor of his state of mind on that last, reflective day:

"Just before I came here I wrote an article in which I said the world is bipolar militarily, multipolar politically and fragmented economically. When you talk of world order you have to take account of each of these realities and also the fact that probably history will record this as one of the philosophical revolutions of history.

"In the nature of things this task could not have been completed—even without Watergate. This is the basic thing. I think in one way or another the relationship between China, the Soviet Union, the industrial democracies, the United States and the developing world, this five-sided aspect is a permanent feature of the future."

This, then, was the essence of the Kissinger strategy: to change the "permanent" features of international politics—no minor achievement in a world where such changes almost invariably have been the product of events rather than the design of statesmen. As a student of those historical moments when statesmen did succeed in changing the international structure, he was compelled to make the effort; indeed he relished it. In 1815 Metternich, Castlereagh, Talleyrand and Alexander I created a new European order: it survived thirty years. Bismarck also created a new European system after the Franco-Prussian war of 1870, and his system also lasted thirty years before it began to disintegrate. Kissinger was often to comment that any system that endures for thirty years must have its merits. It is sixteen years since Nixon's visit to China and Russia.

Of course Kissinger's critics on the right see it quite differently. And they inevitably focus on "détente." The charge is that Kissinger sold an unsuspecting public a phony "generation of peace" with the Soviet Union and then subordinated all aspects of policy, including morality and human rights, to the pursuit of that end. In this charge the description of his methods and tactics almost invariably includes the claim that he sought to buy peace with his economic concessions to the Kremlin, to ensure Soviet adherence through a "web" of bilateral agreements and incentives and to tame Soviet power through arms control agreements and an agreed code of conduct. In all of this he failed, according to his critics.

Thus there has come into being a mythology of détente. Fortunately, as time passes, the worst revisionism will fade, as it does with respect to all historical periods. The first myth is that détente was somehow created in secret. This of course clashes with the opposite charge, that it was oversold to the public. The latter is closer to reality. As the Watergate crisis deepened, there is no doubt that Nixon fell back to his last line of defense: his foreign policy. Détente was indeed oversold, but out of political expediency, not chicanery. It must be remembered that the American public was eager for a relaxation of international tensions; after the disaster of Vietnam, anything that smacked of a purposeful and peaceful foreign policy was eagerly embraced. America needed a respite from failure, and détente provided it. For proof of this one only need reread the evaluations of foreign policy written in 1972 and 1973.

The second charge is that Nixon and Kissinger naïvely believed that formal agreements would tie down Soviet strength. This was the "Gulliverization" of foreign policy, as one critique cleverly described it at the time. This myth has endured, but it does not reflect the reality of the time. No one of any consequence thought that the various agreements with the Soviet Union—even the arms control agreements—had inherent strength to restrain the USSR. They were intended to be linked in a strategy of both incentives and penalties. The economic component was a significant element of the strategy of détente. Perhaps too great an emphasis was placed on the incentives, but it should not be forgotten that the first summit took place after the mining of Haiphong and the bombing of North Vietnam, and that the last Nixon summit took place after the nuclear alert of October 1973. An eminent student of Communist affairs, the German Sovietologist Richard Lowenthal, has written that "Kissinger was no more inhibited than the Soviets by the fatuous document about refraining from unilateral advantages."

In addressing this general charge that SALT was believed to be sufficient to deter the Soviets from their aggressiveness, Kissinger and Scowcroft, writing jointly in *The Wall Street Journal*, stated in 1984: "Another [fable] is that SALT was intended to restrain Soviet behavior and that it did not stop Angola, Ethiopia or Afghanistan. One can accuse Richard Nixon of many sins, but simple-mindedness is not one of them. No serious member of his administration believed SALT by itself, or even primarily, would restrain Soviet conduct. What we did believe was that a web of incentives and penalties might indeed induce restraint. Watergate prevented this from being tested."

This is my view also, but there is another aspect seldom examined. The real defect of détente, and indeed of Kissinger's conduct of foreign policy, was the weakness of its indigenous roots. After decades of anticommunism and of alarms and crises in our relations with the Soviet Union and China, a major realignment in those relations could not quickly take hold in the public consciousness. This was not a matter of selling détente, though that was part of it, but of gaining enough time for the new situation to be understood and absorbed by the American people. Kissinger, a foreign-born national security adviser, was not ideally suited to this task, which, in any case, should be a presidential task. To convince the public of the validity of a policy is preeminently a political effort, which involves considerable sensitivity to the vagaries of popular opinion in the United States. Anyone elected to the presidency has to have some of this talent. Even at the presidential level, however, justifying the policy of détente was a project that required a subtle weaving of intellectual and geopolitical strands into a pattern that would command public support. Before Watergate, Nixon was not very skillful at implanting his policies in a domestic soil; he tended to impose them by fiat. Ford had neither the time nor the talent for it, nor did Carter.

As his own difficulties in office multiplied in late 1975 and early 1976, Kissinger was advised by his subordinates and friends that the country as a whole did not understand his policies, especially détente. Thus, he undertook a number of speaking engagements outside Washington and presented a series of lectures on the fundamental purposes of foreign policy. They were among his best and most thoughtful speeches. The themes were familiar ones, and they provide an interesting contrast with the early defense of détente, which promised more and stressed new initiatives rather than tradition. By the spring of 1976, well into the second phase of Kissinger's policies, his defense was couched both in recognizable Kissingerisms—an "equilibrium of power"—and in mainstream positions—"to contain Soviet power without global war." In Boston on March 11, 1976, he said: "It is our responsibility to contain Soviet power without global war, to avoid both abdication as well as unnecessary confrontation. This can be done, but it requires a delicate and complex policy. We must strive for equilibrium of power, but we must move beyond it to promote the habits of mutual restraint, coexistence, and, ultimately, cooperation. We must stabilize a new international order in a vastly dangerous environment, but our ultimate goal must be to transform ideological conflict into constructive participation in building a better world. This is what is meant by the process called 'detente'—not the hunger for relaxation of tension, not the striving for agreements at any price, not the mindless search for friendly atmosphere which some critics use as naive and dangerous caricatures."

By the time of this speech the "complex and delicate" policy Kissinger called for was impossible to pursue, at least until after the presidential elections. This passage nevertheless remains the best capsule summary of détente, and it accurately reflects Kissinger's basic position, which always included both containment and coexistence.

A third charge, mainly from the left, is that détente was pursued at the expense of moral considerations. In the 1970s, the standard reply was that nothing was more moral than peace. This was clever, but failed to confront the issues. There were two aspects to the criticism. First was the broad, older claim that one could not do any business with Communists; to do so would compromise the moral standing of the United States. By the 1970s, this had less impact than in the early postwar period. The more immediate and operational question concerned the impact of détente on human rights in the Soviet Union: the price for dealing with Moscow should have been an end to repression inside the Soviet Union, or, at a minimum, free emigration.

The critics had a point. Détente was narrowly based, in the sense that it was primarily a political and strategic policy. The human-rights issue struck at the very legitimacy and survival of the Soviet political structure. No one in the Nixon-Ford period believed that the Soviet Union could be bribed by economic concessions or arms control into relief in the area of human rights. The opposite was the working hypothesis that was put into practice: in an atmosphere of détente it might prove possible to gain some internal relaxation, especially with regard to emigration. That was the strategy that worked until challenged in 1975 by the Jackson amendment linking trade and Jewish emigration, which assumed the opposite: that pressures would pay off. It failed.

By far the most serious charge was that Kissinger's détente dangerously weakened the country's defense and jeopardized America's national security. In the early 1970s this charge was usually documented by presenting evidence of the growing Soviet arsenal of missiles; this was inanely attributed to the shortcomings of SALT, as if Kissinger could have charmed the

Soviets into a permanent state of strategic inferiority. The subsidiary charge is more to the point: namely, that because of the narcotic effect of détente, the United States complacently permitted the buildup of Soviet power and neglected a U.S. countereffort, in the mistaken conviction that Moscow could be tamed by diplomacy. This is the essence of President Reagan's accusation of a "decade of neglect." Again, it is nonsense.

During this so-called decade of neglect the United States increased its capability to attack critical Soviet targets from 1,700 warheads in 1970 to 7,000 in 1978. In the 1970s, the United States deployed 500 newer ICBMs with three MIRV warheads each; it converted its sea-based missile force to nearly 500 new Poseidon missiles, each with 10 to 14 warheads, replacing the older single-warhead Polaris missile. The even longer-range and more capable Trident missiles for submarines were under advanced development when Ford left office. The construction of the first Trident submarine began in 1975. The B-52s were modernized with new avionics and new engines and were equipped with short-range attack missiles; the air-launched cruise missile was developed and tested in this same period. The B-1 was developed, though stopped by Carter. Under the détente of the 1970s the United States improved its strategic position far more than under the period of anti-détente, when no new strategic systems were deployed that were not created by Nixon, Ford or Carter.

It is worth considering the judgments of the chairman of the Joint Chiefs of Staff, in a letter to Senator Proxmire, written shortly *after* Kissinger left office: "The Joint Chiefs of Staff do not agree that the Soviet Union has achieved military superiority over the United States. . . . [US strategic forces] are considered sufficient to achieve US objectives today."

Despite the persistence of these myths, there has been some mellowing. One of Kissinger's critics, the writer Norman Podhoretz, even conceded that he did achieve "greatness" as a practitioner of the art of diplomacy. Indeed, as was said of Nixon, Kissinger has been lucky in his successors. His conduct of office seems to grow as his successors compile a less enviable record. Even one of Kissinger's more persistent and incisive critics, a former colleague at Harvard, Stanley Hoffmann, wrote that the questions Kissinger provokes "are not the ones that are asked of trivial figures."

Once, in San Clemente, when his staff was composing one of Nixon's long annual reports that we called the State of the World report, Kissinger told us to use something from Immanuel Kant's essay on perpetual peace. This set off a wild staff search in San Clemente, and not surprisingly, there was no copy of the essay in that pleasant resort town. So we called Washington urgently to dispatch a copy on the next courier flight. This puzzled the Washington staff no end.

Kant's exposition was a simple one: perpetual peace is achievable but it does not come naturally; it must be constructed. This indeed was the key to Kissinger's foreign policy. Despite Vietnam, despite Watergate, Kissinger left American foreign policy in better shape than he found it. Three days before he left office, Kissinger was assessed by the London *Times*: "It is usually better to have a great man in a great position, and whatever his errors of judgement, or his failures, Dr. Kissinger is one of the great American statesmen of the twentieth century."

Kissinger would probably reply, "What errors?"

XI

JIMMY CARTER AND SALT

Historians will have difficulty judging the foreign policy of Jimmy Carter's administration. Its achievements were significant. The Camp David agreement brokered by Carter between Menachem Begin and Anwar Sadat in 1978 was probably the high point. Given the volatile history of the Middle East, however, the conclusion of the treaty turning the Panama Canal over to Panamanian sovereignty may prove an even more enduring accomplishment than Camp David. The strategic arms control treaty signed by Carter and Brezhnev in June 1979, though never ratified, was observed for seven years after Carter left the White House (and even beyond the date of its formal expiration). Yet when the Carter administration departed in January 1981, some surveys of public opinion showed that its foreign policy had been widely discredited, that large segments of the population thought that the United States was in deep and serious trouble abroad. And a majority of the electorate obviously shared this judgment. The immediate cause for Carter's 1980 defeat was, of course, the handling of the Iranian hostage crisis. But the sense that there was a broader strategic collapse was heightened by the Soviet invasion of Afghanistan, only six months after the Carter-Brezhnev summit in Vienna. And President Carter's rather naïve statement of surprise at Brezhnev's actions only compounded the sense of failure.

The Carter administration should have been able to conduct a reasonably effective Soviet policy. It was well staffed with experienced hands. National Security Adviser Zbigniew Brzezinski, was in the first rank of American Sovietologists. The position of chief Soviet specialist (counselor of the State Department) was occupied by one of the most widely respected students of Soviet policy, Marshall Shulman of Columbia University. And the new secretary of state, Cyrus Vance, had had broad experience in the top levels of the American government; after leaving government and becoming a New York attorney, he had continued a strong interest in East-West relations.

Left entirely to their own devices, these three might have carved out a somewhat different foreign policy than the policy actually followed, even though there were some sharp conflicts among them on the substance of policy. But given the momentum of a successful election campaign, and especially considering the campaign's legacy of high moralism, the Carter team gradually adopted a new mode in dealing with the Soviet Union. Initially, the most important difference introduced by the Carter administration was a strong emphasis on human rights, especially in public pronouncements. There was also an increasing preoccupation with strategic arms control, which was to be expected, but which gradually came to be an end in itself. This approach to arms control was related to a third characteristic: a determination to unlink other, lesser, conflicts from U.S.-Soviet relations and especially from arms control. These departures reflected a dogged determination—especially on Brzezinski's part—to distance the administration from Kissinger. In part the new mode also reflected the priorities of the new president himself, who made much more of an impact on foreign policy than he is credited with by his subordinates in their memoirs.

These were not strategic changes but tactical shifts. Had that been all that was involved, probably no significant change from previous policies would have resulted. But underlying this new consensus was a personal dispute. I discussed with Brzezinski the old problem of the White House versus the State Department, but he dismissed it. At the time, in January 1977, he protested so much that I wondered if perhaps there were already some tensions, which would have been natural. Even if there was a friendship between Vance and Brzezinski, their institutional roles guaranteed friction, if not conflict. Unfortunately for the administration, the institutional conflict was not confined to bureaucratic infighting. It eventually took on a major strategic dimension. Brzezinski insisted on giving priority to normalization of relations with China in a sort of rerun of the Nixon-Kissinger performance. This clashed with Vance's view that the Soviet negotiations should be completed first. At a critical moment, Brzezinski won over Carter to his side. The result was to delay the U.S.-Soviet arms control negotiations. By early 1979, the administration had alarmed Moscow by its blatant playing of the China card, including what must have seemed like a policy of collusion in the Chinese "counterattack" on North Vietnam. But the administration nevertheless reached its arms control goal (in June 1979), only to be overwhelmed by the invasion of Afghanistan. At that point none of Carter's genuine achievements—Camp David, Panama or China—could save him from the agony of Iran and eventual defeat.

In January 1977, when Jimmy Carter took office, relations with Moscow took a bad turn. The cause was human rights, which Carter had stressed during the election campaign and again in his inaugural address. This was taken as a signal inside the State Department that the long years of Kissinger's realpolitik were over. Without consulting the White House or waiting for any new directives, the State Department bureaucracy issued a statement of sympathy for the Charter 77 Group in Czechoslovakia, a new human rights monitoring group. Then the department issued a statement of sympathy for the plight of Andrei Sakharov, the well-known Soviet physicist and human rights fighter, who was undergoing one of the KGB's periodic harassment campaigns. This, of course, got immediate press attention; the press was quick to conclude that Carter was embarked on a "striking" departure from the Kissinger policy. The president decided to endorse the State Department's new pronouncements, but for some reason he added that the department may have been remiss in not asking for a clearance from the White House. This confused matters, as did Brzezinski's statement to the press that human rights and arms control were "organically related"; a short time later, the president disavowed this position by denouncing "linkage."

But far more important than this skirmishing was the decision of the White House to answer a letter to President Carter from Andrei Sakharov. This letter used the occasion of Carter's coming to office to appeal for his support for human rights in the USSR and his intercession on behalf of certain individuals. The existence of such a letter was a rumor at first, and I am not sure that an authentic text was ever received at the White House; but the contents were available through several channels and were eventually printed in *The New York Times*. Brzezinski and Vance were determined that Carter should not make himself vulnerable, as Ford had done by refusing to meet with Solzhenitsyn. They decided to reply, even though only a few days earlier Vance, at his first press conference, had denied any intention to be "strident or polemical."

Brzezinski asked me to draft a reply for the president. But I argued that the reply should be from Vance, not Carter, who ought to be free at the outset of his administration to choose when and how to issue policy pronouncements. I thought that the president risked becoming the prisoner of every prominent dissident who chose to write to the White House. How could he refuse to respond in some future instance? Brzezinski disagreed, on the practical grounds that Vance would be the adminstration's chief negotiator and should not have the extra burden of having entered into correspondence with Soviet dissidents. So Carter signed the letter. I then discovered that a strong sentence of sympathy for "prisoners of conscience" had been added, whether at Brzezinski's own initiative or Carter's I never learned.

To make matters more complicated, the White House scheduled a meeting with the recently released dissident Vladimir Bukovsky (whose freedom I had negotiated at Kissinger's behest in December with Ambassador Dobrynin in a trade for the Chilean Communist Luis Corvalan). The Bukovsky visit turned out to be a strange event. He met not with President Carter but with Vice President Mondale; though he was received in the White House (the Roosevelt room), no photos were permitted. All of this activity drew an angry letter from Brezhnev. Brzezinski saw this letter as an ominous portent and

persuaded Carter that he was being tested by Brezhnev. This
seemed unlikely to me since the Brezhnev-Carter correspondence was still private. But in response the administration's
rhetoric was stepped up, and Dobrynin was lectured by President Carter about human rights.

Just as it seemed that Carter might be shaping a wide-ranging
new policy, he encountered the grim realities of all human
rights policies toward the USSR. The brutal reality is that the
Kremlin is in charge, not Western opinion, the White House
or the Congress. In early February the Soviets acted, and began
by arresting several of the leaders of the Helsinki Group,
starting with Alexander Ginzburg, and including its founder,
Yuri Orlov; in early March, Anatoly Shcharansky was arrested
and charged with treason and espionage. This was a shock. No
such charge had ever been made against a dissident. To
underline the gravity of the situation, the Soviets produced a
so-called witness, a Soviet Jew named Lipavsky, who not only
claimed friendship with Shcharansky, but who later claimed
that he had been acting as an agent for the CIA. The Shcharansky case was turned into a broad attack to discredit the
dissident movement. And there was little Washington could
do. Indeed, it did nothing more than protest. Vance proceeded
to Moscow to arrange the SALT negotiations, and Shcharansky
remained in prison for the next nine years, even though his
innocence was vouched for by Carter personally. He was
released in 1986; the speculation was that his release grew out
of a bargain between Ronald Reagan and Mikhail Gorbachev
during their first summit meeting.

All of this simply proves that in the sphere of human rights,
the reality of the Soviet system finally governs. For the West,
the improvement of human rights is a desirable objective, even
a critical one. In the Soviet Union dissidence cannot be tolerated, even in the arts. What is at stake is the domination of the
regime over its citizens. The notion that some deviations are
permissable (say, in music) inevitably undermines the legitimacy
of the system. And emigration raises even more threatening
implications, that there is a valid reason and right to flee. One
American reporter writing from Moscow summed up Carter's
initiation: "President Carter's first lesson from the Soviets seems
to be—as it had been for so many Americans before him—that

protecting the ideology on which the Soviet state justifies itself is a matter of the utmost importance to the Kremlin."

In short, Moscow approaches the question of human rights as an internal political threat; the impact on foreign policy is secondary. Whatever concessions are made or compromises struck, they are carefully calculated, usually concluded in private and scarcely, if ever, the result of a public hue and cry.

For the West this requires almost endless patience, frequent uneasy compromises (such as trading known Soviet spies for Soviet dissidents), quiet diplomacy as well as public pressure— and in the end a willingess to be satisfied with meager progress. This naturally leads to frustrations, and in the United States, occasional emotional outbursts and even punitive legislation. But the basic situation cannot be altered as long as the Soviet system remains what it is.

Another frustrating aspect is trying to find one's way through the maze of opinions expressed by Soviet emigrés themselves, who naturally wish to dictate American policy. Thus, Solzhenitsyn roundly denounced the Helsinki conference but Sakharov supported it. Shcharansky criticizes it and wants it amended; others want it abrogated. Many of the most prominent emigrés have been freed by quiet diplomacy, but immediately upon their release they demanded a campaign of public pressures. The problem is that the United States cannot abdicate its national interests, which are not necessarily consonant with the views of Soviet dissidents and emigrés. This conflict of interests has applied, most of all, to the arms control negotiations, where the very American liberals who are most vociferous in their support of Soviet dissidents recoil in horror at the notion of linking Soviet human rights to the Geneva arms talks.

As a consequence of these realities, the Carter human rights campaign petered out. Only when relations between Washington and Moscow improved did Jewish emigration grow and eventually reach the level of the Nixon period. However, in that improved atmosphere Brzezinski was able to negotiate the release of five major dissidents, and this was not very different from Kissinger's approach. But it must be acknowledged that the improvement in Jewish emigration was achieved by Carter even though the Jackson-Vanik amendment had not been rescinded.

The Carter administration was eager to begin negotiations on strategic arms control. At first I thought that a quick conclusion of the Kissinger negotiations would be the preferred course. It would produce an early agreement, which is always a good omen for a new administration. It would guarantee Republican support from Ford and Kissinger, as well as in the Senate. It would give the administration two or three years to negotiate a follow-up agreement. I briefed Brzezinski and his deputy David Aaron (with whom I had worked on Kissinger's NSC) on the status of the Ford negotiations and wrote a long memorandum on how they might be finished. But this approach did not reckon with the impact of domestic politics or the character of the new president.

Completing the Vladivostok accords seemed to Carter to be an admission of failure. Critics were arguing that it was not "real" arms control, and Brzezinski eventually denounced it for permitting an expansion of armaments. Even those in the administration more knowledgeable about the actual negotiation and about arms control were reluctant to be caught up in finishing the old administration's business. So the Vladivostok option was branded the "If Ford Had Won the Election Option"—not an appellation calculated to get many supporters.

The problem for the new team was that it was not so easy to reinvent the wheel. Most of the variants of strategic arms control had been examined in the negotiations preceding and after the Vladivostok meeting. Moreover, the unsettled issues were genuinely contentious, such as how to overcome Soviet resistance to inclusion of Backfire in the limitations. The election had not ended disputes within the arms control community, both inside and outside the government. And most important, the Soviets considered that the negotiations had been interrupted, but not broken off. For the Soviet Union the starting point was the draft treaty that was still on the table in Geneva. Few in the new administration seemed to appreciate this Soviet attitude, even though Brezhnev made it clear in a major speech in March. Brzezinski too easily assumed that we could start afresh, and I must admit I tended to agree: a new president always has a great deal of leeway and can accomplish more at the outset of his term than later, when he faces reelection. Thus, I had no problem entertaining some new

SALT variants, but I was not prepared for how far Jimmy Carter wanted to go.

I must say that throughout the several months that I remained on the NSC staff President Carter treated me with unfailing graciousness, and at no time did he indicate any problem with the fact that I was a Ford holdover. (Nor did Brzezinski or Vance.) He allowed me into the inner circle of his arms control advisers, and on those few occasions when I substituted for Brzezinski he treated me as a professional. Yet, I never had a good sense of what the new president was really like. He was always quiet and reserved, but one suspected a flintiness beneath the calm exterior, and even a temper, which did occasionally break through. He demonstrated an incredible capacity for hard work and an insatiable appetite for details. In this his staff served him badly; rather than shielding him from the minutiae of interagency studies, they fed him. He became, for example, an expert on the facts of SALT arms control, to the point that he began to lose sight of the forest.

His relish for details was evident in my very first encounter with him. Together with Brent Scowcroft I participated in a very sensitive briefing on the strategic war plans of the United States, presented to him at Blair House shortly before the inauguration. Carter seemed less interested in the horrendous implications of the strategic attack options than in the details of control: how he could order a nuclear strike at any time of the day or night, how the White House and Pentagon communication system operated, and all such details. He seemed to have an obsession with the technical aspects, possibly because he was an engineer. He was appalled at the looseness of the command-and-control procedures. Later, after becoming president, he instructed Brzezinski to order a dry run of the emergency evacuation plan for the president, via a helicopter that would land on the south lawn and whisk the president to a command aircraft at Andrews Air Force Base. When Brzezinski told me of this plan for a test run one evening, about an hour before he ordered it, I decided to go home rather than watch what I knew would be a fiasco. The helicopter would probably not react quickly enough and the procedures to get the "president" (Brzezinski, acting in his place) on his command aricraft would be fouled up. And indeed, I was right. No previous president had taken evacuation very seriously.

Later Carter became intrigued with the idea of how few nuclear weapons would be needed to carry out the strategic mission of assured destruction. His idea was that a force of 200 missiles launched from submarines might be sufficient to deter the Soviets. All of this was hair-raising to the Joint Chiefs of Staff, but good soldiers that they were, they never really complained. I am not at all certain that this 200-missile plan was ever really serious; more likely it was Carter's way of alerting the JCS that he was in charge. When it came to arms control, however, Carter was serious in insisting that the United States propose a major reduction in strategic arms (much as Reagan did later), on the simplistic but appealing notion that fewer weapons are better and safer—as if all of his predecessors had been warmongers who insisted unnecessarily on more and more weapons. Reductions of strategic armaments should be applied to those categories of weapons that are capable of a surprise attack or a first strike; simply reducing numbers is political therapy but could prove dangerous. I was surprised therefore that there was almost no resistance to the idea of proposing large reductions. Brzezinski and Vance, as well as the new arms control negotiator, Paul Warnke, and the secretary of defense, Harold Brown, all allowed the idea of major reductions to become the leading candidate for a new proposal to the Soviets. They surely knew that it was not likely to prove attractive to the Soviet side.

I must admit that I saw no great harm in stressing major reductions, as long as it was understood that this was mainly for show. The real strategy would be to apply some modest reductions to the numerical ceilings negotiated at Vladivostok. This was eventually agreed within the administration: one proposal to the Soviets would be to defer the contentious unresolved issues left over from Vladivostok and reach an interim treaty on those elements already agreed upon. This echoed the last U.S. proposal urged on Ford by Rumsfeld and rejected by Brezhnev. This revival would not go down well in Moscow, but it might look more attractive to Brezhnev if he compared it with potentially rancorous new negotiations over major reductions, which remained the prime Carter proposal. At least this was the rationale, and it gradually became the accepted wisdom in the administration: that the Soviets would agree to a "deferral" proposal, which we would present as an interim step toward a more comprehensive arms control scheme.

After a great deal of infighting and maneuvering, this two-pronged approach was approved by the president for Vance to take to Moscow in March 1977. I did not know that Vance had initially balked at this scheme but had been persuaded to try it. There was an unfounded rumor at the time that he was not informed of the instructions until he left for Moscow: this was not true, although the instructions were written in the White House. To guard against leaks, both Carter and Brzezinski insisted that the SALT decisions be drafted without interagency clearances; thus the delegation's instructions were a virtual secret from the other departments. David Aaron and I had sketched out the proposal for reductions that Carter favored, adding those specific items we thought valid, but without much regard to the previous internal debates. We also drafted the second option, to defer unresolved issues and proceed to an interim agreement. The night before we left for Moscow, Brzezinski enthusiastically predicted to me that Brezhnev would accept the deferral scheme.

I was given the unenviable job of guarding the written instructions from the other members of the Vance delegation. Vance briefed the delegation on the flight to Moscow, but only in broad terms. This caused great consternation in the delegation, which included Leslie Gelb, director of the Bureau of Political-Military Affairs in the State Department, Walter Slocombe, deputy assistant secretary of defense for international security affairs, and General Edward Rowny, who had served in the delegation during the previous administration and still represented the Joint Chiefs of Staff. Paul Warnke, the new director of the Arms Control and Disarmament Agency, was fully informed, but he was in a somewhat sensitive position at that moment because his appointment had provoked a bitter confirmation fight in the Senate.

I was badgered for details, but I had no choice but to deny the various requests to examine the documents. It reached such a ludicrous point in Moscow that in order to show the delegation one part of the instructions, I had to cut out some paragraphs before Xeroxing the remainder. Naturally, when the others saw me cutting up the instructions there was a howl of protest, not to say derision. When I told Vance of my embarrassment, he laughed and said that while he had ordered me to protect the instructions, he had not expected me to get caught. So a Ford holdover was entrusted with the mission of keeping Carter's secrets safe from his own delegation.

This was an amusing sidelight to a deadly serious meeting in Moscow between the Soviet leaders and the new secretary of state's arms control team. The instructions from the president to Vance were so tightly held (as they say in the government) because in fact Carter had authorized two major concessions, if the negotiations seemed to be moving in the direction of major reductions: Vance was authorized to offer to scrap both the B-1 bomber and the Trident submarine. This was a surprise to me, but it had obviously been cleared through the president. Apparently, the White House was justifiably concerned that this fallback position not become widely known, especially since it did not appear too likely that these particular cards would be played, at least not on this trip. What eventually turned out to be even more baffling was that Vance did not feel he actually had the authority to bring any concessions into play without checking with Washington first. This gave the affair a surreal quality.

The negotiations went badly for a variety of reasons. The Soviets were in a sour mood because of the campaign in Washington on human rights. And Brezhnev began the meetings with a lecture that did not bode well for the talks. Then he departed, turning the meeting over to Gromyko, which was another bad sign. Kissinger had always had Brezhnev as his negotiating partner, at least until broad presentations had been made and debated. Vance would have to make his case to Gromyko. Even worse, as it turned out, Vance had not thoroughly gone over our position with Dobrynin beforehand in Washington, which Kissinger had always done to ensure that the Soviets had time to understand and digest what we were proposing. Thus the Soviets had only a general idea of the two American proposals: deferral and deep reductions, as we were calling them. Unfortunately, Carter had talked openly about negotiating reductions. So the Soviets were unsure whether they were dealing with propaganda or a real proposal.

Nevertheless, it was also apparent that, leaving aside some tough talk on human rights, the Soviets still wanted to negotiate about strategic arms. Their complaint was more procedural than substantive; they kept saying that the American government had changed, but there had been no election in Moscow. The Soviet position was as before, and the United States was obliged to go back to the point that had been reached with Ford. Vance did not want to repudiate his predecessors altogether, but he could not accept the Soviet demand either. An impasse developed but was overcome at the last minute when Gromyko and Brezhnev proposed another meeting in Geneva in May (in two months), between Gromyko and Vance, to continue the discussions. This was not a bad outcome. And had matters rested there, the Vance mission would probably have been interpreted as a small step forward.

But fate intervened. The story is one of minor errors mushrooming into a diplomatic blowout. Philip Habib and I had remained behind in the Kremlin after the final session with Brezhnev to go over a brief communiqué with Georgi Kornienko, the Soviet deputy minister of foreign affairs, while Vance returned to the ambassador's spacious residence, Spaso House. Habib, who was very close to Vance and was then under secretary of state, was on his first trip to the Soviet Union; I had settled a dozen communiqués with Kornienko, who was not easy to deal with but always proved accommodating in the end, after carefully arguing every point. Unfortunately, Habib decided to engage in a fencing match with the redoubtable Kornienko. All that was accomplished was to waste about an hour. Meanwhile, back at the ambassador's residence, Vance and Warnke had grown tired of waiting for me and Habib to talk over the outcome, and they held a press conference for the American reporters and the foreign press corps. Their message was that we had run into Soviet resistance and that no real progress had been made on SALT; new working groups on other arms control negotiations had been agreed upon, however, and it would be announced that Vance and Gromyko would meet again. This would have been a rather routine news story, but then Vance and Warnke went into the details of the American proposals and defended them as reasonable—by implication criticizing the Soviets for turning them down. Now the story changed dramatically. The headline would be that the Soviets had turned down Carter's plan for reductions.

I have always felt this was a mistake that could have been

avoided. Both Habib and I would have argued against releasing more than a minimal report before returning to Washington, or no more than a background briefing that emphasized the positive aspects. Now the president would get the impression from the press wires that our mission had failed. And, of course, the Soviets would learn that Vance had made public the details of the negotiating positions.

By the time Habib and I returned, the press conference was over and the reporters were smelling blood. Their question was how could we have been so foolish as to believe that the Soviets would ever accept our proposal for reductions. In the various versions our alternative of deferring some issues and signing a truncated agreement was completely lost. The *Washington Post* reporter wrote that we had "seriously miscalculated the impact and the consequences in the Soviet Union of the U.S. plan for deep cuts. . . . the negotiators were badly taken by surprise." We finally called Washington and alerted Brzezinski to the outcome and the probable press reporting. By the time we arrived in London the next day, Gromyko had lashed back with an unprecedented press conference of his own, attacking the U.S. proposals for hypocrisy and, in general, taking a tough line. That evening I talked long-distance with Brzezinski, who decided to answer Gromyko and asked me to draft some remarks and cable them to the White House. I drafted a statement and suddenly realized that unlike the Kissinger missions, ours had no "back channel" for sending messages to the White House. The new State Department team was dismayed by the very idea of communicating directly to the White House. I had to call a friend at the embassy who knew the old procedures and get him out of bed, and finally I sent my cable. Brzezinski used some of it to good advantage, but the rhetoric was escalating.

Joseph Kraft, commenting in his column on the Moscow trip and especially Brzezinski's briefing, wrote that the briefing showed that the American approach to the Moscow talks was "self-indulgent and irresponsible in almost every respect." I had suggested to Brzezinski that he cite the analogy of the Soviet rejection of ABM controls at the Glassboro summit in 1967, to make the point that this was probably not the last word from Moscow. Kraft, however, thought it was not apt: on both occasions the United States had sought to change the rules in the middle of the game; whereas Johnson had been careful, Carter was "cocky."

For his *New York Times* column James Reston turned to George Kennan, who was quoted as saying that Carter had been "too sudden, too public, too narrow and even too discourteous. . . . the administration has made just about every mistake it could make in these Moscow talks."

Instead of treating the visit as a step toward the resumption of negotiations and stressing the importance of the next meeting between Vance and Gromyko, both sides were suddenly shouting accusations. This was then compounded by loose talk from our delegation and from Washington. By the time of our return flight *The Washington Post,* in a caustic editorial, wrote that it was the most disorderly retreat from Moscow since Napoleon's. I felt so bad about the trip that I called Brzezinski from the aircraft and suggested that Carter meet the plane at Andrews Air Force Base as a gesture of solidarity. And he did.

Looking back at this episode, I have no doubt that it was badly handled by everyone. As the one with the most experience, I had been far too sanguine. I doubt that I could have changed the course of events much, but both Marshall Shulman and I blamed ourselves for not advising Vance of the potential for considerable Soviet hostility. Vance seemed to recognize that we had all miscalculated, and unfortunately he said so after his return. This encouraged even wilder speculation about trouble in the administration. The most lasting result, in my view, was that it strengthened Vance's determination to get on with SALT negotiations, if necessary at the expense of other issues. It also sobered Carter, and to some extent Brzezinski. Both began to talk more about détente and to downgrade any linkage between arms control and geopolitical issues. Brzezinski talked of a "progressive accommodation" with the Soviet Union.

The affair turned out to be of less importance than all the sound and fury suggested. It was not until the SALT treaty was actually signed in 1979 that this visit of March 1977 was resurrected by critics in order to compare the final outcome unfavorably with the original "deep cut" proposals carried to Moscow. The final treaty was portrayed as a retreat from these proposals. But the recovery from the debacle was much easier than had seemed likely on the dreadful return trip to Wash-

ington. At the next meeting, in May in Geneva, Vance and
Gromyko agreed to resume formal negotiations, and to do so
in accordance with a formula Leslie Gelb and I had worked
out to concentrate on three separate agreements: a treaty,
more or less along the Vladivostok lines, but with some reductions in some categories of weapons; a temporary agreement
on those matters that could not be resolved (a protocol to the
treaty), and a statement of general principles that would govern
subsequent talks on more extensive reductions. Thus, the
elements of the original Carter approach were preserved.

The Moscow episode was significant because it brought into
the open the potential for conflict between the White House
and the State Department, and between Brzezinski and Vance.
The last evening in Moscow, Vance had decided he needed
some bargaining room for the final session with Brezhnev. He
wanted to foreshadow—not offer—the concessions of the B-1
bomber and the Trident submarine. But when he cabled the
White House for permission, he was turned down (this fact
was kept from the delegation). Vance was stunned, I believe.
And later he and I talked over the problem of a secretary of
state's relationship to the White House. I think he agreed that
he would have to have a much clearer idea of the degree of
his autonomy in the future. I do not know if he took the issue
up with Brzezinski. But on the basis of this incident, I was not
surprised that tensions began to grow between the two men
and their institutions. In retrospect, I think that it would not
have been a good idea to broach the trading of the B-1 or the
Trident. But since Carter later abandoned the B-1 without
obtaining anything from the Soviets, mentioning the possibility
at this point could not have done much damage. The Trident
is a quite different matter. Offering to scrap it would have been
dangerous because it was intended to be the backbone of the
U.S. strategic force through the end of the century.

Whatever may have been the effect of this initial tilt between
Vance and the White House, to my utter dismay it happened
again, this time during Vance's negotiations with Gromyko in
Geneva in May. Vance asked me to sound out Dobrynin on a
formula to end the dispute over the Soviet Backfire bomber;
the interagency group in Washington had developed a formula
including restrictions on where the Backfire could be based
and its mode of operation, and a tentative ceiling on the

number that could be produced. Dobrynin was intrigued and tentatively agreed, subject, of course, to Gromyko's review. I reported this to Vance, and he cabled to Washington for approval. Again, he was turned down. Washington's rationale was that the idea was still too vague. This time, however, Vance continued to probe for an agreement, despite the White House admonitions (they did not have the nerve to overrule him, so he had some room for bargaining). But Gromyko began to sniff out that we were hedging, and he pulled back.

I took advantage of a talk with Dobrynin—we walked laps around the Intercontinental Hotel parking lot—to discuss several other issues, and to urge him to tell Gromyko that he was risking undercutting Carter with Moscow's tough talk and slippery negotiating. The three-part scheme we were offering was halfway between our position and theirs, I told him, and they would be wise to nail it down. If Vance failed this time, I said, then the right wing would have every reason to move against SALT and kill it when the original agreement expired in October 1977. I doubt that this had much effect on Dobrynin; the Soviets could not help but notice that Carter was trimming the defense budget and abandoning the B-1. But the fact is that after that May meeting in Geneva, relations began to improve. The Soviets began to tone down their language, though it would take several more months before the first significant breakthrough occurred, in late September, when Gromyko visited Washington and met with Carter.

Another troublesome aspect of that first visit to Moscow by Vance was the unusually harsh Soviet behavior. Looking back, I think that the Soviets overreacted. True, the Carter proposal for reductions was a departure from the previous negotiations, and there were grounds for irritation because of the pressure for human rights. In a speech in March, before Vance's arrival, Brezhnev had stressed that Vladivostok should be finished first, and then reductions could be considered. We should have given more weight to this speech as a signal. But I still believe that the essence of the American position should have been more interesting to the Soviets. It would have confirmed the status quo, and after some bargaining, reductions could easily have been accommodated. Brezhnev would have sealed an early bargain with a new administration that had a reputation for being more "liberal" and that was interested in cutting back on defense spending and dropping some key weapons systems. All these tendencies could and would have been enhanced by a softer Soviet response. Instead, the Soviets jeopardized their relationship with Washington at the very start.

The Soviet refusal to consider the Carter offer, in my judgment, represented a lost opportunity. What was in play in the early part of 1977 could have been turned into an agreement that would have endured the trials of the later Carter period. The Soviets were not being asked for reductions greater than they themselves came to propose in the 1980s, in the negotiations with Reagan. (Indeed, the upper limit that Carter proposed was only 250 missiles and bombers below what Brezhnev had tentatively agreed upon with Kissinger.) Had the Soviets moved quickly to consolidate an agreement, even in vague terms, they probably could have created a better foundation for a relationship with Carter; they could have gained a tactical advantage over the Chinese and perhaps they could have avoided the problems of the new American ICBM, the MX, to say nothing of the eventual emergence of the Strategic Defense Initiative. Some Soviets have since admitted to me that they missed a chance.

One reason for these mistakes may have been that Soviet policy was in transition, as was Brezhnev's leadership. In early 1977, Brezhnev had been in power for a little over twelve years; he was seventy-one years old and was faced with the growing economic consequences of his conservative policies. The economy was running down, but there was little Brezhnev could do about it, except seek help from the West. This was the period that Mikhail Gorbachev, in the 1980s, was to criticize for failing to address fundamental problems. As matters became more difficult, Brezhnev characteristically sought a political solution—he took over the presidency of the Soviet Union, pushing out his old friend Nikolai Podgorny, who apparently did not go gracefully.

In foreign policy, however, Brezhnev had made a significant speech just before Carter's inauguration, at the Soviet city of Tula, an ancient center for the production of cannons (and samovars) just outside of Moscow. In this speech Brezhnev had strongly supported détente and had implied some criticism of the burden of the Soviet military buildup. As it turned out, this speech was the forerunner of several policy statements by

Brezhnev that ended in a remarkable denunciation of nuclear war as "mutual suicide."

It is now believed that during this period, Brezhnev began to trim back Soviet military spending, or, more precisely, the rate of growth of Soviet military spending. And this constraint lasted into the early 1980s. At first he may have had the support of the more modern-minded military, such as the newly appointed chief of the general staff, Marshal Nikolai Ogarkov. Ogarkov's appointment was taken as a good omen, since he had participated in the SALT negotiations as a member of the Soviet delegation during an earlier phase (Harold Brown knew him quite well). Finally, Brezhnev knew that the SALT agreement on offensive weapons that he had signed with Nixon in 1972 would expire in October 1977. He had to preserve his option with Carter to extend that agreement. For domestic economic reasons—a major new consumer goods program was in preparation—Brezhnev had almost ruled out the alternative of launching a new round of armaments. These internal pressures led him to want a second SALT agreement, and this explained his eagerness not to break off with Carter after the Vance mission. In other words, Brezhnev still wanted some measure of détente with the United States.

But a different trend was also important: opportunities for strategic gains in the Third World were beginning to develop in the wake of the Soviet-Cuban intervention in Angola. It must have seemed a tempting time for the Soviet Union to make headway at the expense of a new American leadership reluctant to engage in Kissingerian power politics. It was, after all, the new ambassador to the U.N., Andrew Young, who had said that the Cubans in Angola were actually a stabilizing factor. A more aggressive Third World policy must have seemed even more attractive in light of what was emerging as a split in Washington, with Brzezinski in particular leading the way to normalization with China before going further with the Soviets. Thus, Brezhnev was embarking on a dual policy, challenging the United States in various Third World areas, but encouraging a SALT agreement.

This was evident in a minor test in early 1977. A motley collection of Katangese tribesmen invaded Zaire from Angola. Twenty years earlier they had been part of the forces around Moise Tshombe, who ruled Katanga, a remote part of Zaire when Zaire was still the Congo. The province, later known as Shaba, was a rich mining area, and Tshombe had Belgium's support. He was eventually killed, and his force fled into Angola, where they had lived since the mid-1960s. Suddenly, they attacked across the border. It seemed to me then, as now, that this was a Soviet-Cuban operation. But the Carter administration chose to see it as a small, backwater affair of no particular consequence for the United States. Thus, they asked the Moroccans to send paratroopers to help drive out the Katangese, and the episode ended. I thought that this sent a bad signal, though I admired the ingenuity of calling on our own proxies, the Moroccans. My instincts as a Kissingerian holdover were confirmed when Kissinger made a public speech criticizing the handling of the invasion, which he too branded as a Soviet operation. Today it is still a murky affair, but I remain convinced that it was a small Soviet test of the Carter administration. That it was repeated on a much larger scale and with better organization one year later would seem confirmation of my view.

The major test came in late 1977, after I had left the government, in a confrontation in the remote Ogaden desert of Ethiopia. American relations with Ethiopia had steadily deteriorated since the overthrow of Emperor Haile Selassie in 1974. The real power was a Communist faction, led by a colonel with the improbable name of Mengistu Haile Mariam (Holy Mary). At that time, Moscow was supporting Ethiopia's neighbor, Somalia. The two countries are separated by a sort of no-man's-land, the Ogaden desert, claimed by both, but generally recognized as belonging to Ethiopia. In the spring of 1977, Mengistu turned openly to Moscow for military assistance, and the United States was thrown out of its various assistance missions and the communications station in Kagnew was closed.

In the summer of 1977, Somalia invaded the Ogaden and occupied it. Mengistu turned to the Soviet Union for help in October, and to the shock of nearly everyone, Cuban troops began arriving in Ethiopia. A Soviet officer, General Vasily Petrov, organized and led a World War II–type of armored attack that not only drove the Somalis out of the Ogaden but for a time seemed to threaten an invasion of Somalia as well. At this point the United States began to give lukewarm support to Somalia, and to warn Ethiopia against allowing Cuban troops to cross the old border. Deputy NSC Director David Aaron was sent to Addis Ababa with this message for Mengistu. The Cuban troops did, in fact, stop and the crisis receded, but not without leaving a deep scar. Brzezinski had wanted to make a major response: this was a dangerous pattern of Soviet intervention with proxy troops. But Vance and Harold Brown objected. The United States could not support Somalia's claims to the Ogaden; moreover, Somalia had asked for a crisis by invading Ethiopia in the first place. And Harold Brown's position was decisive: he balked at the show of force of sending a carrier into the area.

Therefore no linkage was made between this latest Soviet transgression and any other aspects of Soviet-American relations. Other negotiations with the USSR, including those on strategic arms control, continued without change. The Soviets had scored a strategic coup. There is simply no doubt that the weak American reaction encouraged the Soviets to believe that they had a relatively free hand for that kind of operation. To compensate for this setback, Brzezinski decided to intensify his China option, traveling there himself in the spring of 1978.

Other incidents followed. The Afghan government was overthrown by Communists in April 1978. And, amazingly, the United States offered some limited economic assistance to the new government. Moscow must have read this as a confirmation that the United States had no strategic interests at stake in Afghanistan, and perhaps even in the general area. In May 1978 the Shaba invasion was repeated; this time French and Belgian paratroopers were our proxies. This in itself was not objectionable; but the United States' failure to take the Soviets to task was the real issue. A coup in Yemen followed shortly thereafter and shifted the leadership in Aden even more in the Soviet direction. Finally, in the winter of 1978, the Soviets signed a new treaty with Vietnam that was a blank check for Hanoi to invade and conquer Cambodia, which it did in early 1979. The invasion followed Deng Xiaoping's visit to the United States, when he confided to President Carter his plan to "counterattack" against Vietnam a short time later. Five years before, as we have seen, Brezhnev had tried to tempt Nixon and Kissinger with an alliance against China. Now Deng Xiaoping was making almost the same proposal in reverse to Carter. It is still not entirely clear whether he got a green light from Washington on his Vietnam action, but he certainly encountered no flashing red light.

So in February 1979 the Soviets were confronted by a Chinese attack on Vietnam, which turned out to be a fumbling operation that exposed serious weaknesses in the Chinese military. The Soviet response was to make no move against China, but to draw closer to Washington. Indeed, in retrospect the Chinese attack may have been the apogee of the Sino-Soviet dispute.

The Soviet strategic reaction was to complete SALT negotiations and arrange a summit meeting for Vienna in June 1979. At first glance this would seem to have justified Brzezinski's strategy of moving with China first. But the same period coincided with the collapse of the Shah in Iran and the increasing turmoil in Afghanistan. It may be that in the SALT negotiations the Kremlin was simply buying some insurance for rough weather. Only six months after the summit, the Soviets invaded Afghanistan, the one area where American and Chinese interests seemed to coincide. The invasion did break the pattern of encirclement of the USSR by a new anti-Soviet coalition of the United States, Europe, Japan and China. But it also was costly. The Soviets lost the ratification of Brezhnev's SALT treaty and provoked a chain reaction that ended with the election of Ronald Reagan and the rearmament of the United States.

Looking back at this crucial turning point, Brzezinski and Vance in their memoirs reached opposite conclusions: Brzezinski argued that a tougher response to early Soviet transgressions would have deterred the Afghan invasion and thus ensured the SALT treaty; Vance argued that a more vigorous pursuit of SALT and less antagonism through manuevers with China would have given the Soviets an incentive to pause. Brzezinski would seem to have the better of the argument; the failure to face up to the significance in the shift in Kabul from the old regime of Mohammed Daud to the Communist regime of Noor Mohammed Taraki was a fatal mistake, but in keeping with the general thrust of Carter's foreign policy; despite foreboding and a pessimistic report from Kabul, the administration decided on "watchful waiting."

But both Vance and Brzezinski are probably wrong in their speculations. Afghanistan was not a minor or trivial affair, subject to the whims of American policy. It was a cold-blooded

strategic decision by the Kremlin to end the turmoil in that
country, install a more reliable puppet and, if successful, give
the Soviet Union a geopolitical advantage dreamed of by the
czars. The notion that the Soviets had miscalculated has persisted. Even leading European statesmen foolishly believed that
Moscow could be talked out of Afghanistan. The Soviets may
have underestimated the extent and ferocity of the Afghan
resistance. But nearly a decade later, after more than 30,000
casualties, the Red Army is still there, entrenched for a long
war. The Soviets knew the invasion of Afghanistan was a bold
stroke.

Even though Afghanistan ended any chance for SALT, the
agreement was sound, as far as it went, and earned the rare
distinction of remaining in force even beyond its nominal
duration, despite the fact that it was never ratified by the
Senate. It came to be attacked as "fatally flawed" by candidate
Reagan, but that was wrong. The agreement itself achieved
roughly what had been sought over the years by both Democrats
and Republicans. The individual provisions have stood up
rather well. The treaty limited the number and types of Soviet
ICBMs, considered by all hands as the most threatening Soviet
weapon; it limited indirectly the total number of U.S. and
Soviet missile warheads (which would grow in numbers nevertheless); it put aside for two years the controversial issues
connected with the American cruise missiles, without forcing
us to give them up; it restricted the infamous Backfire bomber's
production rate; and it called for some overall reductions
(about 10 percent) after 1981.

There was a great deal of continuity with the previous
administrations. For example, in early 1970, at the very outset
of the SALT negotiations, the United States proposed a limit
of 1,900 missiles and bombers, and settled for 2,400 at Vladivostok; in March 1977 in the abortive Vance mission to Moscow
the proposal was for reductions to a ceiling in the range of
1,800 to 2,000, but Carter settled for 2,400, to be reduced to
2,250 later; and many years later in the Reagan period, the
United States proposed reductions that would have meant a
ceiling of about 1,800; and the Soviets eventually countered
with a similar plan for a limit of about 1,600.

In the 1979 SALT II debate, the chairman of the Joint
Chiefs of Staff, General David Jones, aptly summed up the

situation when he said the treaty was a modest but useful step. Though designed to last through the end of 1985, it was defended on the grounds that it was to be superseded by a new and supposedly better agreement. It was immediately attacked as defective, unverifiable and unfair. What was surprising was that even putative supporters of arms control were not enthusiastic. There was a diverting debate about verification, because of the loss of electronic listening posts during the revolution in Iran. Kissinger and Ford gave SALT the most guarded, lukewarm support; Haig opposed it and Nixon waffled. One problem was that it had taken too long to complete, and too much had transpired between the Nixon summit of 1972 and the Carter summit of 1979. By the time of the Senate hearings, the political atmosphere was shifting to the right, which made the administration's job even more difficult. There was already a litany taking shape that Carter had "lost" Afghanistan, Yemen, Iran and Nicaragua. Carter's passivity meant that the Soviets had "nothing to fear and nothing to gain"—as one observer put it.

Moreover, as Carter turned to the difficult task of selling his SALT agreement to the Senate, he found himself in a position that other presidents had occupied. In order to sell his disarmament agreements, he had to promise a more extensive armaments program to placate the critics. In Carter's case, the buildup involved pressing for the MX missile. The administration argued that the United States had to go ahead with this missile lest we fall into inferiority in the SALT treaty, which allowed each side one "new" ICBM. The Soviets would certainly go ahead with their new ICBM, so the United States had to match them. But, it was argued, the new missile would be vulnerable to a Soviet strike if emplaced in a fixed ICBM silo; thus it was decided to make it mobile; and the SALT ceiling setting an upper limit on the number of Soviet ICBMs was cited as the guarantee that the Soviets could not build a force large enough to threaten the mobile MX. In sum, it was necessary to ratify SALT in order to limit the threat to a new American ICBM, a threat, however, that was produced by the very deficiencies of the SALT agreement. Quite an irony.

Perhaps most damning was that despite an intricate set of provisions, the net result of the treaty was that both sides would increase their strategic armaments throughout the life of the agreement. This was a severe indictment of a president who had attacked SALT I and Vladivostok for their failure to achieve disarmament. In the end, in some desperation, the administration found itself reduced to arguing that its SALT agreement was better than none at all—a weak reed ten years after the first negotiations had begun, and seven years after the first agreement. Clearly, the SALT agreements were becoming more and more marginal to the strategic competition. The administration had begun with a scheme for major reductions and had settled for a variant of Vladivostok, and all of this had taken almost three years.

This weakened Carter's position, though not irretrievably so. But unlike Nixon, he had not embedded the agreement in a broader relationship with Moscow. The opposite had happened: SALT had been immunized from the currents of Soviet-American conflicts, whether in the Middle East, Africa or even Central America. The failure of SALT would not jeopardize other policies. The critics sensed this vulnerability and bore down hard against the provisions of the treaty during the Senate hearings, which Carter had inexplicably allowed to be delayed into the fall (Senator Jackson attacked the treaty as appeasement). The administration's handling of the ratification process was badly botched; no president should have allowed the Senate to dally over such a critical treaty. It was signed in June, and when the Soviets invaded Afghanistan on Christmas Day, it still had not been voted upon by the Senate.

As the maneuvering over the treaty came down to the final weeks, the administration came under new pressure, in negotiations with Senator Sam Nunn of Georgia and others, to promise that there would be an increase in the military budget of around 5 percent, rather than the 2 to 3 percent the administration preferred. This tentative understanding began to win over some Republican critics; Kissinger and Ford both indicated that they would have supported such a bargain on behalf of SALT.

Then the strange interlude of the "discovery" of a Soviet brigade in Cuba intervened. It was revealed by the administration that an organized Soviet military force of about brigade size had been stationed in Cuba for years, in apparent violation of the Kennedy-Khrushchev understanding of 1962. The implication was that Carter's predecessors had been derelict in not challenging the Soviets on this score. Nothing was more calculated to lose the support of Ford, Nixon and Kissinger for SALT. The incident led to some tortuous explaining that the brigade configuration was in fact a new development in an old situation. The result, however, was confusion and irritation. Whatever the facts, the affair was badly mishandled, alienating almost everyone. The Soviets later claimed that the incident proved that Carter was never serious about SALT, but they said this in defense of their Afghan invasion. The fact is that the Soviet invasion of Afghanistan in December 1979 did kill SALT and brought to an end the era of détente that had begun in 1969. The 1980 presidential election ratified this verdict. A new policy had to be forged, and this was the task entrusted to Ronald Reagan.

But Carter left behind one last accomplishment: his firm handling of the Polish crisis. As the tensions grew over the emergence of the first genuine workers' movement, the trade union Solidarity, it became more and more likely that the Soviets would move, perhaps invading Poland and provoking a major bloodbath. As the crisis mounted Brzezinski, with Carter's support, orchestrated a campaign of public and political pressures. This may have given the Soviets pause. We may never know what the Kremlin intended in December 1980. But the crisis did produce one instructive episode. Brzezinski ordered the compilation of a list of arms that could be sent to *China* if the Soviets should invade Poland—this from an administration that had entered office attacking the power politics of Kissinger and proclaiming a new morality.

XII

REAGAN'S
ROAD TO GENEVA

On November 21, 1985, Ronald Reagan became the ninth American president to meet with the leader of the Soviet Union. Each of President Reagan's predecessors had sought some basis for a peaceful relationship with the USSR. Each left office frustrated and angry at the implacability of his Soviet counterpart. Only Nixon made some significant progress in the early 1970s, but by the time Reagan took office in January 1981, the superpowers were in another cycle of deteriorating relations.

The Soviet leaders had initially thought that the deterioration might be checked by the new administration in Washington. Dobrynin, in various conversations, let it be known that the Soviets assumed they would be dealing with another conservative Republican administration—in effect, a replay of Nixon. In two long preinaugural conversations with Reagan's national security adviser-designate, Richard V. Allen, Dobrynin stressed that the Soviets were ready to do business with the new administration.

Later, after Alexander Haig had taken office as Reagan's secretary of state, Dobrynin's line was that it seemed as if the old pre-Carter policies would be resumed. He urged that new

talks be started between Haig and Gromyko and that SALT
be "rescued." Haig countered with a lecture on unacceptable
Soviet behavior, and the need for the Soviets to earn their way
back into the good graces of the United States. In his memoirs,
Haig claims that his view was that there was nothing to negotiate
with the Soviets at this early date and, above all, there was no
need to make concessions on a strategic arms agreement, which
the Soviets desperately wanted.

Yet the Soviets persisted in acting as if Nixon had returned,
with Kissinger's policies intact. In part this was because of their
profound disillusionment with Carter, and in part it was
Brezhnev's wishful thinking. By 1981, his position had become
more complicated. He was still trying to promote Konstantin
Chernenko as his successor, but the effort was meeting growing
resistance. Chernenko, for his part, was playing the role of
front man for Brezhnev and was arguing for a conciliatory
foreign policy. It was in this period, for example, that Chernenko claimed that nuclear war threatened the end of civili-
zation—the very phrase used by Stalin's short-lived successor
Georgi Malenkov in 1954 and for which he was sharply
criticized.

Thus it is not surprising that Brezhnev kept probing and
hoping for signs of conciliation from Reagan. He wrote a rather
plaintive letter to the new president, angling for a summit
meeting. Haig intervened to kill any moves toward an early
summit, on the grounds that with the Polish crisis still unresolved, a summit would send a signal of weakness: "there could
be no summit while the shadows of Budapest and Prague fell
across Poland." Yet the tone of Reagan's replies to Brezhnev
suggested that he was not altogether averse to a meeting. And
certain American actions must have encouraged a Soviet belief
that Reagan was jettisoning his tough campaign pose. Of major
significance was the White House decision to lift the embargo
on grain sales to the USSR, imposed by Carter in retaliation
for the invasion of Afghanistan. This was a clear gift both to
the American farmers and to Brezhnev. When Dobrynin asked
the new secretary of state if there were any continuing conditions on grain sales, Haig rather sheepishly said only general
Soviet behavior.

A second and equally publicized gesture by the Reagan
administration was the handling of the SALT II treaty, which

had been withdrawn by Carter from consideration by the Senate. It was still unratified. And, of course, Reagan had denounced it during the election campaign. It was widely believed that he would abandon it after taking office. This was the position taken by several of the second-level officials in the administration. But that view was quickly squelched by Secretary Haig, who initiated a new policy known as the "no-undercut" policy. This cumbersome phrase, so characteristic of the government bureaucracy, meant that if the Soviets did not "undercut" the treaty by their actions, the United States would not do so either. This was not quite the same as abiding by the treaty's provisions; at least the administration liked to think that there was an important distinction. Moreover, it had the virtue of putting the burden on the Soviets. Amazingly, this policy survived for over five years: not until May 1986, after the formal date for expiration had passed in December 1985, did Reagan move to end this unusual circumstance by announcing that the United States would not be bound by the treaty's provisions; even then, the entire treaty's status was ambiguous. Preserving the unratified agreement was a shrewd decision by Haig; it immediately removed a potentially explosive issue.

It also permitted the administration to concentrate on a major defense buildup without the distraction of an arms control debate. Thus, the Reagan approach to the Soviets emphasized first and foremost the strength of U.S. national defense. The corollary to the military buildup was the deemphasis of diplomacy, especially arms control negotiations. Later, a third element emerged, the pursuit of an anticommunist counteroffensive, which eventually became the "Reagan Doctrine." The implication of this doctrine was to treat regional conflicts as East-West clashes, and to search for a "strategic consensus" with American clients, a consensus based on opposition to the Soviet Union.

This was more of a mind-set than a set of carefully considered strategies. Indeed, the original military buildup was based on hastily arranged figures and guesses. In his memoirs, David Stockman has revealed that well after the inauguration the new secretary of defense, Caspar Weinberger, had no strategy but only a collection of minor fixes to the budget. These fixes, of course, did constitute a strategy. They reflected an awareness in the new Pentagon that defense was likely to continue to suffer either feast or famine; that it was necessary to "get well" as the phrase went, to pile on increases as a hedge against the day when the cycle would turn and the budget-cutters would take their revenge on defense. So the Defense Department went for large increases in spending. The number of innovative programs, however, was quite limited; indeed, the only addition to the American strategic arsenal in the first four years was the battleship *Iowa*. The remainder of the strategic forces had been developed by Reagan's predecessors: in exasperation over Reagan's attacks on a decade of defense "neglect," both Carter and Ford in public statements finally had to remind the president that his deterrent forces were created by them.

The Reagan administration drew a clean link between the buildup of American military strength and any prospects for arms control. If the Soviets saw the resurgence of American power, then, and only then, would they become interested in legitimate arms control. This was the classic position held by many students more versed in the intricacies of arms control than candidate Reagan. But the new president went considerably further, claiming that the Soviets did in fact have a "margin of superiority" over the United States. He used this assertion to good advantage, insisting first on a military buildup to "catch up" with the Soviet Union, and then on reductions of nuclear weapons to bring the Soviets down to our level.

Yet when confronted with the realities of governing and conducting a foreign and defense policy, Reagan the president began to show a more pragmatic side than Reagan the candidate. The "margin of superiority" magically began to shrink, and the "window of vulnerability" began to close. For some years, as noted earlier, much had been made of the vulnerability of American ICBM silos to a Soviet attack, which could virtually disarm the United States without inflicting the massive casualties of an attack against cities. This would leave the president with the choice of either launching a counterstrike, knowing that American cities could easily be attacked by remaining Soviet missiles, or simply accepting the damage, which would be tantamount to a strategic defeat. This line of reasoning had become almost an article of faith with many strategists who were advising the new administration. It was called the window of vulnerability because it was expected that it would open as soon as Soviet missiles acquired the accuracy necessary to execute such a surgical strike. The window would close when the United States had taken effective countermeasures. One such countermeasure was to build a mobile ICBM that could not easily be targeted. This simple idea led to fantastic schemes: for example, under Carter, there was the plan to build an array of hundreds of silos, moving missiles about from one to another in a deceptive shell game; another proposal, dating to the Ford administration, was to build a "race track" around which missiles would swirl continuously. Under Reagan, there was even a plan to build the silos so close together that the incoming warheads would destroy each other; naturally, it was called fratricide.

Carter had taken the threat sufficiently seriously to propose the convoluted shell game for basing the new MX ICBM. Reagan scrapped this, and to the amazement of critics as well as supporters, Secretary Weinberger proposed putting the MX in fixed silos, the very silos that were the most vulnerable to a Soviet attack. The administration made no particular effort to justify this, other than citing expediency. The president then appointed a commission led by my old mentor, Brent Scowcroft. That commission's report quietly closed the window of vulnerability; it proposed as an interim measure to deploy 100 MXs, but advocated that the United States shift to a smaller, mobile and less vulnerable missile, unfortunately called the Midgetman. Reagan thanked the commission and blithely ignored its recommendations.

But in effect both the margin of superiority and the window of vulnerability disappeared during Reagan's first term. The president was able to execute these turnabouts for two reasons: The fantastic scenario of a Soviet strike did not wear well with the public or the Congress, and it seemed less and less plausible to strategists; the craziness of the new schemes for dummy silos, fratricide, and so forth, made the entire affair appear more and more ludicrous. Second, a right-wing president could cancel the emphasis on the Soviet threat with impunity. Reagan's anti-Soviet rhetoric and his skepticism about arms control gave him unusual freedom to maneuver.

But this cavalier attitude foreshadowed an unwillingness on the administration's part to confront sharp strategic choices. It chose to compromise rather than resolve basic issues. Thus,

Reagan lifted the grain embargo against the USSR without denying the principle of economic sanctions, which was invoked in the case of Poland less than nine months later. He denounced arms control, but in less than a year his administration was involved in negotiations. He denounced SALT II as fatally flawed but lived up to its provisions for five years. He attacked the Helsinki conference but continued to participate fully in the follow-on meetings at Madrid, Stockholm and Vienna. In major strategic matters, Reagan gradually became less distinguishable from his predecessors—until the surprise proposal to build a Star Wars defense.

The Reagan defense buildup was not only about numbers of weapons or intricate balances. What Reagan achieved was a change in the psychological balance. Much of the country supported him in the belief that the Russians had gained an edge over the United States. This attitude, as well as the accumulation of issues from Watergate to Iran before Reagan took office, created a severe crisis of confidence in the country. It was surely one reason for Reagan's election. And his defense buildup was the response. By the end of his first term, it was widely believed that Reagan had reversed the unfavorable strategic trends and that the United States was at least even with, if not ahead of, the Soviets. This resurgence of confidence was nowhere more evident than in the outburst of American nationalism at the Los Angeles Olympics in 1984.

The fact was that the United States was not nearly as weak as Reagan believed in 1980, nor was it as strong as he claimed four years later. Not much had changed, if measured by conventional yardsticks of military power. But the change in the psychology had a telling effect, especially on the Kremlin.

Great powers base their policies not on the current balance of forces but on anticipated trends. Thus in the late 1970s Brezhnev undertook a geopolitical offensive probably because he foresaw that the correlation of forces was becoming favorable for the Soviet Union. This, incidentally, also allowed him to cut back on his military effort in 1976. But by 1982, the Soviets saw that the trends were becoming unfavorable. If they were to affect the future balance, the Soviet leaders would have to take action, either to counter the Americans, or to arrest the trends by diplomacy.

Moscow's problem, however, was that its leadership was

increasingly paralyzed by the question of who would succeed Brezhnev. And the succession problem was becoming incredibly complicated by maneuvering that included various plots and subplots, scandals in the Soviet first family, sudden and unexplained deaths of police officials, the demise of the old guard (Mikhail Suslov, the supremely influential ideology chief, died in January 1982). Finally, a new heir apparent emerged: the former KGB chief, Yuri Andropov. But the confusion and weakness had given the Reagan administration a free ride for almost four years.

It also pointed up a fundamental contradiction in Reagan's foreign policy. On the one hand, the administration insisted that the Soviets were bent on a relentless expansion and had to be checked at every turn. On the other hand, it maintained that the Soviet system was basically weak and had entered a historical decline. Reaganites tried to square the circle by arguing that the Soviets were still expansionist; now they were motivated by desperation and thus doubly dangerous. It was Soviet military prowess that remained valid, not the political or economic system, and American policy had to be geared to countering the military threat. Hence the priority Reagan gave to our military buildup, not to negotiations to take advantage of Soviet troubles. The time was not ripe for negotiating, this argument continued, and might not be for years. But as Alexander Haig pointed out to the White House, if the United States was too weak to negotiate, then it was also too weak to confront the USSR.

Initially, the administration had made no secret of its deep aversion to arms control and to arms control negotiations. Of course, no administration can afford to be seen as purely hawkish, or worse, as initiating an arms race. So the safe position on arms control was to advocate major reductions in armaments. Never mind that under certain circumstances reductions could even be dangerous (if the number of military targets, i.e., ICBM silos, shrinks more rapidly than the number of weapons, i.e., warheads, then a first strike becomes tempting). The Reagan arms control specialists, of course, knew that reductions had to be carefully defined, but they were cynically gambling that there would be no prospect of having to negotiate. They developed extensive proposals for deep reductions, clinging to the concept as a guarantee against having to engage in serious arms control. Even Haig claimed that the result in 1981 and 1982 was a "flawed" position.

At first this was no particular problem as far as the bilateral SALT negotiations were concerned. There was, after all, Carter's treaty in being, and both sides were prepared to live with it for a time. Thus these negotiations could be stalled without much risk, and there were no new SALT negotiations scheduled until mid-1982.

But the administration also inherited a second set of negotiations that involved the NATO allies and European security more directly. These negotiations grew out of the "dual-track" (all tracks are inevitably "dual" in the American government) NATO decision of December 1979. The first track was to deploy 572 new American intermediate-range missiles in Europe starting in 1983 to counter the Soviet buildup of a new family of intermediate-range mobile missiles called the SS-20. This Soviet buildup had led to a growing European concern that Europe might find itself facing a new Soviet threat at a time when the longer-range intercontinental weapons were being regulated in the SALT II negotiations; hence the call for a new European missile balance, initiated by German chancellor Helmut Schmidt in the fall of 1977, which finally led to the decisions of 1979, when Carter was still in office.

The second track adopted by NATO was to negotiate with the Soviet Union for an arms control agreement covering intermediate-range missiles on both sides. The Carter administration had held one round of talks without any appreciable result. Now Reagan had to decide whether to continue this second track of negotiations. His natural inclination was to avoid any talks and concentrate on deploying the American missiles in Europe. But this deployment was still three years away; it was unlikely that such a prolonged schedule could be maintained without some semblance of negotiations to placate public opinion in Europe. All of the European allies faced internal pressures from antinuclear peace movements, and they desperately pressed for negotiations. The danger, of course, was that after the NATO nations had conciliated the European left by opening negotiations, the same pressures would return and then would have to be placated by concessions to the Soviets to prove the West's good faith.

The decision to negotiate was also complicated by internal

divisions in Washington. One school in the Pentagon opposed the original dual track, because they favored using cruise missiles on American ships or submarines to counter the Soviet SS-20s. At sea, the cruise missiles would be truly mobile, under American command and consistent with the new Reagan emphasis on naval power. This idea, however, risked a different crisis: that the Europeans would fear that the Americans were trying to "decouple," that is, to separate their nuclear forces from the land mass of NATO. Moreover, the administration instinctively feared that the negotiations with Moscow, rather than assisting in relieving political pressures in Europe, would in fact stimulate them on the smaller and weaker allies. Indicative of this negative attitude was Secretary Weinberger's caustic comment that if the "movement from cold war to détente is progress, then let me say we cannot afford much more progress." This superciliousness was badly received in Europe, where détente still had a strong attraction. Those officials in Washington who opposed negotiations also sought to link the beginning of talks with Soviet restraint in Poland. The pro-negotiations position was that while an end to the Polish crisis was not a precondition to arms control, Soviet action in Poland might make the talks impossible.

In the end, allied sentiment persuaded Reagan to negotiate on the intermediate-range weapons, but he decided to hold off on reviving SALT. This decision opened the door to a sweeping new U.S. proposal, namely to get rid of all intermediate-range missiles on both sides—the zero option, as it was inevitably called in Washington. This option, revealed on November 18, 1981, foreshadowed a Reagan pattern: effective public-relations positions that would catch the Soviets unawares and put Moscow on the defensive. Haig, with his long experience, recognized the risk in the shallowness of such proposals and opposed the gimmick of a zero option; but it appealed to the public-relations-conscious White House and to the opponents of negotiations in the Pentagon, who assumed the Soviets would reject it. Eventually, the new American position had to be modified to permit missiles on both sides. And, even later, there was an extremely embarrassing incident in which the American chief negotiator, Paul Nitze, proposed a compromise to his Soviet counterpart. Under Nitze's scheme, the Americans would give up the 100 Pershing ballistic missiles scheduled to be deployed in Germany, and would settle for an even level of the remaining cruise missiles and SS-20s. In September 1982 both governments, after much squirming, turned down the walk-in-the-woods bargain, as it was called (the woods being Johann Strauss's Vienna Woods).

Some deal on intermediate-range missiles was probably feasible, but in the end no bargain was struck. This turned out to be a stroke of luck. The Kremlin was then in turmoil. Brezhnev died in November 1982, and Andropov took power. At first he tried to reactivate Soviet diplomacy, but then he began to falter. He fell ill in September 1983 and died in February 1984. In any case, Soviet diplomacy failed to crack the Western alliance. All countries held steady, and the missile deployment began in December 1983. The Soviets withdrew from both sets of negotiations, but still there was no Western sense of crisis. The Soviets were thus confronted in the spring of 1984 with a geopolitical disaster, just at the time when Andropov died and the aged Chernenko took power. This would prove to be a turning point. Reared in the school of détente, Chernenko gradually reopened the dialogue with Washington, finally sending Gromyko to see President Reagan in September to propose the resumption of arms control negotiations.

In the fall of 1984, shortly before his reelection, Ronald Reagan could proudly point to the vindication of his strategy. At home he had reestablished confidence, and abroad he had won a great victory. But the administration's involvement with the NATO allies had changed American policy. The Reagan administration encountered reality in the attitudes of the Atlantic allies, and this clash had altered the Reagan opposition to arms control. The second clash with reality was over the Polish crisis.

Poland had been simmering throughout 1981, as the Reagan administration settled into office. After some alarms in the spring, the situation seemed to be calming down, and Washington even decided to display the carrot rather than the stick, contradicting the prevalent conservative theory that the Soviets should bear the economic consequences of their policies. Washington decided to offer a loan to the regime in Warsaw for grain purchases. At the same time, anticipating that the Soviets might crack down, the administration approved a contingent policy of potential economic sanctions against the USSR, and

Poland as well. The Soviets were warned repeatedly by Haig that Soviet intervention would lead to the "gravest consequences" (it is too bad that this once potent diplomatic phrase has degenerated into a throw-away line). Whether out of concern over the American reaction or otherwise, the Soviets finally hit upon a Polish solution: they selected General Wojciech Jaruzelski, the "strongman" of Polish politics, to lead the imposition of martial law in December 1981, and miracuously the plan worked. The Solidarity movement was caught unawares and could not respond effectively. The initial American reaction was hesitant; but in the face of domestic right-wing criticism, the administration's reaction hardened, leading to a decision to apply economic sanctions.

Yet, as the secretary of state noted, in the end the United States applied sanctions not to the Soviets, or to the Polish regime, but to our allies (not quite true but a good phrase to make the point), because they refused to go along with Washington's desire to deal more harshly with the Jaruzelski regime. The Europeans argued that Jaruzelski's martial law was preferable to an outright Soviet invasion, and that the West should therefore withhold any severe punishments. In the debate some Europeans cruelly cited Yalta to rebut American pressures to take some counteraction. The United States was dismayed and embittered by the persistent European rationalization of Soviet pressures, first in Afghanistan in 1980 and then in Poland in 1982. Washington wanted to take a strong position, but to do so it had to face a fundamental issue: whether to break off the intermediate-range nuclear force (INF) arms control negotiations in Geneva. It decided against invoking this linkage but then chose to demand a major European sanction: that is, for the Europeans to renege on their arrangements to supply gas pipe to the Soviets to complete a pipeline that would deliver natural gas from the USSR to Western Europe. In the face of European refusal to accept this demand, Washington retaliated by forbidding subsidiaries of American companies from supplying parts to the pipeline project.

This brought on a full-scale Atlantic crisis that overshadowed the question of Poland. Eventually, after Haig resigned, the new secretary of state, George Shultz, smothered further controversy and the crisis began to fade away. It had finally dawned on Washington that the price was becoming too high.

There was little that could be done immediately to affect the situation in Poland, but the feckless debate over sanctions could deeply damage the Western alliance. There was a historical footnote to this crisis over the gas pipeline. In 1986, the Europeans decided to buy Norwegian gas in large quantities and reduce their dependence on the Soviet Union. This is precisely what Washington had proposed in 1982. And at almost that very moment in 1986, when the Europeans shifted their source of gas supplies, Poland was admitted into the International Monetary Fund, vindicating the European argument against isolating the Jaruzelski regime.

The Atlantic crisis over arms control and Poland left a bitter aftertaste. It widened the growing gap between what the Europeans came to believe was America's penchant for unilateralism, and what Americans believed was a European tendency toward pacifism or neutralism. Before the West German and British elections of 1983 it seemed that the missile controversy might even threaten the existence of NATO. A false dilemma was presented to the Reagan administration: either placate the Europeans by offering major concessions to the USSR or demand the deployment of missiles as a test of alliance solidarity, even at the expense of a worsening crisis. Fortunately, the Reagan administration refused this Hobson's choice and steered a middle course.

The Polish crisis was also instructive. What was at issue in the West was not simply whether to impose sanctions but the larger question of the nature of the threat from the East and how to deal with it, in particular, whether arms control should be subordinate to other aspects of the East-West struggle or be treated independently. In the background there was the issue of whether the Western alliance should apply a policy of increasing pressures or seek a progressive reconciliation with the USSR. Reagan eventually chose the latter.

On both of these major issues, the Reagan administration finally accommodated its allies. No linkage was imposed between the INF arms control negotiations and the Polish crisis. Reagan was sharply attacked for this lapse in right-wing theology, which held that the Soviets had to be forced to suffer for their actions. But he was undoubtedly correct; his prudence (actually urged by Haig before he resigned) ensured the success of the strategy of denying the Soviet Union a veto over Western strategic decisions. The American missiles were deployed in Europe and the onus for disrupting the negotiations fell on Moscow.

Another myth fell in this period: that the Reagan administration could or would pursue a policy toward Eastern Europe different from that of its predecessors. Criticism of Yalta had become a staple of Republicanism in the United States in the 1950s. But the reality was that the West did not have the option of "liberation" in Eastern Europe after the Hungarian crisis of 1956. Thus the policy of differentiating among the East European regimes evolved during the 1960s and 1970s, and was given a strong impetus by Nixon. This policy meant differentiating between Stalinist regimes and those that were more liberal or more autonomous and offering favorable treatment to the latter; this was originally applied to Yugoslavia, and then, in 1956, to Poland, and finally, in 1969, to Romania. The policy survived the Soviet invasion of Czechoslovakia, and, under Reagan, it survived the Solidarity crisis. Again Reagan resembled his predecessors.

As the Reagan administration strengthened its strategic position, and Moscow's position deteriorated, it behooved the United States to try to translate these conditions into permanent geopolitical gains. How to do so was the problem that the administration had difficulty in facing from the start. By 1984, the pending elections began to cast a different light on Soviet relations, making them not a test of strength but a test of statesmanship. Reagan had built up American defense for over three years; now he had to cash in on his achievements. To do so meant reliance on diplomacy and, eventually, a summit meeting. This progression, from a position well to the right to a position almost in the center of the road, took four years: it was a journey that many of Reagan's predecessors had made.

At first the new conciliatory attitude toward Moscow in Washington seemed a fruitless gesture, perhaps even a cynical one. But Moscow also began to reappraise its policies when faced with the wreckage of its diplomacy in Europe. Both superpowers may have been sobered by the clashes over Euromissiles; Reagan wanted some political dividend for his policy of strength; Chernenko wanted to recover some of the initiative lost in the Euromissile contest. These parallel reassessments provided a common ground. Much to the surprise of all concerned, by the fall of 1984, shortly before the election—which conventional wisdom claimed the Soviets would wait out—Andrei Gromyko was in Washington chatting amiably with the man who had attacked his "evil empire." Thus, in dealing with the Soviet Union over the core issues in Europe, the Reagan administration was within the mainstream of American foreign policy.

But on two other issues—the struggle in the Third World and SDI (Star Wars)—the administration broke sharply with its predecessors.

In effect, Reagan reversed Carter's priorities. Following the lead of his ambassador to the United Nations, Jeane Kirkpatrick, the new president adopted a differentiated approach to Third World regimes: more aggressive opposition to left-wing dictatorships and more toleration of right-wing ones, on the theory that the rightists could be reformed or even changed, but that the Communist or Marxist regimes would yield only under severe pressure. There was also the more positive policy of supporting democracies forthrightly, and even covertly in some cases. These themes established the intellectual basis for the Haig policy of forging a "strategic consensus" in various regions to oppose Communist or Soviet influence. Whereas the Carter administration had tried to relegate the Soviet problem in the Third World to a secondary position, the Reagan administration elevated it. North-South issues were seen by the new administration as an indirect Soviet challenge; even old issues in the Middle East were reevaluated on the basis of the new drive for a strategic consensus.

At first, it was not immediately apparent that a broad strategic shift in policy was developing. Indeed, there may have been no grand design. Haig's memoirs do not suggest there was any particularly coherent plan beyond elementary linkages of Third World conflicts to broad policy. Eventually the new set of policies was christened the Reagan Doctrine: it was virtually a claim to the legitimacy of American intervention in the Third World. It received a strong fillip from the successful intervention in Grenada. The Reagan Doctrine came to embrace active support for the anticommunist "freedom fighters" in Afghanistan, the "contras" in Nicaragua, some of the anti-Vietnamese groups inside Cambodia, and, later, in 1985, aid to Jonas

Savimbi in Angola. These policies raised so many fears that a resistance developed in the Congress, especially focused on Nicaragua. But there was no broadly based objection to the implications of the interventionist Reagan Doctrine. This in itself was an indicator of the change in mood since 1976, when the Congress cut off all funds to anticommunist forces in Angola. A decade later this prohibition was lifted by the Congress, and it was not even a hard-fought vote. Indeed, the Democrats took the lead in advocating assistance to the anti-Vietnamese forces in Cambodia—again a startling shift from the previous decade, when even a hint of involvement in Southeast Asia would have provoked a tidal wave of protest.

The Soviets, of course, resisted the notion of making restraint in their policies a precondition to a more normal relationship. Brezhnev at first countered by saying that the Soviets would be "simpletons" if they were to insist that the United States abandon its foreign bases before talks could begin. Yet a new Soviet pattern began to take shape, and a modification of superpower relationships also emerged. The great fears of 1980—a virtual war scare after Afghanistan—proved to be groundless. The Red Army did not sweep through the Afghan passes to the Persian Gulf; indeed, the Soviet Union is bogged down in a war that it cannot win without extensive escalation and cannot end without costly concessions.

Others of its acquisitions also began to look less inviting. Ethiopia turned into a nightmare of starvation and famine. Yemen refused to settle down into the role of stable client and was plagued by constant factional fighting, even an open rebellion in 1986. The Vietnamese puppet regime in Cambodia could not gain recognition of its legitimacy. And in Angola, Savimbi could not be liquidated, nor could the South Africans be deterred from constant intervention. Other clients, especially Libya, were unpredictable and dangerous and had to be kept at arm's length (Libyan leader Muammar Qaddafi repeatedly failed to get a friendship treaty with Moscow, which used to be standard fare for Soviet clients). And the cost of this new empire was growing, reaching perhaps $40 billion each year. These instabilities and uncertainties led to a review of Soviet policy, after Brezhnev, that pointed toward a more cautious Soviet approach to the Third World: consolidation of its empire, to be sure, but not a relentless search for new clients. The paramount Soviet policy as a result of this reexamination was to tend to matters closer to home.

This Soviet shift was evident in superpower relations. In a number of major and minor crises—the Lebanese and Falklands wars, the Iran-Iraq contest, Grenada, Nicaragua and Libya—the Soviets behaved with a studied prudence. One might think that the landing of American troops in Lebanon, for the first time since the 1950s, would provoke a Soviet reaction. Brezhnev merely warned that in such cases the Soviet Union would "build its policy with due consideration of the fact"—a far cry from Khrushchev's rocket-rattling in the Suez crisis, or for that matter, from Brezhnev's pointed warnings in the Yom Kippur war in 1973. Even in the Persian Gulf, there almost seemed to be a tacit understanding between the superpowers. The United States, for example, swept mines in the area with no Soviet harassment. On the other hand, the Soviets intervened with the Palestine Liberation Organization (PLO) to kill the Reagan Middle East peace plan in late 1982. But in 1986, the Soviet foreign minister met with the Israeli prime minister and the discussion was regarded by the rest of the world community as almost routine.

Soviet behavior could well be explained by the Kremlin's need for a period of consolidation. But it was also true that a new viewpoint emerged in Moscow, especially under Andropov, that held that the superpower relationship should not be held hostage to the vagaries of the Third World contest. There was even a hint by Andropov in April 1983 of a possible division of spheres of influence, i.e., Nicaragua for Afghanistan.

Thus by 1984 the Reagan administration, having revived a policy of strong linkages and having then abandoned it, nevertheless created approximately the situation it had sought. Soviet policy was restrained, and in some measure it was because of Moscow's fear of the consequences of its behavior on the central relationship with the United States. Reagan had changed the rules in the Third World, and successfully. Indeed, he was counting on what he called "the basic prudence of the Soviet leaders." The real danger was that this new, highly tentative relationship and a basic Soviet prudence—newly discovered by the man who had said these same leaders would lie, steal, cheat—had yet to be tested by a major crisis in which the

Soviets were confronted by a target of irresistible opportunity. The Reagan first term had been notably devoid of any such irresistible temptations.

Even in the Reagan Doctrine one could recognize fragments of older American policies. But in one area Reagan broke out of the established bounds: his advocacy in March 1983 of the new, foolproof strategic defense of the United States, which quickly became known as Star Wars because it would be based in outer space.

The origin of this initiative is still somewhat mysterious. Unlike past programs, it did not develop out of a new technology or an established Pentagon plan, or even a brilliant new concept. The strategic situation had apparently been troubling the president and he finally decided to raise the question of defense in a speech on national security. He did not merely lift the lid of Pandora's box, he blew it off completely. For twenty-five years, the United States had been willing to remain defenseless in the face of growing Soviet intercontinental attack forces. The nation was content to remain vulnerable because its leaders reassured them with a simple but persuasive idea: that it would be suicidal for the USSR to launch a general attack on the United States as long as the United States could strike back with enough power to destroy the Soviet Union. The introduction of strategic defense would upset this equilibrium of mutual deterrence. Defense, even a relatively ineffective one, could encourage one side to believe that it might actually gain from launching a first strike; if the other side's missiles were severely damaged, then the inevitable counterattack might be effectively defeated by the new defensive system. Such a situation would obviously be dangerously unstable; it was this analysis that supported the Nixon decision to give up any significant defense in the ABM treaty of 1972. It had not been challenged seriously since then.

Suddenly President Reagan raised not a technical objection but a strategic and moral challenge. Could the United States afford to rely on the ever-increasing power of offensive forces to prevent war? Would not a defense be a safer policy? Defending the United States from outer space was an incredibly simple and compelling concept, not far removed from the concerns and fears of his opponents who favored a nuclear freeze. They too argued that relying indefinitely on the power of offensive deterrence was too dangerous. The odds were against deterrence working forever, and a failure would be catastrophic. Thus the right and left seemed to be converging to raise serious doubts about American strategic policy. The Reagan solution found immediate popular support at home but, as was to be expected, raised serious alarms in Europe.

But its most serious impact was in Moscow. The Soviet leaders—at that point in 1983 Yuri Andropov was general secretary—instantly recognized the challenge and rejected it with some plain language. Such a system would "disarm" the Soviet Union, and, of course, this was its essence. If one side should in fact develop and deploy a strategic defense, even if not leak-proof, before the other side, it could gain a decisive strategic advantage for a policy of blackmail if not outright war. Neither side could afford to lose such a race. American critics might not take the Star Wars idea seriously, but the Soviet leaders could not indulge in such a luxury. Failing to defeat it by pressures and threats, after walking out of the talks on arms control in late 1983, the Soviets wisely switched tactics and sought to defang the issue by linking it to Reagan's other favorite scheme, the reduction of strategic weapons. Thus, once again, a Reagan initiative seemed to have paid off.

In the spring of 1985, the Soviets were back at the bargaining table, in effect talking in the same language as the Americans. Both sides were proposing roughly the same reductions that Carter first had in 1977, and even larger cuts, up to 50 percent, were suggested. But there was a major difference. It seemed that Reagan was not using the SDI merely as a bargaining chip, as many had thought. He was profoundly convinced that defense had to be created to achieve a new offensive-defensive equilibrium—an age-old dream but an incredibly intricate process even between friendly countries, let alone between two hostile adversaries. This was the underlying challenge: to devise a new strategic equation between the United States and the USSR, to balance the offense and the defense on both sides. The immediate consequence in 1985 was to accelerate the movement toward a summit meeting between President Reagan and the new Soviet leader, Mikhail Gorbachev. On November 21, 1985, when Ronald Wilson Reagan and Mikhail Sergevich Gorbachev walked across a small stage to grasp hands beneath the Stars and Stripes and the Hammer and Sickle, their gesture symbolically ended the era that had begun when the Soviet army invaded Afghanistan. At last, the long interregnum in Moscow was over. President Reagan had a counterpart to deal with. The question was, Could a deal be made after five long years of near total hostility? The question remains open.

XIII

THE NEXT PHASE

Ronald Reagan and Mikhail Gorbachev agreed in Geneva that a nuclear war could not be won and must never be fought—echoing Eisenhower and Khrushchev thirty years earlier. Traveling widely different routes, the superpowers seemed to have arrived at a common destination.

It may be that the conflict between the United States and the Soviet Union is unique. Never before has such a broad and deep struggle lasted so long without a major war. More than forty years of peace have accustomed us to the idea that a general war is unthinkable and virtually impossible: the mere existence of nuclear weapons guarantees that they will never be used. Moreover, the balance of forces works against war between the United States and the Soviet Union. The collapse of the Sino-Soviet alliance has fundamentally altered the strategic position of the Soviet Union. All of the major powers are aligned against the USSR. Moscow is confronted by the probability that it would have to fight on two or three fronts if war came. The danger of war has also diminished in recent years as the balance of military power has shifted more in favor of the United States and its allies; the Soviet leaders cannot expect that the outcome of a major war would be advantageous to them. Finally, in almost every major respect the Soviet Union's position has been deteriorating. Whereas thirty years ago the USSR still had a special political, economic and ideological appeal in the world, this broad threat has been progressively reduced. The Soviet Union now poses a basic military threat but not much more.

The dangers of war have receded since the early days of the cold war. Peace is by no means guaranteed, but it seems more likely to endure now than twenty or thirty years ago, when there were constant crises over Berlin or Cuba.

We must take care that this optimism does not turn out to be a dangerous delusion. To expect prolonged peace between two deeply hostile rivals runs against all the lessons of history. A small area of common ground has developed between the two superpowers, but it is very unstable. Despite some comforting rhetorical flourishes, the nuclear equilibrium has become not more reassuring but more fluid, more uncertain and therefore more dangerous.

Nuclear weapons and the attitudes toward them have changed radically over the past forty years and are likely to continue to change. In the development of their strategic forces and doctrines the two superpowers have usually moved in quite different directions. The United States has stressed deterrence and relied on the threat of retaliation; the Soviet Union has emphasized the critical importance of striking first. Whatever their declared doctrines, both sides have moved toward making nuclear weapons technologically more usable while vociferously denying any such intention.

Technology is outstripping the ability of diplomacy to ensure strategic stability. At the time of the Cuban missile crisis, both sides had a few dozen strategic missiles capable of reaching each other's homeland. Ten years later the figure was at least ten times as great. In the next decade the number of warheads on these missiles more than doubled. President Kennedy feared nuclear annihilation in 1962 when Khrushchev clandestinely emplaced 60 missiles in Cuba; now, roughly the same number of warheads can be carried by only 6 Soviet ICBMs. In that crisis the United States decided to withdraw about 40 missiles from Turkey; twenty years later the United States emplaced nearly 600 far more effective missiles in Germany, England and Italy. But this was to counter a Soviet buildup of a new generation of 400 missiles regionally targeted to cover all of Western Europe and much of the Far East.

Citing such numbers is a staple fare of the nuclear debate. Supposedly they prove that the arms race is becoming more dangerous. Pure numbers, while not in themselves decisive, cannot be summarily dismissed, because they do create a psychological climate. Both sides tend to see in the growing numbers not an effort to reach or maintain a balance, but an attempt to gain some advantage. A preoccupation with numbers of weapons may also obscure other, more ominous, developments: weapons are becoming smaller, more accurate, easier to move about and conceal; and with the advent of "stealth"— the bomber invisible to radar—weapons will become more and more difficult to defend against; innovative technologies, such as lasers, offer new possibilities for both offense and defense.

The chances of controlling technology through negotiated agreements will diminish. Consider one case: the United States plans to develop a small, mobile ICBM which would be difficult for Soviet forces to locate and attack; but arms control theory argues that all mobile missiles should be banned because their illegal existence in small numbers probably could not be verified and this would offer an incentive to cheat.

Dilemmas of this kind are bound to multiply. The next generation of nuclear weapons may well be "dual"-purpose: they could be armed with either a conventional warhead or a nuclear one. The accuracy of weapons will be so phenomenal that the ability to deliver a high-explosive charge precisely on target will once again make so-called conventional weapons effective in their own right and as nuclear carriers. The proliferation of small weapons could mean the practical end to verifiable arms control, at least as it has been conceived over the past decades. To limit, reduce, ban or otherwise control new weapons may well require intrusive inspections and a high degree of cooperation, which can only be the product of a significant improvement in political relations.

Most important, defense has returned, after years in the strategic wilderness. Just as it seemed that offensive weapons were invincible, President Reagan began to lay claim to the technological revolution in the name of defending the entire United States. If there was ever a modern genie, it is the

Strategic Defense Initiative; it is not likely to be returned to its bottle. President Reagan touched the same nerve as had the advocates of a nuclear freeze. His rationale was that long-term reliance on nuclear retaliation as the guarantee against war was simply not safe enough. In his epigram "It is better to defend than avenge," the president also raised the moral issue of offensive retaliation as a national policy. And he drew instant and strong popular backing for shifting to defense.

The morality of nuclear deterrence has come under a new assault. American churches have begun to raise extremely complex philosophical questions: Could the use of nuclear weapons in any circumstances be considered "just," or was the entire strategy of threatening nuclear use immoral in itself? The policy of using nuclear weapons first in a European war has also been attacked by prominent strategists. Scientists have added to the growing alarm by discovering that given certain conditions, the entire human race might be extinguished by a "nuclear winter." Thus an explosive coalition has been formed of strategic, moral and political forces, all arrayed against the status quo. The old nuclear consensus has been collapsing. And what will replace it, no one can say.

Nuclear war, however, is not an abstract exercise. Changes in weaponry, or in attitudes toward the weapons, will affect strategic and tactical calculations, but even though nuclear weapons have revolutionized warfare, they have not suspended all of the laws of history. Nations still fight for a cause, however mistaken or ill-defined. Wars are still rooted in conflicts of interests.

The British historian Michael Howard has speculated that if there is a nuclear war, a future historian will explain it by writing that the Soviet Union grew in power and the United States feared it. He had in mind a British analogy: in the late nineteenth century Britain was confronted by the rise of German sea power; London abandoned its splendid isolation in favor of coalitions to block the kaiser's ambitions. The parallel with the United States and Russia is indeed eerie. Britain insisted that Germany restrain its naval power before German political grievances about colonies could be addressed; Germany, however, insisted on a political settlement first. There were a number of important negotiations, but in the end the two nations failed to agree and both slid further down the path to war. Germany was determined not to be denied its place in the sun, and Britain was determined to support her allies.

In some respects the United States finds itself in the same position as Britain did. Washington abandoned its hostility toward China in the name of an anti-Soviet coalition. It has adhered to an increasingly incredible strategy of threatening nuclear escalation in Europe in the name of preserving its anti-Soviet Atlantic alliance. It has repeatedly intervened in distant regions to block Soviet expansion and, under the Reagan Doctrine, even to reverse it. Surrendering one's freedom of action, of course, is a classic recipe for war. Indeed, there is a widespread belief among strategists and statesmen that a Soviet-American war as a consequence of a deliberate choice is a very marginal possibility. But war through "inadvertence" is still possible. The specter of Pearl Harbor had been replaced by the specter of Sarajevo.

In 1980, after the Afghanistan invasion, fears of another 1914 appeared. But the fears were not justified. During the worst period of superpower relations (1980–1985), both sides, as mentioned previously, carefully avoided turning regional conflicts and small wars into confrontations. Thus, the British navy sailed unobstructed to fight in the Falklands; the United States put American forces into Lebanon twice, without a Soviet reaction. Iran and Iraq fought a seemingly endless war, and both the United States and the Soviet Union have supported Iraq. The United States invaded Grenada and overthrew a tinpot Leninist, and shot up Libya, without even a hint of a clash between the United States and the Soviet Union. Some analysts concluded that the superpower rivalry was moderating. In the 1970s the limits of détente had been defined; in the 1980s the limits of confrontation were being defined. Within these boundaries, the two superpowers could coexist.

The conflict has indeed changed in character since the 1940s. There is little left of the ideological crusade of the early American policy of containment. Instead, we are engaged in a struggle for power and influence along more traditional lines. Ideological conflicts brook no compromises, but power and interests are negotiable commodities; they can be limited, in mutually acceptable ways. This is the essence of international politics. The change from an ideological struggle to a conflict of interests explains much about the recent history of Soviet-American relations—why clashes can arise, even in sensitive areas, without automatically producing an East-West confrontation. All of this is ground for reassurance.

Does the change in the nature of the Soviet-American contest also mean that the conflict may well begin to wither? There is little historical precedent to suggest that a conflict of this scope and depth will fade away. Occasionally such conflicts have been transcended as new threats have arisen. England and France fought for hundreds of years, only to join in an alliance in two wars against Germany. The only prospects for such a transformation of the Soviet-American rivalry would be the rise of an Asiatic power center arrayed against the occidental world. There has been periodic speculation along this line in the Soviet Union. Both Brezhnev and Solzhenitsyn seemed to have arrived at the same conclusion: that the main danger to Russia was in Asia; some in the United States muse over the dangers of a Sino-Japanese axis. There may be something to this speculation, but it is too fanciful to influence practical policy.

If nuclear war is to be avoided, we cannot idly wait for history to transform the Soviet-American struggle. We will have to settle it, or at least make some significant progress toward settling it. This means the revival of and greater reliance on politics and diplomacy, and diplomacy that goes beyond the obsession with arms control.

We are entering on the fourth major period in which progress toward settling our conflict with the Soviet Union is possible. Since the war there have been three moments for such progress: after Stalin died in 1953, after the Cuban missile crisis in 1962 and 1963, and during the early period of détente, from 1969 to 1972. Each period has yielded some improvement in relations, and consequently the conflict has become less volatile. But each period has ended in failure. It is this inability to stabilize the relationship that is dangerous and that challenges the current American and Soviet leaders.

In retrospect, it is surprising how little was demanded of the Soviet Union. In 1955, Eisenhower settled for an improvement in the atmosphere and the withdrawal of Soviet troops from Austria. After the Cuban crisis, Kennedy and Johnson let Khrushchev escape with only a small penance. Khrushchev feared he would be asked for major concessions in Europe, and he even offered a partial payment by offering to negotiate a nonaggression pact. Rather than recognizing this as a sign of weakness if not desperation, Washington treated it as propaganda. Thus Khrushchev was never really tested. Within a year he was gone, along with John Kennedy, and East-West diplomacy ground down to the pedestrian projects of the mid-1960s. The bankruptcy of the West was confirmed in 1968, when once again the Soviet Union invaded Eastern Europe with impunity. The only response the NATO powers could agree on was a diplomatic freeze. And by April 1969, when NATO celebrated its twentieth anniversary in Washington, most of those who attended pleaded with Nixon to resume East-West contacts.

One accomplishment of this period has grown in significance: the idea that there could be arms control between East and West. This was Kennedy's major contribution. His speech at the American University in April 1963 was the first flickering of détente. The actual result—a ban on nuclear testing—was not decisive; by 1963 public opinion would not have tolerated much more atomic testing in the atmosphere. The major accomplishment was not only stopping tests but initiating the strategic arms control process: formal negotiations, complex provisions, adequate verification, a solemn treaty, duly ratified, and a promise of more to come. It was a halting start but nevertheless a start.

Détente sought to extend the relationship much further. In Europe the division of Germany and of the continent, implicitly agreed to in 1955 and 1956, was formalized between 1970 and 1975, not merely to ratify the status quo but in the name of a new pan-Europeanism. In strategic arms control, the implications of the Kennedy period were codified by Nixon in the first SALT agreement and the ABM treaty. Both sides would continue to accept their vulnerability to a strategic attack, but in the name of détente. In the end these agreements also proved to be only partial settlements, but the period of détente was far more significant than the brief episodes of progress in 1953 and 1963.

American freedom of action has been rather narrow, given our responsibilities as a world leader. There have been brief periods when we could have been more assertive. On the whole, however, we have made the right decisions at the right time.

The Marshall Plan, the Truman Doctrine, the creation of NATO, the Cuban confrontation, the opening to China, were assuredly the right policies. So too were the periodic efforts, from Truman to Reagan, to explore a more constructive relationship with the Soviet Union. By and large it has been the Soviet Union that has thwarted these efforts, not misguided American policy, as is too often charged in revisionist history.

Yet that is no particular comfort in present circumstances. We now have to deal with current realities, not the record of the past.

The current reality is that the accession of Mikhail Gorbachev to the leadership of the Soviet party marks the beginning of a new historical period in Soviet-American relations. The transition from Brezhnev to Gorbachev also marks a genuine change in generations. Brezhnev was a young man in 1917, when the Bolsheviks took power; Gorbachev is the first postrevolutionary leader; he was born a full generation after the October Revolution. Indeed, he is in reality a postwar leader. He was only ten at the time of Hitler's invasion. But the freedom of action of each successive Soviet leader has become more and more constrained. Gorbachev's generation cannot resort to terror to dismantle the system and rebuild it as Stalin did. They will have to have considerable self-assurance to gamble as Khrushchev did, but they are the products and inheritors of a huge bureaucratic system. Thus, Gorbachev has limited freedom of action. The Soviet system can be changed and reformed, but not radically, drastically or quickly. Yet the domestic crisis in the Soviet Union cries out for just that—radical and urgent changes.

This is the dilemma facing Gorbachev. His only hope of pulling the Soviet Union out of the stagnation of the Brezhnev era is to strike hard at the system and continue the pressures. This means growing opposition at all levels, even in the Politburo; and this gamble in turn means that he is risking his political survival. His predicament has led Westerners to speculate that his reforms are mainly cosmetic, and that after a campaign or two, he will settle back into the comfortable groove of his predecessors.

I doubt this—at least that is not the impression I carried away in early February 1987, after meeting with Gorbachev for three hours as a member of a group of Americans that included Kissinger and Vance. Gorbachev was impressive: self-confident, articulate, obviously intelligent and sophisticated. He seemed to be a man who knew what he wanted and was determined to achieve it, even at high risk. His commitment to "revolutionary change," however, is an invitation to a severe struggle within the Soviet party. He freely acknowledged such opposition and the resistance is apparently greater than he anticipated. My guess is that he will persist with his reforms but, at some point within the next two to four years, will face an internal crisis. The odds of prevailing seem no better than sixty to forty in his favor. If he does overcome his opposition, as Khrushchev failed to do, he may well change the Soviet Union profoundly; if he fails, another time of troubles will follow that could be dangerous for the United States. The temptation to try foreign adventures to compensate for internal failures may prove irresistible, as it did for Khrushchev in the Cuban missile crisis.

In our conversations, one thing became clear. He will give domestic policy priority, and his clear preference is to buy some time in foreign policy. He explained what is called "new thinking" in foreign policy, which turns out to be Orwellian for "greater pragmatism." Gorbachev seems to recognize that the Soviet Union's global position has gradually weakened. The Soviet state now is forced to play the role of a more conventional world power. It no longer leads a revolution; it can no longer offer ideological inspiration to the world; it can no longer pose as the model for economic development. It is still the master of a European empire, but an empire that is decaying from the virus of diversity and democracy.

It turns out that the champions of a universalist doctrine have been poor imperialists. The British had the wit to devise the commonwealth. The Soviets have only the threat of intervention. The rise of Solidarity in Poland was the watershed for the Soviet empire; the decline of that empire is only a matter of time. In this sense the lands behind the old Iron Curtain have become the new sick man of Europe—the area where the danger of a future war may be greatest. Recognition of this danger is one reason why détente in Europe has survived the collapse of superpower relations in the early 1980s, and why the diplomacy of détente remains Eurocentric.

The accumulation of internal crises for Moscow has led many

observers to proclaim the "historical decline" of the Soviet Union: to speculate that the present period is not merely a passing phase but the beginning of a long-term secular trend.

This is surely debatable and probably wrong. After two hundred years of growth, it is highly unlikely that Russian power has begun to decline because of a decade of adversity. Only a few years ago there were equally confident predictions of a new era of Soviet expansion. It is difficult to believe that the situation has changed radically: in the 1970s the challenge was to manage the emergence of Soviet power; the task in the 1980s is to deal with a "sick Bear." Even if the Soviet Union has entered what historians will see as the beginning of a long-term decline, it will be a matter of many decades, perhaps fifty years, before this decline is fully evident. This does not mean that the internal crisis and the crisis of empire are not serious. Indeed, if the Soviet leaders themselves become convinced that they are entering a truly historical decline, it may be the beginning of a period of danger for the West. The Soviet Union will not simply acquiesce in the disintegration of its power position. Gorbachev was not elected to preside over the dismantling of the Soviet empire. If pressed, the Soviet Union will fight back, politically, ideologically, economically and, in the end, militarily.

Yet there is a strong view in the United States that contends that the best American strategy is to apply increasing pressure on the Soviet Union. The theory is intriguing. It holds that if faced with external containment and defeats, the Soviet Union will turn inward; then the regime will have to change, and it will liberalize internally and will become a legitimate partner for negotiations. This view is an enormous gamble for which there is virtually no supporting evidence in Soviet history. The Soviets, when confronted by adversity abroad, have retreated, they have compromised and have even made concessions, but they have always returned to the fray.

The first objective for American policy is to create the circumstances that will make it difficult for the Soviet Union to resume the offensive after Gorbachev or his successors have rebuilt Soviet power. Gorbachev wants a "breather" in world affairs. But we have to be clear about his purposes; he wants to gain time to rebuild Soviet power in all of its dimensions. It is the task of Western strategy to make him pay a price for this interlude—a price in concessions that will advance strategic stability and the settlement of regional conflicts.

To deal effectively with the Soviet Union we must realize that much more is involved than developing clever schemes to solve the latest problem of negotiations. The starting point has to be the clear recognition of the source of strength of our international position—our alliance with Europe and Japan. Somehow we refuse to learn how to live with the undeniable success of American foreign policy since World War II. Despite all the setbacks, failures and outright catastrophes, the Western cause has grown in strength. Few alliances have been more successful than NATO; rarely have major powers so quickly put behind them the animosities of a great conflict. And rarely has one of the victorious powers come to dominate the world to the extent that the United States has. The United States must continue to support and lead a powerful coalition of forces to contain the Soviet Union, but it will have to do so in an era vastly different from the period of the coalition's creation.

We have won the ideological war; we are close to winning the political contest in the Third World, except for the Middle East. We long ago won the economic competition. Yet there is a nearly irresistible strain of isolationism in America.

And this is reflected in the obsessive concern in the United States with altering the Atlantic alliance and withdrawing from Europe. We must resist this constant temptation to tinker with a successful alliance, to play with various forms and types of American involvement. There is nothing more encouraging to the Soviet leaders in their time of troubles than the hope that sooner or later the United States will disengage from Western Europe. The struggle for the mastery of Europe, to paraphrase A. J. P. Taylor, continues and will continue as long as the Soviet Union remains one of Europe's great powers. The balance of world power could still be changed by shifts in this vital area. Thus, preserving the European alliance remains the cornerstone of American policy.

Maintaining an anti-Soviet coalition has become more complicated by our tentative alliance with China; the natural course for Sino-American relations is to move toward a closer military relationship. This is bound to be seen as a major threat by the Soviet Union. While we cannot grant Moscow a veto over American policy, the American connection to China needs to be handled with extreme care. We have no genuine common interests with China (whether that country "modernizes" or not) beyond the common opposition to Moscow; and Sino-American relations will weaken as both the Soviets and the Chinese try to moderate their strategic differences. Nor will the new generation of Soviet leaders continue Brezhnev's bitter anti-Chinese hostility. They will seek freedom to maneuver, and sooner or later there will be a new generation in power in Peking that will not have experienced the debates and clashes of the 1960s and 1970s; all of this, in turn, will be unsettling for Washington.

A successful alliance policy cannot ignore the fact that the industrial democracies will not support a foreign policy that does not include an effort at détente. Our Western allies and Japan obviously want both containment and coexistence. This is even the crude basis on which the Chinese are prepared to join with the United States. In practice this means that the United States has to engage in the process of negotiations with Moscow, including arms control arrangements.

Arms control has had a checkered history. Much of what seemed important has turned out to be misleading or ephemeral. And there have been some deep disillusionments. But time and again, arms control negotiations and the idea of limiting or otherwise controlling nuclear weapons have returned to the forefront of East-West relations. This is not accidental; it simply reflects the imperatives of the nuclear era. Some American administrations have made arms control a centerpiece, and others have become engaged more reluctantly. But a pattern seems to have been fixed, despite the setbacks and failures. East-West relations are in large measure about the control of strategic and nuclear arms.

Indeed, the Reagan experience demonstrates that the American public will not tolerate a policy of deliberate disdain or benign neglect of arms control. President Reagan found that public and congressional pressures insist on a serious and active effort. Moreover, it is also clear that something of the same process is at work on the other side. The Soviet Union has been reluctant to abandon the arms control process. It has been drawn back to it, even under humiliating circumstances.

Nevertheless, arms control has changed since the Nixon agreements of 1972. Arms control can no longer be justified as the catalyst for détente. Flawed arms control agreements will not be supported in the name of some other, distantly related, aim. This puts an even greater burden on the negotiations. Support for arms control will require a far more meticulous concern for the details of verification to prevent cheating and, above all, a constant concern with broad strategic results; simply limiting or reducing weapons cannot be the basis for a long-term strategic stability. This is a formidable task, if only because there is no agreement on what constitutes stability. It has become even more difficult with the revival of strategic defense: defining a durable balance between offense and defense is the very essence of stability. Yet the Reykjavik summit demonstrated the inherent difficulty of reaching any agreement.

If the American public demands arms control, it also insists on an adequate defense, and will hold its leaders liable for failures and defeats that arise from weaknesses in our defense capability. But in order to gain support for the strong defenses that remain the bulwark of the anti-Soviet coalition, every administration has to be seen as actively pursuing a peaceful relationship with the Soviet Union. This potential contradiction is becoming more and more serious in the clashes between the White House and the Congress. Increasingly, the Congress has made its appropriations for defense dependent on arms control measures. In effect, the Congress has tried to micromanage foreign relations at long distance.

The result has been to create even greater confusion and to complicate the actual conduct of foreign policy. But congressional intervention is a permanent new reality: the Congress will persist in trying to limit the operational conduct of foreign policy, as compared with the 1950s and 1960s; this is a consequence of Vietnam, Watergate, and, more recently, Irangate. The ability of the executive branch to conduct truly clandestine activities has virtually ended. Any use of force, no matter how limited, or indeed, however successful, provokes another round of constitutional debate about war powers and leads to new limits on the president's freedom of action. Even a highly popular president like Reagan had to fight through almost every national security issue, even before the Iranian arms fiasco. And all of this is further complicated by the fact that the boom-and-bust cycle of defense spending continues.

Thus, as the Reagan administration reactivated its East-West diplomacy from 1984 to 1986, its defense budget started to slide drastically.

Another trend is the weakening of the idea of linkage, of making arms control negotiations or agreements dependent in some degree on political issues. This weakening was probably inevitable: as the size and sophistication of nuclear arsenals has grown, intricate Kissingerian strategies of linkages have carried less and less conviction. Ford did not really practice linkage after Angola. Carter invoked linkage only after the crisis of Afghanistan, and Reagan formally abandoned it, only to try to revive it when confronted by summit meetings.

The decoupling of arms control from the geopolitical contest is bound to limit American policy in a dangerous way. For it remains clear that the chief threats to Soviet-American relations are not weapons alone but regional conflicts as well as arms competition. Afghanistan should have demonstrated the dangers of de-linking arms control. The current reality is that linkage has become almost impossible, except perhaps in a major crisis. If this situation is not changed and some degree of linkage reestablished, it is inevitable that the United States and the Soviet Union will be drawn into major clashes.

Whether in arms control or regional negotiations, a serious American diplomacy will finally have to decide how to define and deal with legitimate Soviet interests, and how to gain public support for a policy that inevitably involves some American concessions. Does the Soviet Union have a right to strategic parity, or is this too dangerous a state of affairs for the United States? What is the legitimate security interest of the Soviet Union in the areas on its periphery: in Eastern Europe, in Afghanistan, in China? Does it have an implicit right of intervention in its sphere of influence; if so, does it include intervention with armed forces? Can the United States tolerate such a permanent threat to peace? What of the link between the nature of the internal Soviet regime, which will never be acceptable to the United States, and the content of Soviet foreign policy? Can the two be separated?

These are not academic questions. During the period of détente an effort was made to resolve some of these issues. Concessions were made in the name of establishing a more general international equilibrium. Strategic parity was con-

ceded, but not a Soviet advantage. A Soviet sphere was acknowledged, but not an exclusive one: the right of direct
intervention was challenged, in China, in Poland, in Afghanistan. The right of intervention beyond the Soviet periphery
was actively resisted. Concern with the unacceptable character
of the internal Soviet regime was subordinated to foreign
policy, but human rights were not abandoned.

To deal with the question of legitimate Soviet interests
involves a policy in which contradictions must be reconciled
almost constantly and tactics and strategy must be finely tuned.
A policy that requires such a consistent and careful management in a democratic society is not doomed to fail, but it is
extraordinarily difficult to carry out. It is bound to fail, however,
unless it can command the public support necessary to sustain
it when challenged in a crisis. It is exactly on this point, the
unwillingness of the public to continue supporting the general
strategy when confronted by setbacks or disappointments, that
all previous efforts have foundered.

To sum up: the danger of war with the Soviet Union has
diminished, but two of the three obstacles to war, the existence
of nuclear weapons and the balance of power, are inherently
unstable: nuclear weapons and strategic doctrines will change,
as will the global balance. In the end, we must rely on the
prudence of our leaders—unless a world order can be built
that minimizes the chances of human failing. Such an order
demands both the control of nuclear arms and a process for
resolving regional conflicts. The effort to achieve these two
aims is bound to be protracted and to require strong public
support and understanding. Every American leader has recognized this predicament. Despite different approaches in
different periods, the United States has no reason to be ashamed
of its efforts. Nonetheless, the historical record is not encouraging.

To return to Kant: the natural order for states is war; peace
must be created.

INDEX

Aaron, David, 185, 186, 187, 208, 211, 221
Abrams tank, 40
Acheson, Dean, 5, 31, 185
Adenauer, Konrad, 16, 31
Afghanistan, 11–12, 123, 143, 164, 197, 202–203, 204, 221, 222–223, 225, 226, 240, 241, 242, 245, 250, 259, 260
Akalovsky, Alex, 92
Albania, 114
Alexandrov-Agentov, Andrei, 71
Allen, Richard V., 168, 227
Allende, Salvador, 133, 137
Allison, General Roy, 53
"America in a Hostile World" (Brzezinski), 174
Andropov, Yuri, 73, 122, 233, 236, 242
    SDI and, 244
Angolan civil war, 10–11, 129, 131, 132, 135–147, 148, 158, 163–164, 166, 197, 219, 259
    Reagan and, 240–241
Antiballistic missiles (ABMs), xv, xvi, 9, 14–15, 40–47, 214
    of Soviet Union, 14, 15, 27, 37, 38, 40–41, 83

ABM treaty, 47–50, 53–54, 72, 243, 252
Antunes, Melo, 134
Arab-Israeli war (1967), 17
Armed Forces Movement (Portugal), 132
Arms Control and Disarmament Agency (ACDA), 38, 40, 42
Austria, 251

B-1 (long-range bomber), 40, 54, 87–88, 90, 94, 156, 200, 212, 216, 217
B-52 (long-range bomber), 94, 102, 156, 169
Backfire bomber, 101–102, 123–125, 153, 156, 157–161, 162, 208, 216–217, 233
Bahr, Egon, 31
Baker, James, 176, 181
Begin, Menachem, 202
Berlin talks, xv, 9–10, 13, 16, 20, 26, 27, 28, 29–33, 34, 35, 46, 47, 55, 105
Berlin Wall, 19, 29
Biden, Joseph, 142
Big Bird (airborne ICBM), 87
Bismarck, Otto von, 5, 194, 196

Bombers (missile-carrying), 88, 90, 92, 94, 95, 98, 101–102
  See also B-1; B-52; Backfire bomber; F-111; "Stealth" bomber
Botha, Roelf ("Pik"), 146
Brandt, Willy, 28, 30, 31–33, 34, 51, 118
Breaking with Moscow (Shevchenko), 26
Brezhnev, Leonid, xiii, xv, 4, 5, 10, 47, 166, 228, 253
  ABM treaty and, 50
  Angolan civil war and, 143–144, 145
  Backfire bomber and, 157, 158–159
  Crimean summit and, 61, 62–63, 64, 65–67, 70–71, 73–74
  détente and, 8, 55, 56–61, 74, 78, 85–86, 127, 218–219
  Helsinki conference and, 33, 99, 117, 118, 122, 123, 124–128, 140
  human rights and, 205, 206
  Kissinger and, 8, 21, 58, 77, 87–91, 102, 155, 158–162
  military policy of, 81–82, 84, 85, 218–219, 232–233
  Moscow summit and, 6, 8, 10, 11, 12, 21–22, 35, 47, 51–54, 55, 58–59
  peace program of, 46–47
  Reagan and, 228
  SALT negotiations and, 66, 72, 77, 78–80, 87–91, 155, 156–161, 212, 213, 216, 218
  SALT II treaty and, 128, 202, 222
  Sino-Soviet relations and, 28–29, 57, 60–61, 63–66, 77–78, 82
  Soviet MFN status and, 107–108
  succession problems for, 228, 233, 236
  Third World crises and, 241, 242
  Vienna summit and, 123, 202–203
  Vladivostok summit and, 6, 11, 70, 76–77, 85, 91–97, 98, 99–100, 118–119, 173
  Watergate and, 69, 78
  West Germany and, 32, 51
  Yom Kippur War and, 69

Brezhnev Doctrine, 13
Britain, 16, 115
Brown, George, 155–156, 185, 210, 219
Brzezinski, Zbigniew, xiv, 163, 174, 175, 183–184, 186, 189–190, 203
  on Afghanistan invasion, 222
  human rights and, 205–206, 207
  Kissinger and, 184–185, 203
  Polish crisis and, 226
  SALT negotiations and, 208, 209, 211, 214, 215
  Sino-U.S. relations and, 221, 222, 226
  strategic arms reduction and, 210
  Third World crises and, 221
  Vance and, 204, 216
Buchanan, Pat, 167
Bukovsky, Vladimir, 205
Bush, George, 84, 148, 150–151

Caetano, Marcello, 131
Cambodia, 18, 28, 112, 113, 240, 241
  North Vietnam invasion of, 11, 29, 221
Camp David accord, 175, 202, 204
Carlucci, Frank, 134
Carter, Jimmy, xiv, 11, 58, 163, 230
  Camp David accord and, 175, 202, 204
  détente and, 74, 175, 215
  and Ford, television debates between, 120, 173, 176–179
  foreign policy of, 173–176, 184
  grain sale to Soviet Union and, 12
  human rights and, 204–207, 212
  Iranian hostage crisis and, 202, 204
  NATO's "dual-track" strategic arms decision and, 234
  Panama Canal Treaty and, 175, 202, 204
  Polish crisis and, 226
  presidential campaign of, 168, 173–175
  SALT negotiations and, 175–176, 204, 208–226, 228, 229
  SALT II treaty and, 11, 12, 66, 103, 128, 202, 224–226, 229
  strategic arms reduction and, 210–211, 212

Third World crises and, 240
Vienna summit and, 123, 202–203
Carter Doctrine, 180
Case, Clifford, 141
Castro, Fidel, 155
Ceausescu, Nikolai, 115, 121
Central Intelligence Agency (CIA), xiv, 5, 6, 110, 155, 158
    Angolan civil war and, 135, 136–141, 144–145, 146
    Chilean elections and, 133
    missile gap intelligence of, 82, 83
    Team B of, 84–85
Chernenko, Konstantin, 122, 228, 236, 239
Cheney, Richard, 148
Chile, 133, 137, 142
China, 3, 4, 15, 193
    Japan and, 251
    North Vietnam support by, 14, 23, 25, 29
    and Soviet Union, 4, 10, 11, 13–14, 15, 24–29, 33, 34–35, 40, 60–61, 63–66, 77, 82, 96, 192, 251, 257
    and United States, 4, 5, 8, 10, 35, 51, 60, 75, 77, 78, 104, 172, 221, 222, 226, 256–257
China and the Superpowers (Medvedev), 26
Chou En-lai, 27, 28, 35
Chuikov, Vasili, 17
Church, Frank, 155
Clark, Dick, 141, 145
Clark amendment, 145, 147
Clements, William, 155–156, 159, 170
Colby, William, 85, 110, 138–139, 140, 148, 149, 150, 151
Cold war, 10
Conference on Security and Cooperation in Europe (CSCE), see Helsinki conference
Congress
    ABMs and, 15, 49
    Angolan civil war and, 141–142, 145–146
    Jackson-Vanik amendment and, 99, 100, 104–108
    MIRVs and, 44–45
    SALT negotiations and, 44, 45, 53, 54, 99–104, 258
    South Vietnam aid and, 110
    Third World crises and, 241
    Vietnam War and, 17–18
Connally, John, 181
Containment, see Détente
Corvalan, Luis, 205
Crimean summit meeting (1974), 61, 62–63, 64, 65–68, 70–72, 73–74
Cruise missiles, 102–104, 153, 156, 157–161, 162, 200, 223, 235, 236
Cuba, 10–11, 33, 133
    Angolan civil war and, 129, 142–147
    Soviet military forces in, 225–226
    Soviet submarine base in, 32–33
Cuban missile crisis, xv, 4, 20, 29, 81, 247, 251, 253, 254
Cunhal, Alvaró, 132
Czechoslovakia, xvi, 4, 9, 10, 13, 15, 16, 38, 204

Daniloff, Nicholas, 158
Davis, Lynn, 186
Davis, Nathaniel, 137, 141
Dean, John, 68, 70
Defense Department, 7, 39, 161, 230
    SALT negotiations and, 40–41
De Gaulle, Charles, 15, 16, 17
Deng Xiaoping, 221–222
De-Stalinization, 46, 57
Détente, xiii, xiv, xv, 3–12, 20–23, 55–61, 251–252, 257
    Brezhnev and, 8, 55, 56–61, 74, 78, 85–86, 127, 218–219
    Carter and, 174, 175, 215
    criticism of, 196–201
    Ford and, 11, 79, 83, 120, 123, 126, 147, 163, 164–165, 166, 168, 171, 173, 174–175, 176
    Johnson and, 10
    Kennedy and, 10, 252
    as Kissinger policy, 4, 8–9, 10, 11, 12, 20–23, 67, 74–75, 109–110, 115, 126–127, 135, 147, 185, 193–200
    Nixon and, 4, 8–9, 10, 11, 12, 20, 23, 67, 74
    Reagan and, 12
    strategic parity under, 259–260

Détente (continued)
  U.S. strategic arms system under, 200
  waning of U.S. support for, 74–75, 99
  Watergate's effect on, 6, 11, 67, 68–75, 78, 118, 190–191, 201
  Western Europe and, 10, 55–56, 254, 257
Dobrynin, Anatoly, 35, 69, 108, 227–228
  ABM treaty and, 48, 49, 50
  Angolan civil war and, 145
  Berlin talks and, 29, 34, 46, 47
  fall of Saigon and, 112
  human rights and, 206
  SALT negotiations and, 46, 47, 212, 216–217
  Sino-Soviet relations and, 24, 25, 27
  Vladivostok summit and, 101, 104
  Watergate and, 68
Douglas-Home, Alec, 19
Dual-purpose missiles, 248

Eanes, General Ramhlo, 135
Eastern Europe, 239, 252
  Helsinki conference and, 120, 121, 127, 177, 178
East Germany and, 31–33
  West German recognition of, 28
Easum, Donald, 137
Egypt, 17, 28, 68, 69
Eisenhower, Dwight D., xiv, xv, 10, 17, 246, 251
Ervin, Sam, 68
Ethiopia, 11, 146, 197, 220–221, 241
Europe, see Eastern Europe; Western Europe
European Economic Community, 16
Evans, Roland, 154

F-111 (fighter-bomber), 102, 169
Falklands war, 242, 250
Fallaci, Oriana, 188
Ford, Gerald, xiii, xiv, 73, 75
  Angolan civil war and, 138, 140, 141, 145, 146
  and Carter, television debates between, 120, 173, 176–179
  détente and, 11, 74, 83, 120, 123,
    126, 147, 163, 164–165, 166, 168, 171, 173, 174–175, 176
  fall of Saigon and, 112
  foreign policy of, 11, 166
  Halloween massacre and, 148–155
  Helsinki conference and, 11, 120–129, 140, 173
  Kissinger-Brezhnev preliminary SALT negotiations and, 161, 162
  Mayaguez incident and, 113
  MFN status for Soviet Union and, 106, 107, 108
  Nixon pardon by, 78, 173
  North Korean crisis and, 170
  Panama Canal treaty and, 164–165
  Poland gaffe made by, 173, 176–179, 181
  Portuguese revolution and, 134, 141
  reelection campaign of, 158, 163, 166–171, 173–183
  SALT negotiations and, 77, 78–80, 85, 104, 164–165, 231, 259
  SALT II treaty and, 225, 226
  Sino-Soviet relations and, 77, 96
  Vladivostok summit and, 6, 11, 70, 76–77, 85, 91–97, 98, 99–104, 118–119, 173
  Watergate and, 9, 78, 173, 183
Foreign Intelligence Advisory Board, 85
Fosdick, Dorothy, 100
France, 117
Franco, Francisco, 86
Frankel, Max, 177, 178
Fulbright, J. W., 74–75
Furtseva, Katerina, 59

Gallup, George, 173
Gallup Poll, 182
Garagiola, Joe, 181–182
Gelb, Leslie, 211, 216
Geneva summit meeting (1955), xv
Geneva summit meeting (1985), xv, 206, 227, 244–245, 246
Glassboro, New Jersey, summit meeting (1967), xvi, 14–15, 214
Goldwater, Barry, 172
Gomez, General Costa, 132, 133
Gomulka, Wladyslaw, 31, 34

Gonçalves, Vasco, 131–132, 134
Gorbachev, Mikhail, xiv, 60, 71, 73, 218
  Geneva summit and, xv, 206, 227, 244–245, 246
  military policy of, 85
  political dilemma facing, 253–256
Graham, General Daniel, 110
Grechko, Andrei, 93
Greece, 135, 146
Grenada, 240, 242, 250
Gromyko, Andrei, xiv, 35, 51, 60, 61, 109, 236, 240
  Crimean summit and, 62, 67, 68, 72
  Helsinki conference and, 117, 118, 119, 125
  Jewish emigration and, 106, 107
  SALT negotiations and, 88, 212, 213, 214, 216–217, 228
  Vladivostok summit and, 91, 93

Habib, Philip, 111, 112, 213, 214
Haig, Alexander, 7–8, 53, 62, 68, 69, 149, 233, 238
  "no-undercut" policy of, 229
  Polish crisis and, 237
  SALT negotiations and, 227–228, 229, 235
  Third World crises and, 240
Haile Selassie, 220
Haiphong harbor, mining of, 50, 55
Haldeman, H. R., 53
Halloween massacre (1975), 148–155
Halperin, Morton, 39, 97
Helms, Richard, 25
Helsinki conference (1975), 10, 11, 20, 33, 99, 109, 114–129, 140, 173, 177, 178, 207, 232
Hersh, Seymour, 144
Hitler, Adolf, 22, 46, 57, 64, 193
Ho Chi Minh, 14, 27
Hoffman, Stanley, 200
Honecker, Erich, 121
Human rights, 204–207, 212, 260
Humphrey, Hubert, 18, 45, 172
Hungary, invasion of (1956), xv, 34, 239
Hussein, King, 32

Intercontinental ballistic missiles (ICBMs), 37, 38, 42–43, 45, 48, 49, 50, 81, 82–83, 85, 87, 88, 90, 91, 92, 223, 224, 231, 247
  with MIRV warheads, 37–38, 43, 45, 88, 92, 94, 95, 159, 200
  MX missiles, 42, 90–91, 218, 224, 231
  "window of vulnerability" problem of, 42, 230–231
ICBM silos, 38, 42, 82, 224, 230–231, 233
Intermediate-range nuclear force (INF) missiles, 103, 234–236, 237–239
International Monetary Fund, 238
Iran, 224, 232, 250
  arms fiasco, 258
  hostage crisis, 180, 185, 202, 204
Iran, Shah of, 222
Iraq, 250
Israel, 28, 32, 97
  Arab-Israeli war and, 17
  Yom Kippur war and, 68, 69

Jackson, Henry, 53, 80, 74, 93, 99–100, 101, 104, 105–109, 225
Jackson-Vanik amendment, 99, 100, 104–108, 109, 143, 147, 177, 199, 207
Japan, 4, 60, 64, 251, 256, 257
Jaruzelski, General Wojciech, 237, 238
Javits, Jacob, 75, 107
Jewish emigration from the Soviet Union, 75, 99, 100, 105, 106–109, 207
Johnson, Lyndon, xv, 9, 24, 172, 251
  ABMs and, 37
  détente and, 10
  Glassboro summit and, 14–15
Joint Chiefs of Staff (JCS), 39, 155, 200
  SALT negotiations and, 72, 90–91, 96
Jones, General David, 223–224
Jordan, Hamilton, 183, 184
Juan Carlos, King, 86

Kant, Immanuel, 201, 260
Kaunda, Kenneth, 138
Kennan, George, 10, 215
Kennedy, Edward, 103, 104

Kennedy, John F., xv, 24, 92, 122, 247, 251
détente and, 10, 252
Khrushchev, Nikita, xiv, xv, 4, 20, 46, 57, 58, 60, 92, 242, 246, 247, 251–252, 253, 254, 255
military policy of, 81, 84
Kirkpatrick, Jeane, 240
Kissinger, Henry A., xiii, xiv, 186, 254
ABM treaty and, 47, 48–49, 50
Angolan civil war and, 137, 138, 139, 140, 141, 145, 146, 158, 163–164
Berlin talks and, 20, 29–33, 34, 46
Brezhnev and, 8, 21, 58, 77, 87–91, 102, 155, 158–162
Brzezinski and, 184–185, 203
Carter's campaign attack on, 174
China and, 4, 5, 8, 10, 35, 77, 78, 104
cited for contempt of Congress, 154–155, 191
Crimean summit and, 62, 63, 67, 71, 72
détente as policy of, 4, 8–9, 10, 11, 12, 20–23, 67, 74–75, 109–110, 115, 126–177, 135, 147, 163–164, 185, 193–200
fall of Saigon and, 111–112
Halloween massacre and, 148–155
Helsinki conference and, 114, 117, 118, 119, 120, 121, 125
Jackson-Vanik amendment and, 106–108
Mayaguez incident and, 113
Moscow summit and, 51, 52, 53
North Korean crisis and, 168–169, 170
NSC and, 5–6, 7–9, 70
Portuguese revolution and, 133, 135
"precaution" policy of, 22
preliminary SALT negotiations (Moscow) of, 87–91, 155, 158–162
Rhodesian crisis and, 166–167
SALT negotiations and, 8, 20, 34, 36, 39–43, 46, 47, 48, 66, 72, 79, 80, 101, 103, 104, 197
SALT II treaty and, 225, 226

Sino-Soviet relations and, 24–29, 34–35, 60, 61, 64
Solzhenitsyn and, 140–141, 168
on strategic arms superiority, 72–73, 80
style and substance of "Kissinger-era" diplomacy, 188–201
Vietnam War and, 5, 8, 18–20, 23, 39
Vladivostok summit and, 77, 91, 92, 93, 94, 95, 96, 97, 98
Washington press corps and, 189–192
Watergate and, 68, 190–191, 201
"Year of Europe" project of, 115, 127
Yom Kippur war and, 68–69
on Zaire crisis, 220
Knoche, Eno, 151
Konev, Marshal Ivan, 17
Kornienko, Georgi, 95, 97, 231
Kosygin, Alexei, xv, xvi, 14–15, 27, 28, 59
Kozlov, General Mikhail, 92–93, 124, 159
Kraft, Joseph, 45, 126, 214
Kulakov, Fyodor, 73

Laird, Melvin, 40, 49, 54
Laos, 18
Lebanon, 242, 250
Lehman, John, 153, 154, 185
Libya, 241, 242, 250
U.S. bombing of, 102
Lisagor, Peter, 72
London Economist, 179
London Times, 201

McCloy, John, 31
McFarlane, Robert, 150
McGovern, George, 45
McNamara, Robert, 14–15
Malenkov, Georgi, 228
Malta, 119
Mansfield, Mike, 16
Mao Tse-tung, 63, 64–65, 68
Marshall Plan, 3, 253
Martin, Graham, 111, 112
Mathias, Charles, 103, 104
Mayaguez incident, 113–114
Medvedev, Roy, 26
Meir, Golda, 69
Mengistu Haile Mariam, 220, 221

Metternich, Prince Klemens, 194, 196
Middle East, 10, 17, 28, 32, 240, 256
  Vladivostok summit and, 97
  See also names of Middle Eastern countries
Midgetman (mobile missile), 231
Mintoff, Dom, 119
Missiles, *see* names and types of missiles
Mobutu, Joseph, 137, 139, 141, 142
Mohammed Daud, 222
Mondale, Walter, 103, 104, 185, 187, 205
Molotov, Vyacheslav, 114
Moscow summit meeting (1972), 6, 8, 10, 11, 12, 21–22, 35, 47, 51–54, 55, 58–59
Most-favored nation (MFN) status, 105–108
Mozambique, 132
Multiple independently targetable reentry vehicles (MIRVs), 37–38, 40, 41–45, 54, 66, 72, 73, 88, 89–92, 94, 95, 159, 200, 223
  of Soviet Union, 41, 45, 54, 66, 87, 89, 90
MX missile, 42, 90–91, 218, 224, 231

National Front for the Liberation of Angola (FNLA), 136, 139, 141, 142, 145
National Security Council (NSC), xiii, 5, 7–8, 13
  Berlin talks and, 13, 26, 29, 33, 34
  Kissinger and, 5–6, 7–9, 70
  SALT negotiations and, 9, 13, 26, 39–40, 41, 47, 82, 161–162
  Sino-Soviet relations and, 13, 14, 25–26, 27, 33
  Vietnam War and, 25
  White House attitude toward, 6–7
National Union for the Total Independence of Angola (UNITA), 136, 139, 142, 145
Nessen, Ron, 104, 181
Neto, Angostinho, 136
New Republic, 167, 180, 181

New York Times, The, 45, 48, 74, 144, 177, 183, 189, 195, 205, 215
Nicaragua, 164–165, 224, 240, 241, 242
Nitze, Paul, 48, 53, 236
Nixon, Richard, xiii, xvi, 3, 172, 227, 252
  ABMs and, 15, 37, 49–50, 243, 252
  Berlin talks and, 16, 20, 29, 32–33, 35, 105
  China visit of, 51, 60, 75, 172
  Crimean summit and, 61, 62–63, 64, 65–68, 70–72, 73–74
  détente and, 4, 8–9, 11, 12, 20, 23, 67, 74
  experience in Soviet affairs of, 7, 47
  NATO and, 15–16
  MFN status for Soviet Union and, 105
  Moscow summit and, 6, 8, 10, 11, 12, 21–22, 35, 47, 51–54, 55, 58–59
  NSC and, 7
  resignation of, 9, 74, 75
  SALT negotiations and, 36, 41, 43, 46, 65, 72, 79–80, 252, 257
  SALT II treaty and, 226
  Sino-Soviet relations and, 24, 27, 28–29, 35, 60–61, 63–66, 192
  "State of the World" reports of, 34, 35, 201
  Vietnam War and, 3–5, 17–20, 23, 50
  Washington press corps and, 189
  See also Watergate
Noor Mohammed Taraki, 222
North Atlantic Treaty Organization (NATO), xvi, 3, 15–16, 17, 115, 187, 252, 253, 256
  "dual-track" strategic arms decision of, 234–239
  "flexible response" policy of, 16–17
  Portuguese revolution and, 134, 135
North Korea, 168–170
North Vietnam, 13, 18
  fall of Saigon and, 99, 110–114, 119, 143, 145, 191
  invasion of Cambodia by, 11, 29, 221

North Vietnam (*continued*)
  Kissinger negotiations with, 8, 23
  Soviet support for, 14, 23, 25, 29
Novak, Robert, 154
Nuclear submarines, 40, 54, 81, 83,
    87, 89, 90, 91, 92, 102–103,
    156–157, 160, 200
  U.S. base in Spain for, 86, 87, 93,
    94
Nuclear testing, underground, 72,
    165
Nuclear weapons, *see* Strategic
    arms; SALT negotiations

Ogarkov, Marshal Nikolai, 219
Organization of African Unity
    (OAU), 137, 138
Orlov, Yuri, 206
Osborne, John, 167–168, 180, 181,
    182

Packard, David, 49
Pakistan, 26, 35
Palestine Liberation Organization
    (PLO), 32, 97, 242
Palma Carlos, Adelino da, 132, 134
Panama Canal treaty, 164–165, 175,
    186, 202, 204
Pentagon, 83, 84, 155
  ABMs and, 49
  MIRVs and, 45
  NATO's "dual-track" strategic
    arms decision and, 235
  SALT negotiations and, 40, 43,
    44, 101
Pershing missiles, 156, 235–236
Pike, Otis, 154–155, 191
Podgorny, Nikolai, 59, 218
Podhoretz, Norman, 200
Poland, 33–34, 105, 120, 126, 173,
    176–179, 181, 260
  Solidarity crisis in, 127, 178, 226,
    228, 232, 235, 236–238, 239,
    254
Polaris missile, 200
Popular Movement for the Libera-
    tion of Angola (MPLA), 136,
    137, 138, 139, 141, 143, 144,
    145
Poseidon missile, 86, 200
Portugal
  Angolan civil war and, 136, 138
  revolution in, 131–135, 139, 141

Qaddafi, Muammar, 241

Reagan, Ronald, xiv, xv, xvii, 11,
    85, 147, 151, 158, 164, 222,
    226
  attack on Ford's détente policy
    by, 164–165, 166, 168, 171,
    173, 174–175
  Brezhnev and, 228
  détente and, 12
  Eastern Europe and, 239
  foreign policy of, 176, 232, 233,
    239
  Geneva summit and, xv, 206, 227,
    244–245, 246
  grain sales to Soviet Union and,
    232
  ICBM silos and, 231
  INF missile control in Europe
    and, 234, 235, 236, 238, 239
  Iran arms fiascao and, 258
  military buildup under, 229–230,
    232–233
  Panama Canal treaty and, 164
  Polish crisis and, 236–237, 238
  SALT II treaty and, 223, 228–
    229, 232, 233, 235
  SDI (Star Wars) program of, 54,
    232, 240, 243–244, 249
  strategic arms reduction and, 210,
    233–234, 257
  Third World crises and, 240–242
Reagan Doctrine, 229–230, 240–
    41, 243, 250
Reston, James, 215
Reykjavik summit meeting, xv, 258
Rhodesia, 166–167
Ribicoff, Abraham, 107
Richardson, Elliot, 68, 148
Roberto, Holden, 136, 137, 138,
    139, 141, 144
Roberts, Chalmers, 44, 126
Rockefeller, Nelson, 139, 148, 149
Romania, 125–126, 239
Rumsfeld, Donald, 148, 149, 150,
    151, 153, 154, 155, 159, 191,
    210
Rusk, Dean, 24, 185

Sadat, Anwar, 69, 202
Saigon, fall of, 99, 110–114, 119,
    143, 145, 191
Sakharov, Andrei, 204, 205, 207

Sandinistas, 164–165
Savimbi, Jonas, 136, 138, 139, 141, 142, 144, 240–241
Schlesinger, James, 69, 96, 119, 148–156, 161
Schmidt, Helmut, 121, 234
Schorr, Daniel, 155
Scowcroft, Brent, 92, 113, 120, 146, 148–149, 154, 161, 168, 169, 170, 178–179, 180, 186, 197, 209, 231
Sentinel (ABM system), 37
Shcharansky, Anatoly, 206, 207
Shelest, Pyotor, 58–59
Shevchenko, Arkady, 26, 143
Short-range attack missiles, 200
Shulman, Marshall, 203, 215
Single Integrated Operational Plan (SIOP), 93
Smith, Gerard, 40, 42, 44, 48, 53
Smith, Ian, 166
Solidarity movement, 127, 178, 226, 228, 232, 235, 236–238, 239, 254
Solzhenitsyn, Aleksander, 126, 140–141, 168, 205, 207, 251
Somalia, 11, 220, 221
Sonnenfeldt, Helmut, 6, 7, 69, 70, 95, 106, 120, 149, 158, 161
South Africa, 141–147
South Korea, 168
South Vietnam, 23, 110, 111, 112
Soviet Union, xiv, 3
    ABMs of, 14, 15, 27, 37, 38, 40–41, 83
    Afghan invasion by, 11–12, 123, 143, 164, 197, 202–203, 204, 221, 222–223, 225, 226, 240, 241, 245, 250, 259, 260
    Angolan civil war and, 138, 143, 146–147, 219
    China and, 4, 10, 11, 13–14, 15, 24–29, 40, 60–61, 63–66, 77, 82, 96, 192, 251, 257
    Cuban military and submarine bases of, 32–33, 225–226
    Czech invasion by, xvi, 4, 9, 10, 13, 15, 16, 38, 204
    grain sales to, 12, 125, 126, 228, 232
    Hungarian invasion by, xv, 34, 239
    ICBMs of, 81, 82–83, 85, 91

    internal crisis within, 253–255
    intermediate-range missiles of, 103
    Jewish emigration from, 75, 99, 100, 105, 106–109, 207
    MFN status for, 105–108
    Middle East and, 17, 28, 32
    MIRVs of, 41, 45, 54, 66, 87, 89, 90
    natural gas supply line to Europe from, 237–238
    North Vietnam support by, 14, 23, 25, 29
    nuclear submarines of, 81, 83
    shift in superpower military power balance, 246–247, 250–260
    Sino-U.S. relations and, 256, 257
    Solidarity crisis and, 226, 228, 232, 235, 236–237
    Third World crises and, 10–11, 219–222, 241–242
Spain, 135
    U.S. nuclear submarine base in, 86, 87, 93, 94
Spínola, António, 131–132, 134
Sputnik, xv
SS-9 (Soviet ICBM), 82
SS-18 (Soviet ICBM), 82
SS-20 (Soviet intermediate-range missile), 103, 234, 235, 236
Stalin, Joseph, 10, 46, 57, 58, 66–67, 251
Star Wars, see Strategic Defense Initiative (SDI)
State Department
    Angolan civil war and, 137, 138, 139, 141
    Berlin talks and, 29–30
    détente and, 163
    human rights and, 204–207
    NSC and, 7, 39
"Stealth" bomber, 248
Stevenson amendment, 99, 109
Stockman, David, 229
Stockwell, John, 139, 140
Strategic arms (nuclear weapons), xiii, xiv, 9, 12, 37
    moral and political forces against, 247–249
    nuclear war dangers, 247, 249–250, 251, 260

Strategic arms (*continued*)
  See also names and types of strategic arms
Strategic arms limitations treaty (SALT) negotiations, 8, 9, 13, 15, 21–22, 62, 74, 154, 252
  ABM treaty, 47–50, 53–54, 72, 243, 252
  ABMs and, 27, 41–42, 43, 45–46, 47, 214
  B-1 bomber and, 40, 54, 87–88, 90, 94, 156, 200, 212, 216, 217
  Backfire bomber and, 101–102, 123–125, 153, 156, 157–161, 162, 208, 216–217, 223
  Brezhnev and, 66, 72, 77, 78–80, 87–91, 155, 156–161, 212, 213, 216, 218
  Brzezinski and, 208, 209, 211, 214, 215
  Carter and, 175–176, 204, 208–226, 228, 229
  checkered history of, 257–258
  Congress and, 44, 45, 53, 54, 99–104, 258
  Crimean summit and, 61, 62–63, 64, 65–68, 70–72, 73–74
  cruise missiles and, 102–104, 153, 156, 157–161, 162, 200, 223, 235, 236
  deferred proposal agreement, 162, 211, 212
  détente policy and, 199–200
  Dobrynin and, 46, 47, 212, 216–217
  Ford and, 77, 78–80, 85, 104, 164–165, 231, 259
  Glassboro summit and, 14–15
  Gromyko and, 88, 212, 213, 214, 216–217, 228
  Haig and, 227–228, 229, 235
  Helsinki conference and, 124–125, 128
  ICBMs and, 37, 38, 42–43, 45, 48, 49, 50, 81, 82–83, 85, 87, 88, 90, 91, 92, 223, 224, 231, 247
  ICBM silos and, 38, 42, 82, 224, 230–231, 233
  intermediate-range missiles and, 234–235, 237, 238–239
  JCS and, 72, 90–91, 96
  Kissinger and, 8, 20, 34, 36, 39–43, 46, 47, 48, 66, 72, 79, 80, 87–91, 101, 103, 104, 155, 158–162, 197
  linkage with political issues, 8, 237, 259
  MIRVs and, 37–38, 40, 41–45, 54, 66, 72, 73, 88, 89–90, 94, 159, 200, 223
  missile-carrying bombers and, 88, 90, 92, 94, 95, 98, 101–102
  Moscow summit and, 51–54, 55, 58–59
  Nixon and, 36, 41, 43, 46, 65, 72, 79–80, 252, 257
  NSC and, 9, 13, 26, 39–40, 41, 47, 82, 161–162
  nuclear submarines and, 81, 83, 87, 89, 90, 92, 93, 94, 102–103, 156–157, 160
  Pentagon and, 40, 43, 44, 101
  Reykjavik summit and, xv, 258
  Soviet-U.S. preliminary SALT talks, 43–44, 50–53, 87–91, 158–162
  Trident submarine and, 54, 87, 90, 91, 200, 212, 216
  underground testing and, 72, 165
  Vance and, 206, 211–219
  Vladivostok summit and, 78–80, 92–96, 97, 98, 99–104, 159, 160, 208, 217, 218, 223, 225
SALT I treaty, 80, 83, 165–166, 225
SALT II treaty, 11, 12, 66, 103, 128, 202, 215, 222, 223–226, 228–229, 232, 233, 235
Strategic Defense Initiative (SDI), 15, 54, 218, 232, 240, 243–244, 249, 258
Submarine-launched missiles, 45, 48, 49, 50
Submarines, *see* Nuclear submarines
Suslov, Mikhail, 233
Syria, 32

Taiwan Straits crisis (1950s), 27
Thieu, Nguyen Van, 11
Third World, 10–11, 55, 147, 219–222, 241–242, 256
  See also names of Third World countries
Trident submarines, 40, 54, 87, 90, 91, 200

Truman Doctrine, 3, 146, 253
Tshombe, Moise, 219–220
Turkey, 247

Underground nuclear testing, 72, 165
U-2 spy flight, downing of, xv

Vance, Cyrus, xiv, 183–184, 185, 186–187, 203, 254
  on Afghan invasion, 222
  Brzezinski and, 204, 216
  human rights and, 205
  SALT negotiations and, 206, 211–219
Vanik, Charles, 105
Vienna summit meetings, 123, 202–203
Vietnam War, xvi, 3–5, 8, 10, 13, 23, 39, 50, 172, 185, 196, 201, 258
  mid-1980s attitude toward, 18–19
  national division over, 3, 17–20, 133, 143
  Paris peace agreement, 56
Village Voice, 155
Vladivostok summit meeting (1974), 6, 11, 70, 76–77, 78–80, 85, 91–97, 98, 99–104, 118–119, 156, 157, 160, 173, 177, 208, 217, 218, 223, 225

Wall Street Journal, The, 168, 197
Warnke, Paul, 210, 211, 213
Washington Post, The, 37, 44, 45, 74, 126, 165, 188, 189, 191, 192, 214, 215
Washington press corps, 189–192

Watergate, xvi, 7, 9, 55, 98, 133, 143, 173, 183, 185, 188, 197, 232, 258
  effect on détente of, 6, 11, 67, 68–75, 78, 118, 190–191, 201
Weinberger, Caspar, 229, 231, 235
Western Europe, 4, 16–17, 256
  détente and, 10, 55–56, 254, 257
  NATO's "dual-track" strategic arms decision and, 234–239
  natural gas supply line from Soviet Union to, 237–238
West Germany, 28, 30–31, 60
  Berlin talks and, 16, 28, 29, 30, 33
  Helsinki conference and, 114, 116, 117
  recognition of East Germany by, 31–33
  Soviet Union nonaggression treaty with, 32, 51
"White Revolutionary, The, Reflections on Bismarck" (Kissinger), 194
Will, George, 140
World Restored, A (Kissinger), 193

Yemen, 221, 224, 241
Yom Kippur war (1973), 68–69, 242
Yugoslavia, 105, 239

Zaire, 136, 141, 219–220
Zamyatin, Leonid, 71
Zero option (for intermediate-range missiles), 235

ABOUT THE AUTHOR

WILLIAM G. HYLAND, editor of *Foreign Affairs* magazine, has pursued a long career both in government and in academic life. During the years of détente, Mr. Hyland served on the National Security Council staff at the White House under Henry Kissinger from 1969 to 1973 and was director of intelligence at the State Department from 1973 to 1975, when he became a deputy assistant to the president for national security affairs. After he left government service in 1977 he joined the Georgetown Center for Strategic Studies and subsequently became a senior associate at the Carnegie Endowment for International Peace. He was named editor of *Foreign Affairs* in 1984 and lives in New York City.